AF360073

BÉARN AND THE PYRENEES
(VOLUME II)

LECTOR HOUSE PUBLIC DOMAIN WORKS

This book is a result of an effort made by Lector House towards making a contribution to the preservation and repair of original classic literature. The original text is in the public domain in the United States of America, and possibly other countries depending upon their specific copyright laws.

In an attempt to preserve, improve and recreate the original content, certain conventional norms with regard to typographical mistakes, hyphenations, punctuations and/or other related subject matters, have been corrected upon our consideration. However, few such imperfections might not have been rectified as they were inherited and preserved from the original content to maintain the authenticity and construct, relevant to the work. The work might contain a few prior copyright references as well as page references which have been retained, wherever considered relevant to the part of the construct. We believe that this work holds historical, cultural and/or intellectual importance in the literary works community, therefore despite the oddities, we accounted the work for print as a part of our continuing effort towards preservation of literary work and our contribution towards the development of the society as a whole, driven by our beliefs.

We are grateful to our readers for putting their faith in us and accepting our imperfections with regard to preservation of the historical content. We shall strive hard to meet up to the expectations to improve further to provide an enriching reading experience.

Though, we conduct extensive research in ascertaining the status of copyright before redeveloping a version of the content, in rare cases, a classic work might be incorrectly marked as not-in-copyright. In such cases, if you are the copyright holder, then kindly contact us or write to us, and we shall get back to you with an immediate course of action.

HAPPY READING!

BÉARN AND THE PYRENEES
(VOLUME II)

LOUISA STUART COSTELLO

ISBN: 978-93-90294-89-3

Published: 1844

© 2020
LECTOR HOUSE LLP

LECTOR HOUSE LLP
E-MAIL: lectorpublishing@gmail.com

VIEW OF AGEN (LITHOGRAPH)

BÉARN AND THE PYRENEES (VOLUME II):

A LEGENDARY TOUR TO THE COUNTRY OF HENRI QUATRE.

BY

LOUISA STUART COSTELLO,

AUTHOR OF
"THE BOCAGES AND THE VINES," "A PILGRIMAGE TO AUVERGNE," ETC.

WITH NUMEROUS ILLUSTRATIONS.

IN TWO VOLUMES,
VOL. II.

1844.

CONTENTS

CHAPTER XVI.

CHAPTER XVII.

LIST OF ILLUSTRATIONS

The Drawings in this work were made on the spot, by Miss Costello, Mr. Dudley Costello, Madame Francisque Michel, of Bordeaux, and other friends; and the Wood-cuts and Lithographs are executed by Mr. Thomas Gilks.

BÉARN AND THE PYRENEES.

Castle of Pau

COURT-YARD OF THE CASTLE OF PAU

CHAPTER I.

Renown Of Pau—Lectoure—The Labourer-Duke—Auch—Tarbes—
The Princess And The Count—Costume—Arrival At Pau—The
Promenades—The Town—Improvements-First Impressions—
Walks—Buildings—Hotels—The Magnificent Baker—The
Swain—Tou-Cai!

We left Agen on our way to Pau, where we proposed taking up our winter quarters, having so frequently heard that it was one of the best retreats for cold weather in the South of France: its various perfections casting into the shade those, long-established, but now waning, of Montpelier, Nice, &c. At Lectoure we changed horses, and remained long enough to admire the fine view from its exalted position, and a few of the humours of its population of young ragged urchins, whose gambols with a huge Pyrenean dog diverted us for some time. Lectoure is situated on the summit of an immense rock, surrounded by hills and deep valleys. It was formerly very strongly fortified, as the remains of its Roman and Middle-Age walls attest.

The tower of the church, partly Roman, partly English, is a very striking object, from its extreme height and apparent fragility, which is, however, merely imaginary; for it has resisted the efforts of time and war for centuries: it once had a steeple of stupendous height; but as it was continually attracting the stray lightnings, and was, besides, much dilapidated, it was demolished. The episcopal palace, now the Mairie, is near it, bought for the town by Marshal Lannes, Duke de Montebello. The statue of this hero of Napoleon is in the grand square, and his portrait, as well as those of other great men born in Lectoure, adorn the walls of the interior. There are many fine promenades, from whence delicious views can be enjoyed; from that of Fleurance it is said that, on a clear day, the towers of the cathedral of Auch are seen; and the view is bounded by the snowy giants of the Pyrenees. Although the day was fine, we could not, however, distinguish either. This public walk was made at the time when Lannes was a simple labourer in his native place; and he, with others, received six sous a-day for his work. The Duke de Montebello is said afterwards to have sat beneath the trees which overshadow it, and told his companions in arms how his youth was passed, and what his pay was at that time. This is a trait which does the brave soldier's memory infinite honour.

The country is agreeable and diversified on the way to Auch, and the two towers of the cathedral are seen at a great distance, crowning the height on which the town stands. They have so much the aspect of a feudal castle, that it is difficult to believe that one is looking on a church. The nearer you approach, the more determined seems the form: and walls, and bastions, and turrets, and ruins, seem rising out of the hill: all, however, as you come quite close, subside into a huge mass, which gives a promise of magnificence and grandeur by no means realized; for there is more of Louis XIV. and XV., than Charles VIII., who began the building, about the architecture; and the towers, which appeared so grand at a distance, have a singularly poor and mean appearance attached to the façade, and compared to the enormous bulk of the fabric.

The boast and glory of the cathedral of Auch are the series of painted windows in the choir, of remarkable beauty, and in wonderful preservation: the colours vivid, and the size of the figures colossal; but though extremely gorgeous, they cannot compare, in purity of effect, to earlier specimens, where less is attempted and more accomplished. I never saw such large paintings of the kind: the nearest approach to it being those of the same period at Epernay, amongst the vines of Champagne. There is a great deal of rich sculpture, both in the stalls and in the surrounding tombs, but the taste did not accord with mine, and, on the whole, I felt but little interest in the cathedral: we were spared the usual fearful exhibition in the winding staircase of one of the towers, where a little child, to earn a few sous, is in the habit of suspending itself by a rope, over the well, formed by the twisting steps, and sliding down to the bottom with terrific celerity.

The town of Auch did not please me enough to induce us to stay longer than to wait for the diligence, which was passing through to Tarbes; and, having secured the *coupé* we continued our journey. Before we had travelled half a league, on descending a hill, suddenly, a line of singularly-shaped objects, quite apart from all others in the landscape, told us at once that the purple Pyrenees were in sight; and we indeed beheld their sharp pinnacles cleaving the blue sky before us. For some distance we still saw them; but, by degrees, they vanished into shade as evening came on, and we lost them, and all other sights, in the darkness of night; in the midst of which we arrived at Tarbes.

"Tharbes is a large and fine town, situated in a plain country, with rich vines: there is a town, city, and castle, and all closed in with gates, walls, and towers, and separated the one from the other; for there comes from the heights of the mountains of Béarn and Casteloigne the beautiful *River of Lisse*, which runs all throughout Tharbes, and divides it, the which river is as clear as a fountain. Two leagues off is the city of Morlens, belonging to Count de Foix, and at the entrance of the country of Béarn; and beneath the mountain, at six leagues from Tharbes, is the town of Pau, also belonging to the said Count."

This is Froissart's description of Tarbes, in his time; and, as far as regards its beautiful sparkling river, which is *not the Lisse*, but the Adour, might apply to it now; for the streams that appear in all directions, in and round the town, are as clear as crystal, and run glittering and murmuring through streets, roads, and promenades, as if the houses and squares had no business there to intercept its mountain-torrent.

We were much struck, when we first issued from our hotel in the Place-Maubourguet, to behold, opposite, framed, as it were, in a square opening between the streets, a gigantic mass of blue mountains shining in the sun. They appeared singularly near; and one cannot fail to regard them with a certain awe, as if a new nature had dawned, different from any one had known before. This is the most interesting spot in Tarbes; and its beautiful promenade by the river is also attractive. There are no monuments, — no buildings worth notice. The once fine castle may be traced in a few solid walls, and its moated position; but this tower was one of the first indications we had that all specimens of architectural art had ceased, and in future, with a few exceptions, it must be nature alone which was to interest us. The red *capelines* of the market-women, and their dark mantles (*capuchins*), lined with the same colour, give their figures a strange, nun-like appearance, which always strikes a stranger, and at first pleases. As these shrouded forms flit about amongst the trees, they look picturesque and mysterious; but the eye soon wearies of this costume, which is totally devoid of grace. The cloak, being so cut as to prevent its falling in folds, hangs stiffly round the wearer's limbs; concealing the shape, and producing a mean effect. It is a sort of penitential habit; and the peaked hood looks like the dress of the San Benitos, or a lively image of the appropriate costume of a witch who might be an inquisitor's victim. We could not help contrasting it with the beautiful and graceful cloak worn by the charming Granvillaises, — those Spanish-looking beauties whose appearance so delighted us in that distant part of Normandy. The Granville girl has also a black camlet mantle, or *capote*; but the stiff hood is not peaked: it is lined with white, and is worn in the most elegant and coquettish manner; showing the figure to great advantage, and setting off the invariably pretty face, and its snow-white, plaited, turban-like cap, never to be seen in the South. There are so few pretty countenances in the Pyrenees, that perhaps even the Granville drapery would not make much difference; but, certainly, nothing can be uglier than to see the manner in which this scanty shroud is dragged over the form; giving more the idea of a beggar anxious to shield herself from the inclemency of the season, than a lively, smart, peasant girl pursuing her avocations. The scarlet gleams of its lining alone in some degree redeem its ugliness; as, at a distance, the vivid colour looks well amongst more sombre tints.

It is difficult, at the present day, to picture Tarbes as it was at the period when the Black Prince, and his Fair Maid of Kent, came to this city of Bigorre, in all the splendour of a conqueror, to see the Count of Armagnac, who was in debt to the magnificent Gaston Phoebus, for his ransom, two hundred and fifty thousand francs.

The manner in which the count managed to get off part of his debt is not a little amusing. He had represented his case to Edward, who saw nothing in it but a very ordinary event: "You were taken prisoner," said he, "by the Count of Foix; and he releases you for a certain sum. It would be very unreasonable to expect him to waive his claim. I should not do so; nor would my father, the king, in similar circumstances: therefore, I must beg to decline interfering." The Count of Armagnac was much mortified at this straight-forward answer, and began to devise what could be done. He bethought him of the power of beauty; and applied to the right person.

Gaston Phoebus arrived at Tarbes, from Pau, with a retinue of six hundred horse, with sixty knights of high birth, and a great train of squires and gentlemen. He was received with much joy and state by the prince and princess, and entertained with infinite honour.

The fair princess chose her moment, and took occasion to beg a boon of the Count of Foix, whose gallantry was proverbial; but, just as he was on the point of granting it without condition, a momentary light made him cautious "Ah! madam," said he, "I am a little man, and a poor bachelor, who have not the power to make great gifts; but that which you ask, if it be not of more value than fifty thousand francs, shall be yours."

The princess talked and cajoled, and was as charming and insinuating as possible, in hopes to gain her boon entire; but Gaston began to feel certain that the ransom of the Count d'Armagnac was the object of her demand; he, therefore, kept firm, in spite of her fascinations, and she was obliged to name her request that he would forgive the count his ransom.

"I told you," replied he, "that I would grant a boon to the value of fifty thousand francs; therefore, I remit him that sum of what he owes me."

And thus did the fair Princess of Aquitaine obtain a remission of part of the ransom of the Count d'Armagnac.

We took a carriage from Tarbes to Pau,—our intended resting-place for the winter. The drive, for several leagues, was extremely charming; the banks were covered with rich purple heath; the oak and chestnut growing abundantly and luxuriantly. But though, in our certainty of seeing some *new* growth as we approached nearer to the sunny South, we transformed the round, thick oaks into *cork trees*, we were obliged to submit to disappointment when we were assured that there was not a cork-tree till the Spanish side of the Pyrenees was reached. Long before we arrived at Pau, the hitherto pleasant, bright day had changed, and a sharp, drizzling, chilly rain accompanied us on the remainder of our journey—mist shutting out the prospect, and all becoming as dreary as a wet day makes things everywhere. We were a little surprised to find that there was no amelioration in this particular, since we looked forth upon the streaming streets of Lisieux!

We drove into Pau through an ugly suburb, which gave a sufficiently mean idea of its appearance; but we imagined that the town would repay us for its approach. Still the grey, unpainted shutters of the slovenly-looking houses were not replaced by others of brighter and cleaner aspect: still ruined, barrack-like buildings, dilapidated or ill-constructed, met our view; and, when we drove through the whole of the town to the Grande Place de Henri Quatre, and paused at the Hôtel des Postes, instead of a handsome, flourishing inn, we were astonished to see a wretched, ancient, red, low-roofed tenement, adjoining a somewhat ambitious-looking house without taste or grace. Here we could not find accommodation; and, considering the appearance of what we had heard was the best inn, we did not much regret the circumstance.

We were equally unsuccessful at several others; having looked at dirty, dingy, black apartments on a fifth floor as the only ones left: so full was the town of visitors returning, in all directions, from the different baths in the Pyrenees, where, as *it had rained all the summer*, invalids and tourists had been lingering for fine days, until patience was exhausted, and "all betook them home."

At length we got housed in very tolerable but desolate cold rooms, with furniture as scanty, and accommodations as meagre, as we had ever met with in towns where no English face had been seen, except *en passant*. This surprised us, as we had heard *comfort* abounded in Pau, as well as every luxury and beauty which wearied travellers would be glad to call their own; add to which, a soft, mild climate, *which could be depended on*, and the only drawback *too little wind* and too continuous warmth.

This was the third of October, and it was as cold as Christmas; the rain continued without ceasing; and, in spite of our impatience, we were obliged to remain in our inn. The next day, however, brighter skies revived us; and when we stepped forth on the rugged pavement, we felt in better spirits; no change, however, did the fine sun and sky operate on the town, which, it is sufficient to say, is one of the ugliest, worst-paved, "by infinite degrees," and most uninteresting that exist in France. The castle, of course, was the first attraction; and—though without the slightest claim to notice on the score of architecture; though dirty, and slovenly, and rugged, and dilapidated, more than could possibly be expected in a region which is immortalized by the name of Henri Quatre, and being, as it is, the goal sought by all travellers, consequently forming the riches of Béarn, the cause of such a host of travellers and tourists visiting Pau; the subject of all boast, the theme of all pride; though it is neglected and contemned by the ingrates of its neighbourhood,—the castle is, from its recollections, almost worth the long journey which is to find it at its close.

We returned to the Place Royale, after lingering long, on this our *first* visit, in the chambers now in the course of restoration by the most thoughtful and beneficent of sovereigns; and there we lost no time in securing an abode in one of the beautifully-situated pavilions of the Bains de la Place Royale,—a new and well-arranged building, let in *suites* of apartments, well furnished, and perfectly clean and inviting, having been recently renovated. From the windows of the rooms allotted to us, we beheld the whole of the long chain of the magnificent Pyrenees, from the Pic de Bigorre to the giant du Midi, and the countless peaks beyond. Our first impression was almost wild delight at the prospect of living long in a spot with these splendid objects always before our eyes, in uninterrupted grandeur; with a glowing sun always shining, sheltered from the north wind by the high promenade at the back of the house; with a beautiful little rapid stream running along at the base of our tower, the murmuring, sparkling, angry Gave[1] meandering through the meadows beyond; the range of vine-covered and wooded hills opposite, dotted with villas, which glittered white amidst their luxuriant groves; and, at the back of all, the everlasting awful mountains, purple and transparent and glowing with light.

View from the Baths, Pau.

VIEW FROM THE BATHS, PAU

We were not deceived in the enjoyment we anticipated in this particular, for,

---

[1] *Gave* is the generic name of all the mountain streams in this region, but that of Pau is called *"the Gave,"* par excellence.

to make amends for the unwilling *discoveries* we made as to the reputation of Pau, our mountains seemed to devote themselves to our pleasure, assuming every form of beauty and sublimity to satisfy and enchant us.

When we took our first walk in the promenade, improperly called *the Park*, we were fascinated with the extreme beauty of this charmed grove, which is planted in terraces, on a *côteau* bordering the Gave, and is *one of the most* charming possessed by any town in France: there is the same glorious view of the range of giant mountains even more developed than from the Place Royale; the paths are kept clean and clear and neat; the trees are of the finest growth, and everything combines to make it a most attractive spot, though the usual somewhat Gascon mode of describing it, adopted at Pau, as *"the most beautiful in the world,"* appears to me rather hyperbolical when I recollect those of Laon, Auxerre, Dijon, Dinan, Avranches, and others; which have not, however, the Pyrenees as a back-ground, it must be confessed.

The only part of the town of Pau which will bear mention, is that portion which borders the Gave, above a fine avenue of trees, which extends to a considerable distance along the banks of the small clear stream of the Ousse: that is to say, *the houses* which face the mountains; but the street in which their entrances are found is narrow, dirty, slovenly, and worse than *ill*-paved. These mansions—for some of them are large and isolated—have a magnificent position, and, seen from the Bois Louis, as the grove below is called, have a very imposing aspect. The principal street, Rue de la Prefecture, is extremely mean, and the shops of the least inviting appearance. It is very badly paved throughout its great extent, for it reaches from one end of the town to the other; but here and there a few flagstones serve to make their absence elsewhere regretted. There is one good square, which might be fine if, as seldom happens in France, the intention had been carried out, or success had attended it. There are two rows of good houses, with paved colonnades, but very few of the shops, which should have made it a *Palais Royal*, are inhabited; consequently, the appearance of poverty and desolation is peculiarly striking. One or two houses are taken, and some windows filled with goods, very different from those, doubtless, originally expected to appear; grocers, sadlers, and wine-merchants occupy the places which should have been filled by *marchandes de modes*, jewellers, toysellers, and ornamental merchants. The Place Henri Quatre is, therefore, a half-executed project, and impresses the stranger with no admiration. Another large, desolate space, called the Place Grammont, contains the Champ de Mars, and is dedicated to the military, whose barracks form one side of the square. A walk, called the Haute Plante, is near this, and, descending from it, the baths of Henri Quatre and the Basse Plante are reached, and the approach to the Park.

The great horse fair of Pau is kept in the Haute Plante; but it is by no means an inviting spot: the park is, in fact, the only place where one can walk pleasantly; for the pretty Bois Louis is principally devoted to the washerwomen of the town, and soldiers; and the drains of the streets running down in this direction, generally cause so unpleasant an odour, that a stroll there can rarely be accomplished with pleasure. To reach the park and to return from it, is a work of great pain; the pointed and uneven stones making the walk intolerable, and there is no way by which to arrive there, but through the damp, dirty streets.

If, as was once projected, a terrace walk was made to extend from the Place Royale—which is a small square planted with trees in rows, to the castle court, it would be an incalculable advantage; and such a means of arriving at the only objects of interest, would be the saving not only of many a sprained ankle, but many a severe cold, as, at all times, the streets are cold and damp; and the less a visitor sees of the town of Pau, and the more of the mountains, and *côteaux*, and streams, the less likely is he to dissatisfied with a residence in this most favoured and misrepresented of all ugly towns.

I am told that Pau is greatly *improved* from what it was seven or eight years ago; if such is the case, the town must then have been in a deplorable condition indeed: that those who are residents from so early a period should be content with the changes which have relieved them from inconvenience, I can easily understand; but that persons who, in Paris or in Normandy, have been accustomed to superior accommodation can be satisfied with Pau, surprises me. Taken in general, those who reside here all the year round, are Irish, Scotch, or from distant country towns in England, many being quite unused to London or Paris; therefore, they can make no comparisons, and from long habit get accustomed to things which must annoy others; but when persons of wealth and condition, forsaking the great capitals and beautiful watering-places at home, and their own splendid and comfortable establishments, come to Pau, to stay for some months, they must surely find that the representations they have heard of it are strangely at variance with truth. Invalids, of course, are glad to submit to whatever may tend to re-establish their health; and, as several persons speak of having derived benefit during their stay, doubtless there is a class of invalids to whom the climate does good: the only question is, would they not have been as well off nearer home, without the enormous expense of so long a journey, and enduring so complete an expatriation?

If one must necessarily go to Pau to meet with charming people and hospitality and attention, I should recommend all the world to hasten thither; but, since this can be found at home or elsewhere, from the same persons, I would not, for that reason alone, counsel a residence there. The accident of finding agreeable society amongst one's own countrymen has nothing to do with the Pyrenees; and we have so usurped the place of the original inhabitants, that only a very few French are left; in the same manner as at Boulogne or Tours. Almost all advantages, therefore, to be derived from foreign society are denied, and the frequent parties at Pau are nearly exclusively English.

More than one family whom I saw arrive, amused me by their raptures, similar to our own on the first view, on a fine day, of the mountains from the Place Royale or the park; and their subsequent discontent, when the absence of the fitful sun had entirely changed the scene, leaving only the damp dirty town, and a grey space, where the concealed giants shrouded themselves, sometimes for weeks together. People generally are so impressed at first, by the fascination of the *coup d'œil*, that they hasten to take a house which they cannot engage for less than six months, or, if for three, the price is advanced; fearing to miss the opportunity of settling themselves, they seldom hesitate about the terms, which are generally very high, and, when once placed, they begin to look about them, and regret that they were so precipitate; for they find themselves condemned to a long, dismal winter, in a very uninteresting, expensive town, without any resource beyond their windows, if they face the mountains; or their fire-side, if their chimney do not smoke—which is a rare happiness. There is scarcely a town in Italy, where numerous galleries are not ready to afford a constant intellectual treat, or where fine buildings cannot present objects of admiration; but in Pau all is barren: there is nothing but the mountains to look at—for the view of the hemmed-in-valley is extremely confined—and the park to walk in; which, after all, is a mere promenade, of no great length and no variety, in spite of its convenience and beauty. The ramparts of most towns in France, which are situated in a fine country, present great changes, and consequent excitement in the view; but at Pau it is always from the same spots that you must seek one prospect.

The walks out of the town are unpleasant; for almost every way you must traverse a long, dusty, or dirty suburb, and generally follow a high road to a great distance, before you arrive at the place which is to repay your toil: this is annoying, as—though climbing up *côteaux* and threading the mazes of vineyards is pleasant—two or three miles of dusty road, encumbered with bullock-carts and droves of pigs on the way and *on the return*, is by no means refreshing.

If pedestrians are not to be thought of, this is of no consequence, and, indeed, it is a circumstance which frequently occurs in French towns; those who take rides on horseback and venture a long way off, are more fortunate; for they come upon beautiful spots, and can reach sublime views amongst the mountains: a mere two hours' *drive* does not change the scene from that which is beheld from Pau, and the great similarity of all the views near greatly reduces their interest.

On the Bordeaux road, as Pau is approached, the sudden burst of the mountains on the sight is very fine; but there are no meadows, no lanes, nothing but a broad, *grande route*, from which the pedestrian can behold this. To reach the pretty *côteaux* of Jurançon and Gelos, one must walk for a mile and a half along a high road, and through a slovenly suburb; to reach the height of Bizanos, where a fine view of the mountains can be obtained, it is necessary to go through the whole straggling village of Bizanos, and run the gauntlet of a whole population of washerwomen, while every tree and hedge is hung with *drapery* bleaching in the air. Bizanos is called a *pretty village*; but those who so designate it can only be thinking of utility, like our hostess at La Rochelle, when she took us to a grand sight, which turned out to be no other than a washing-establishment. The French have, it is acknowledged, no taste for the picturesque, and it appeared to me as if the complaisance of the English abroad led them to agree that anything is pretty which pleases their foreign friends.

No doubt, there is infinitely better accommodation at Pau, than at any other town in the neighbourhood of the baths of the Pyrenees, and those who really require to attend them for several seasons—for it seems that it is generally necessary to do so—are quite right to make Pau their headquarters; but that those who seek amusement should remain at Pau in preference to Italy, or even other towns in France, is inexplicable. I do not know whether many return after they have once departed; but there are seldom fewer than six hundred English and Americans here in the winter. One English family arrived during our stay, took a large house, and made every arrangement for the winter; but, frightened by the continued bad weather, they left it in haste for Paris. I confess I was surprised others did not do the same.

All modern French writers describe Pau as "a *charming town*" alluding, of course, to the *society*, which is to them the great desideratum everywhere; besides, they are accustomed to ill-paved streets, and are not fastidious about cleanliness. The guide-books of these parts cite the descriptions of early writers in order to compare its present with its former state; two are given, which are certainly as much at variance as those obtained by strangers at the present day. In a work printed in 1776, the following passage occurs:

"The town of Pau is of an ordinary size; the greatest part of its houses are well-built, and covered with slate. It is the seat of a parliament, a university, an academy of *belles lettres*, and a mint. The greatest part of the *noblesse* of Béarn make it their usual abode; the Jesuits have a large college founded by Louis XIII. There is a seminary under the direction of the brothers of St. Lazare, a convent of Cordeliers, another of Capuchins, and four nunneries. At the western extremity of the town, is an ancient castle, where the princes of Béarn resided, and where King Henry IV. was born."

The intendant Lebret said of Pau, in 1700: —

"The town of Pau consists of two streets, tolerably long, but very ill-constructed; it possesses nothing considerable. The *palais* is one of the worst kept possible—the most incommodious, and the most dirty; the *maison de ville* is still worse. The parish church cannot contain a quarter of the inhabitants, and is, besides, as ill-supported and as bare of ornament as one would see in the smallest village."

Something between these two accounts might serve to give an idea of what the town is now: the public buildings are totally unworthy of mention, indeed, the only one at all remarkable is the new market-place, which is very large, and solidly built. The churches are more in number, but quite as insignificant as when Lebret wrote; the protestant *"temple"* has not more claim on observation as a piece of architecture, and, being built over the bed of a water-course, is supposed to be in some danger, and is extremely chill in winter. Through the midst of the town runs a deep ravine,—the bed of a stream called the Hédas—which divides it into two, and gives it a very singular effect; a bridge over this connects the two parts; the castle rises from one side, a venerable object; which, whenever seen, excites interest from its history rather than appearance; from this point it looks like an old prison, and the host of grim, dirty houses which clothe the steeps are anything but worthy of admiration.

The quarter of the Place Royale is called by the French, *the Chaussée d'Antin* of Pau—a somewhat ambitious distinction, which must a little surprise a Parisian when he enters it, and observes a shabby row of small low houses and cafés for the soldiery, on one side of the square space planted with trees, where the *élite* of Pau are supposed to walk. On the opposite side, a large hotel spreads out its courts, and a house with unpainted shutters and weather-stained walls; at the extremity, is what seems a ruined church, but which is, in fact, a building left half-finished to fall to decay, where the wood for the military is kept; nothing can be so desolate as the aspect on this side, and the stranger is amazed at the slovenly and dilapidated scene; but he must suspend his judgment, and walk along one of the short avenues till he reaches a parapet wall, where he forgets Pau and its faults in a single glance; for there the grand prospect of the mountains bursts upon him, and its magnificence can scarcely be exceeded.

As soon as the fine weather begins, this place, on a Sunday, is crowded with promenaders, principally tradespeople of the town. A military band is stationed here, and thunders forth peals of music much to the delight of the listeners. A very gay scene is presented on this occasion; but there is little characteristic, as no costumes are to be seen, and the *élégantes* of Pau are exactly like those of any other town.

Along the rugged, damp street, which runs from the back of the Place Royale, are most of the best houses in Pau: those on the side next the valley have the same glorious view as the promenade allows, and are generally taken by the English: one or two of these are fitted up in very good style, and made extremely comfortable; indeed, from this point mansion after mansion has been built, each of which has peculiar attractions; and, though not handsome or elegant, are good, square, large dwelling-houses, sufficiently convenient. These are designated by *French describers as magnifiques hôtels*, &c.; and fortunate are the English families who possess them as dwellings: they have all good gardens, and may boast of one of the finest views of the mountains that it is possible to obtain.

The college, founded by Henry IV., is a large and airy building, without grace or beauty, and enclosed in high walls: it has an imposing effect, from the height of the village of Bizanos, on the opposite side of the Gave.

The Hôtel de la Prefecture, and that where the valuable archives of the town are kept, possess neither beauty nor dignity: the space opposite is now occupied by the new market-house—which appears never to be used, for all the goods are spread out on the stones before it, as if it was only there for ornament: in this space, the guillotine was erected in the time of terror, and the murders of the great, and good, and respectable inhabitants took place. Unfortunately, this is a record, too recent, which every town in France can furnish.

It appears to me that the people of Pau are quiet, honest, simple, and obliging; at least, we never saw an instance to the contrary, except on our first arrival, when our driver took off the horses from the carriage in the inn-yard, and refused to go a step further to seek for accommodation for us; but I suspect he was not a native of the town. The landlady of the inn—who came from Bordeaux—with a mysterious wink, assured us we should find all the common people the same—"*Ces Béarnais sont tous brutals!*" was her remark; but we did not find her in the right.

The Gascon character, though here a little softened, prevails a good deal, as the continued boasting about their town proves, and a certain pomposity in their demeanour, which, however, is harmless and amusing. We were in the habit of employing a baker, who made what was called English bread, and the magnificent manner in which he paid his visits to our domicile was very comic. Our maid, Jeannotte, being out of the way, we were one day disturbed by a vociferous knocking at our parlour-door—for in general all the passage-doors are left open—and hurrying to admit the clamorous visitant, we beheld the baker's assistant, M. Auguste, with a tray of loaves on his head and one in his hand, which he thrust forth, accompanying the action with a flourish and a low bow, exclaiming, "De la part de César!" We were not then aware that such was the name of our baker, and were much awed by the announcement.

Another of our domestic visitors was a source of considerable entertainment to us, and became still more so through the *espièglerie* of our attendant, Jeannotte, who took occasion to mystify him at our expense. This object of mirth was a little stout mountaineer, who came every week from his home in the mountains—between the valleys of Ossau and Aspe—with a load of butter and cheese, with which his strong, sure-footed horse was furnished. In the severest weather this little man would set out; and on one occasion his horse had to be dug out of the snow in one of the passes; but the desire of gain, which invariably actuates these people, and a carelessness of hardship, made him treat all his dangers lightly. He was in the habit of coming to us every week, and generally made his way to our part of the house, as he appeared amused to *look at us* as much as we were to converse with him, and ask him questions about bears, wolves, and avalanches.

His stock of French was small, and he had a peremptory way of demanding what he required, as he divided his neat pieces of butter for our service. He could not be more than five feet high, but was a sturdy, strong-built man, though of very small proportions. One day when delivering his charge to Jeannotte, she asked him in *patois*,—her own tongue—if he was married; he started at the question, and begged to know her reason for inquiring; she informed him it was for the benefit of Mademoiselle, who wished to know. The little hero paused, and presently, in rather an anxious tone, demanded of Jeannotte what mademoiselle's reason could possibly be for requiring the knowledge. "There is no telling," said she, archly, "Mademoiselle thinks you very amiable."

"Is it possible!!" said he, musing; "you don't surely imagine—*do* you think she would have me?"

The laughter of Jeannotte quite abashed the gallant mountaineer, and he replaced his load of butter on his brown *berret* and disappeared, nor would he for some time afterwards pay us a visit. At length he did so, and I found his modest confusion apparent in his forgetting to take the full change of his money, actually on one occasion abandoning *half a sous* of his just due, and retiring with a "C'est égal." When we told him we were going away he was much struck, and stayed longer than usual gazing at us, till we thought he intended to open his mind, and declare his intentions to share his mountain-home with one of our party. I therefore gave him a note of recommendation for his butter to a friend, and he retired apparently more satisfied, though with a heavy sigh and a murmured hope—expressed half in *patois*—that we would come back to the Pyrenees in the summer.

There is still a good deal of simplicity left amongst this people, and certainly but little wit. Strong affection seems to be felt by them towards their relations, and quarrels seem rare; the Béarnais are said to be drunkards; but I never remember to have seen any instances of this in the streets. They are slovenly, and the lower classes extremely dirty; the market-women, in their white flannel peaked hoods of a hideous form, or their handkerchiefs loosely tied, without grace and merely for warmth, have in the cold season a very unpicturesque appearance, and the shrill shrieking voices of those who scream hot chesnuts to sell about the streets, uttering their piercing cry of *"tou cai, tou cai!"*[2] is anything but pleasing to the ear.

The servants, however, seem good, industrious, honest, and very civil; and, as far as our own experience went, we saw only good conduct; while from our hostess at the Bain Royal we met with liberality and extreme courtesy; she, it is true, is from the refined city of Toulouse, but has long resided at Pau, and I should certainly counsel any stranger, whom, they would suit, to choose her apartments as a residence; for her pavilions are situated in the most agreeable position, out of the noise and dampness of the town, and with the whole range of Pyrenees constantly in uninterrupted view.

------

[2] All hot! all hot!

CHAPTER II.

The Climate Of Pau—Storms—Fine Weather—Palassou—Reasons
For Going To Pau—The Winter.

ONE of the chief inducements to foreigners, particularly the English, to visit
Pau for the winter, is the reputation of its climate for mildness and softness. When
we arrived, in October, in a storm of rain, it was, we understood, the continuation
of a series of wet weather, which, throughout the year, had made the whole country desolate, and the company at all the baths had, in consequence, left a month
sooner than usual; for a fortnight after our establishment at Pau, nothing could
be more agreeable than the season, precisely answering to the beautiful weather
which my letters announced from different parts of England. During this time the
mountains were rarely visible, and when seen appeared indistinctly. This charming fortnight, during which Pau seemed to deserve all the commendations so pro-
fusely bestowed on it, was a promise of the calm and peaceful winter which I was
told was always to be found in these favoured regions; I bore the sarcasms against
the fogs and, above all, the uncertainty of the climate of gloomy England, as well
as I could; and my assertion that, till the first week in November, I had last year
bathed in the sea at Brighton, was received with indulgent smiles of pity at my
nationality, both by French and English; but of course not believed, for the air of
France, I have always observed, has such a property of effacing the remembrance
of sunny days passed on the other side of the channel, that, by degrees, our countrymen arrive at the belief that nothing but fog and rain are ever to be seen in our
ill-fated island, and they imagine that, till they came abroad, their knowledge of
blue sky or bright sun was obtained only in pictures, but had no existence on the
banks of the Thames or elsewhere, in the desolate regions they had quitted.

The morning of the 18th of October rose brilliantly, and was succeeded by a
burning day; in the afternoon ominous clouds suddenly appeared, and brought
a storm of rain and hail, whose effects were felt in the extreme cold of the atmosphere for some days, when another change came over the face of things, which
brought forth the character of this calm, quiet place, where the excessive *stillness*
of the air is cited as almost wearying, in quite a different light. It has been said,
and is frequently cited, that a certain sea-captain left Pau in disgust, after passing
some months there, because he could never obtain a *capful of wind*. If that anony-
mous gentleman had had the good fortune to be at Pau on the night of the 23rd
of October, I think he would have fixed his domicile for the rest of his life there;
for such a furious hurricane he could seldom have had the good fortune to enjoy.
For four hours in the dead of night, without intermission, the howling of the wind

through the gorges of the mountains, the rush and swell amongst the hills, vales, and across the plains, was perfectly appalling. Every moment seemed to threaten annihilation to all within its reach; chimneys were dashed down in every direction, trees torn up by the roots, and the triumph of the tempest fiend complete. Furious rain and hail succeeded on the following day, with occasional gleams of sun; and then came a calm, beautiful, summer day again, and the mountains shone out as brightly as possible. This gave place to thick fog and a severe frost on the very next day, lasting for several days; rain then diversified the scene, and on the 29th a wind rose in the night almost as furious as the last, which continued the whole of the day following: a cold gloomy morrow, and the next bright, hot, and pleasant, ended October.

The next day was a triumph for Pau:—"When," asked every one we met—"when, in *England*, would you see such a 1st of November?" All my vivid recollections of charming strolls on the beach and downs in Sussex, and in Windsor Park, were looked upon as figments. I heard no boasting on the 2nd, nor for three more days, for it was foggy, and rained hard, and no one could stir out. On the 6th, a heavy fall of snow had clothed the whole country in white; and now, for three days, a sharp, frosty wind prevented any more remarks about the softness of the climate. The frost and snow had disappeared, as by enchantment, on the 11th, the night of which was so sultry that to keep windows shut was impossible. The Fair of Pau was ushered in by rain, on the 12th; the 13th was as hot as the hottest day in July, accompanied by a good deal of fog, for several days: then came violent wind, hail-storms, wind again—louder and more furious—fog, cold, occasionally bright; and November disappeared on a misty morning, which ended in a burning day, without a breath of air, all glare and faintness.

We were now told that, though St. Martin had failed to keep his summer at the right time, he was never known to desert his post; and as in almanacks a day before or a day after makes no difference, we were content to accept his smiles for nine days in the beginning of December. Again came the question—"When, in England?" &c. and I began to think we were peculiarly favoured, when, lo! letters arrived from that vexatious clime, speaking of "days perfectly lovely," "new summer," and all precisely like a plagiarism on Pau. Fortunately for the reputation of the Pyrenees, no one would, of course, credit this fact; and the English invalids, who had been covering their mouths with handkerchiefs, and shutting themselves up from the variations of the atmosphere, breathed again, and at once generously forgot all but the bright sun and warm air which had come once more to greet them.

It was true that every leaf had long since disappeared from the trees in the park, and that the sun glared fearfully on the high, unsheltered walks; but the partisans of salubrity hastened to disport themselves in its rays, till *three cases in one week* of *coup de soleil* began to startle even the most presuming; and the expected death of one of the patients, together with *another change* of weather to wet, cold, and fog, silenced further remark.

We were assured that the extraordinary alternations of climate we had experienced for two months, was a circumstance quite unheard-of before in Pau, and we looked on ourselves as singularly unlucky in having, by chance, chosen a season so unpropitious. A few simple persons, who ventured to remark that the winter of last year was very similar, were told that they must have been mistaken; and some who recollected high winds were considered romancers. We looked at the strong *contre-vents* placed outside the windows of our dwelling, and wondered why such a work of supererogation should have taken place as to put them there, if the hurricanes we had witnessed were unusual, when I one day, during a high wind, as I sat at home, happened to take up Palassou's Mémorial des Pyrénées, and read as follows:—

"TEMPERATURE OF THE LOWER PYRENEES—
ITS EFFECTS OFTEN DANGEROUS.

"It is well known that divers places differ in their temperature, although they are situated in the same degrees of latitude; the vicinity of the sea, of great rivers, mountainous chains, &c. renders the air more or less hot or cold, serene or cloudy; the modifications which these circumstances occasion are principally remarked in the countries adjacent to the Pyrenees. Snow, frost, and abundant rains, are, for instance, more frequent than in Languedoc or Provence, although these climates are placed beneath the same degree of latitude as the former.

"It is easy to believe that vegetable nature feels this influence. If we except the plains of Roussillon, and some small cantons situated at the foot of the eastern Pyrenees, where a mild temperature may be found, it is to be observed that nowhere, contiguous to this chain, are seen the odoriferous plants and trees common to the South of France. The eye seeks in vain the pomegranate, with its rich crimson fruit; the olive is unknown; the lavender requires the gardener's aid to grow. The usual productions of this part are heath, broom, fern, and other plants, with prickly thorns: these hardy shrubs seem fitted, by their sterility, to the variable climate which they inhabit.

"In effect, the snows of winter, covering the summits of the Pyrenees for too long a time, prolong the cold of this rigorous season sometimes to the middle of spring; then come the frosts which destroy the hopes of the vine-grower.

"'*Storms are very frequent in Béarn,*' says M. Lebret, intendant of Béarn in 1700; he might have added," continues Palassou, "to the list of dangers to the harvests— *the frequent and destructive fogs* to which the country is subject.

"In the landes of the Pont-Long, I have often seen, in the environs of Pau, fogs rise from those grounds covered with fern, broom, and other naturally growing plants, while in parts more cultivated it was clear. * * * The agriculturists of Béarn have not attempted to till the lands in the neighbourhood of Pau, finding them too stubborn to give hopes of return, and *the climate being so very variable*; cultivated produce being peculiarly sensible to the effects of an air which *is one day burning and the next icy.*

"One might write whole volumes if it was the object to relate all the effects of storms which, accompanied with hail, devastate the countries in the neighbourhood of the Pyrenees. It will be sufficient to recount what has come under my own observation. During one violent storm of thunder and lightning, the hail-stones were *as large as hens' eggs*, and desolated the whole range over which it swept. It was immediately followed by a second, less furious, but which did immense damage; and others, little less terrific, followed in the course of the month—June."

Palassou here goes on to describe several dreadful storms of peculiar fury, which were more than usually destructive, and are common in these regions. He considers, that the cutting down of the forests on the mountains, which formerly sheltered the plains and valleys, has contributed to increase the storms in latter years. Summer in the midst of winter, seems by no means uncommon, and winter in summer as little so. The *autun*, or south wind, generally brings the burning days which so much surprised me; but, according to this author, *it is extremely unwholesome* and dangerous to persons inclined to apoplexy; as, indeed, its effects during our stay at Pau led me to imagine.

I cannot feel much confidence, I confess, in a climate where you are told that so many precautions must be taken: for instance, you are never to walk in the sun; you must avoid going out in the evening, at all seasons; you must be careful not to meet the south wind; in fact, you can scarcely move without danger. I ask myself, what can possibly induce so many of my countrymen to travel so far for such a climate,—to put themselves to so great an expense for such a result? for, if England is not perfect as to climate, it has at any rate few unhealthy spots from which you cannot readily escape to a better position: we are never in terror of a *sirocco*,—nor need wrap up our mouths in handkerchiefs to avoid breathing *malaria*. Our climate is variable, but less so than in the Pyrenees; and it is scarcely worth while to go so far to find one worse, and more dangerous to life. Hurricanes are rarer with us than there. We may not often have such hot summers in winter, but neither do we *often* have such cold winters in summer. It frequently rains with us, but it rains as often at Pau; and, however annoying are the variations of which we complain at home, we assuredly do not escape them by travelling eight hundred miles to take up our abode close to icy mountains, in a dirty, damp town, in an uncomfortable house: add to which, we gain little in economy; for Pau is as dear as Paris, without any of the advantages of the capital.

Altogether, the more experience I have of the climate of Pau, the more surprised I am at the crowds of English who resort to this town for the winter: the greatest part of them, it is true, are not invalids, but persons seduced into this nook by its reputation, and arriving too late in the season to leave it. They grumble, and are astonished to find themselves no better off than if they had stayed at home; but they are, it would seem, ashamed to confess how much they have been deceived, and, therefore, remain silent on the subject of climate, content to praise the beauty of the country in fine weather, and enjoy the gaieties and hospitalities which they are sure to meet with. If people came only for the latter advantages, I should not be surprised at their trooping hitherward, provided they were robust enough to bear the *mildness* of climate; but that is not the avowed reason, and those they give are altogether insufficient to account for the mania of wintering at Pau.

Perhaps the best means of ascertaining the nature of the climate is by occasionally looking over old newspapers. In a French one of Jan. 10, 1841, I was struck with this announcement: "Pau.—On Thursday last, in the night, the snow fell so abundantly that it was half-way up the legs, in the morning, in the streets. On Friday morning the *porte-cochère* of one of the *splendid hotels in our Chaussée d'Antin (!)* opened, and forth issued an elegant sledge, drawn by two *magnificent* horses, crowned with white plumes. This novel spectacle attracted the attention of the whole town. The elegant vehicle darted along till it reached the Rue de la Prefecture, &c. &c. and the Pont-Long."

It must be confessed that it is seldom in any part of our *cold climate* that we have the power of such an exhibition in the streets. It is reserved for the invalids who fly to the South of France to avoid a severe winter.

"23rd Dec. 1840. A great deal of snow has fallen between Bayonne and Peyrehorade: the road is become almost impassable."

But I must continue the winter as I found it at Pau in 1842 and 1843. December, with intervals of two days' wind and rain, was extremely pleasant, bright, and clear, and the days very long; for till half-past four one could see to write or read: a circumstance which does not often occur in England during this month. Christmas Day differed but little from many I have known at home: pleasant, bright, sunny, and clear; rather cold, but more agreeable, from its freshness, than the unnatural heat which sometimes accompanies the sun. All the accounts from England proved that the weather was precisely the same. For the two next days, it was fine and very cold, with a high, *easterly* wind; two days warm and pleasant; then succeeded a sharp frost and bright sun; and December closed, dull, cold, and dark.

January began cold, sharp, and gusty—some days biting, and some black and foggy; and from the 5th to the 12th it blew a perfect hurricane, with thunder, one fine day intervening, and occasionally a few bright hours in the course of some of the days. The storm on the night of the 11th was terrific, and it lasted, equally violent, with hail and thunder, all the next day—bright gleams of sun darting out for a moment, and revealing the mountains, to close them in again with mist and rain before you had scarcely time to remark the change. About the middle of the day the wind increased in violence, and the hail came down with fury, thick grey clouds gathered over the sky, the lightning flashed vividly, the thunder echoed far and near, and the gusts howled as if hundreds of wolves were abroad. King Arthur and all his *meinie* must have been out, for the appearance over the mountains was most singular. A broad space of clear *green-blue* sky was seen just above the white summits of several of the mountains, clearly showing the large fields of snow which extended along their flat surfaces, which are broken at the sides by projections, like buttresses, of purple rock, on which dark shadows fell; gleams of sun illumined the edges of the snow on the highest peaks, for a brief space, while, by degrees, the other mountains were sinking away into a thick haze which had already covered the nearest hills. The marshy fields on the banks of the murmuring Gave, and the little Ousse, now swelled to large rivers, and as thick and clay-coloured as the Garonne itself, were covered with a coating of hail, and the snow and transparent mist were seen driving along from peak to peak with amazing rapidity, as if they had been smoke. Presently, the narrow space of blue sky was dotted with small grey specks, as if showers were falling from the heavy canopy above, and, shutting closer and closer, the great mass suddenly sank down, concealing the glittering peaks which strove to shine out to the last. Then all became black; the thunder roared, the wind howled, the hail beat, and winter and storm prevailed. I watched all this with delight; for it was impossible to see anything more sublime, and I could not but congratulate myself that the abode we had chosen, just above the valley and detached from the town, at the foot of the promenade of the Place Royale, gave us an opportunity of seeing such a storm in perfection. It was true that we often thus had our rest disturbed at night, by the sweep of the wind along the whole range of the valley between the *côteaux*; but its melancholy sound, bringing news, as it were, from the mountains and the sea, was pleasant music to my ears, and startling and exciting, when it rose to the ungovernable fury with which I became so well acquainted during our winter at this *quiet place for invalids*!

If Pau were recommended as a place where storms could be seen in perfection, I should not wonder at persons crowding there, who delight in savage nature. The gales from the 5th to the 15th continued furiously, night and day; the wind howled from all points, rocking the houses, and strewing the ground with ruins—then came a change to hot quiet days for a week.

In England, and in all parts of France, the season I am describing was equally violent, but this only proves that Pau has no shelter on these occasions.

January ended with fine weather, and occasional fogs, not so dense as in London, certainly, but as thick as in the country in England. The sun, in the middle of the day, being always dangerously hot. My letters from England still announced the same weather, *without the danger*.

In February, we had a few days like August, then a heavy fall of snow, which for eight days covered the ground, and was succeeded by burning days; and the month ended with heavy rain and floods. March began with cold winds and rain and sharp frost; and when I left Pau the ground was encrusted with frost in all directions.

EXTERIOR OF THE CASTLE OF PAU.

CHAPTER III.

The Castle Of Henri Quatre—The Furniture—The Shell—The Statue—The Birth—Castel Beziat—The Fairy Gift—A Change—Henri Quatre.

"Qui a vist le castig de Pau
Jamey no a viat il fait."

When Napoleon, in 1808, passed through the town of Pau, the Béarnais felt
wounded and humbled at the indifference he showed to the memory of their hero,
Henri Quatre: he scarcely deigned to glance at the château in which their cherished countryman was born; and with so little reverence did he treat the monument dear to every heart in Béarn, that his soldiers made it a barrack; and, without

a feeling of regard or respect for so sacred a relic, used it as cavalierly *as if it had been a church*. They stabled their steeds in the courts of Gaston Phoebus, they made their drunken revelry resound in the chambers of Marguerite de Valois; and they desecrated the retreat where *La brebis a enfanté un Lio*—where Jeanne d'Albret gave birth to him, who, in the language of his mountains, promised that every French-man should have a *poule au pot*[3] in his reign.

That Napoleon should not care for a royal soldier, whose fame he desired his own deeds should eclipse; and of whom, as of all illustrious men, living or dead, the *little* great man was jealous, is not surprising. He had nothing in common with Henri Quatre; and the Revolution, which had brought him forward, had swept away antique memories. The statue of their once-adored Henri had been cast into the Seine with ignominy, by the French, and his name was execrated, as if he had been no better than the legitimate race whom popular fury condemned to obliv-ion: Napoleon's policy was not to restore an abandoned worship; and he would have seen the last stone fall from the castle of Pau without notice. But that the long line of kings, who were always boasting of their descent from the immortal Béar-nais, should have neglected, contemned, or pillaged his birth-place, reflects little honour on the memory of any. The son of Mary de Medici came only to Béarn after his father's death, to carry off all that was precious in art, collected by the kings and queens of Navarre, for centuries—treasures which, according to the historians of the time, had not their parallel in the sixteenth century. The palace of the Louvre became rich in the spoils of Béarn: tapestry, pictures, furniture, objects of *virtu* of all kinds were borne away, and nothing left in its original place. Louis the Four-teenth and his successor occupied themselves little with the country, except to levy subsidies upon it: they knew nor cared nothing for Navarre; except as it supplied them with titles or gave them funds. Louis the Sixteenth, the last of the Bourbons who took the oath to observe the *Fors*[4] of Béarn, promised to act differently, and to occupy himself with this forgotten nook of his dominions; but the fatal events, prepared by his profligate predecessors of the last two reigns, which hurled him from his throne, prevented the accomplishment of his intentions.

As for the sovereign people, when they became rulers, the contempt with which they overwhelmed everything aristocratic, was bestowed in full measure on the abode of him who had been their friend: and the triumph of vengeance, ignorance, and ingratitude, was complete, here as elsewhere.

The neglected castle of the sovereigns of Béarn,—for none of whom, except the immediate family of the brave and bold Henry, need one care to be a champi-on—remained then a mighty heap of ruin, which every revolving year threatened to bring nearer to utter destruction; when another revolution, like an earthquake, whose shock may restore to their former place, rocks, which a preceding convul-sion had removed, came to "renew old Æson:" Louis Philippe, to whom every nook and corner of his extensive kingdom seems familiar, so far from forgetting the *berceau* of his great ancestor, hastened to extend to the castle of Pau a saving hand, and to bring forth from ruin and desolation the fabric which weeds and ivy

---

[3] The *poule au Pot* is a general dish with the Béarnais.

[4] The celebrated Laws of Béarn are called *Les Fors*.

were beginning to cover, and which would soon have been ranged with the shells of Chinon, Loches, and other wrecks of days gone by.

When the architect, employed by the king to execute the Herculean labour of restoring the castle of Pau, first arrived, and saw the state of dilapidation into which it had fallen, he must have been appalled at the magnitude of his undertaking. Seeing it, as I do now,[5] grim, damp, rugged, ruined, and desolate, even in its state of transition, after several years of toil have been spent upon its long-deserted walls; I can only feel amazed that the task of renovating a place so decayed should ever have been attempted; but, after what has been done, it may well be hoped and expected that the great work will be, in the end, fully accomplished; and ten years hence, the visitor to Pau will disbelieve all that has been said of the melancholy appearance of the château of Henri Quatre.

What must have been the state of things before the pretty bridge, which spans the road and leads from the castle terrace to the walk, called La Basse Plante, existed? I am told that a muddy stream, bordered with piles of rubbish, filled up this portion of the scene; but, in less than a year, all was changed, and the pleasant terrace and neat walks which adorn this side of the castle are promises of much more, equally ornamental and agreeable.

Some of the tottering buildings attached to the strangely-irregular mass, were, it seems, condemned by the bewildered architect to demolition, as possessing no beauty, and encumbering the plans of improvement; but the late Duke of Orleans came to visit the castle, and had not the heart to give consent that any of the old walls, still standing, should be swept away. He looked at the place with true poetic and antiquarian feeling, and arrested the hand of the mason, who would have destroyed that part called *La Chancellerie*, which extends between the donjon of Gaston Phoebus to the Tour Montauzet. The prince represented to his father his views on the subject, which were instantly adopted—a question of taste in that family meets with no opposition—and all was to have been arranged according to the ideas of the heir of France, who seemed inclined to make Pau an abode at a *future day*: the King was to have visited the interesting old castle: much animated discussion and much enthusiasm prevailed on the subject in the interior of the royal circle, and the Berceau of Henri Quatre seemed destined to proud days again.

"When, hush! hark! a deep sound comes like a rising knell!"

The wail of a whole nation tells that that *anticipated future* may not come! A cloud has again gathered over the valley of the Gave, and a sad pause—the pause of blighted hopes—has chilled the expectations in which Béarn had ventured to indulge.

But the castle is not, even now, neglected: the architects are still there; workmen are still busy, chiseling and planing; the beautiful arabesques and reliefs are coming forth to view, restored with all their original delicacy: the ceilings are glowing with fresh gilding, the walls are bright with fresh tapestry, and the rooms are newly floored. But for the dreadful event which must cast a gloom over France for some years, the castle would, probably, have been sufficiently put in order for

---

[5] This was written on the spot.

a royal visitor this year; but all the magnificent furniture, sent down from Paris to fit up the *suite* intended for use, now stands unarranged, and a stop is put to embellishment. Amongst the most curious and interesting pieces of this furniture, are the bed and chair of Jeanne d'Albret, her screen—perhaps worked by her own hand—and the bed of Henry II.: all fine specimens of art in this style; the latter, in particular, is quite unique, and is one of the most curious I have ever seen: the sculpture is very elaborate; at the foot reclines, in relief, a Scotch guard, such as always lay at the threshold of the sovereign, at the period when this piece of furniture was made. An owl of *singular expression* sits watching, opposite, surrounded by foliage and poppies, quite in character with the sleepy scene: the posts of the bedstead are beautifully turned: it is so formed as to draw out and close in, forming a *bed by night, a cabinet by day*; and the carved arch at the back is sculptured in the most exquisite manner. A *prie-Dieu* of the same date is near; but all this furniture is merely *housed* for the present, as nothing is arranged; one, of course, looks at these specimens with an admiration which has nothing to do with Henri Quatre's castle, as they would be equally well placed in M. de Somerard's museum, at the delightful Hôtel de Cluny.

A tapestry screen, said to be of the time of Charles VII., has a place in this heterogeneous collection: it represents the Maid of Orleans, crowned by victorious France, whose *lilies* are restored, and her enemies trampled under her feet; in the back-ground is the sea, with strange-looking monsters huddled into its waves, in apparent terror: these are the Leopards of England taking flight from the shores of France. The colours are well preserved in this piece of work, and the whole composition deserves to be remarked, if not for the correctness of its drawing, for the *naïveté* of its details.

It might have been better to have filled the castle with furniture belonging exclusively to the time, or anterior to that of Henry IV.; and it struck me that much which has arrived from Paris, of the period of Louis XIV., is out of keeping with the *souvenirs* of the castle of Pau. I almost hope that, if ever it is entirely restored, these pieces of furniture will be banished, and others, more antique, substituted. The tapestry with which the walls are covered is very curious and appropriate; it is chiefly of the time of Francis I.; and some beautiful Gobelins, of modern date, representing different scenes in the life of Henry, equally so.

The most, indeed the only, beautiful portions of the castle, are the ceilings of the principal staircase and passages leading from it; the medallions of which present the heads of Marguerite de Valois and her husband, Henry d'Albret, with their interlaced initials and arms on the walls: these again occur on the mantel-pieces, in the midst of very exquisite arabesques, which the skill of the modern sculptor is restoring with singular delicacy.

The object which excites the most interest in the castle, is the famous shell of a tortoise, of immense size, said to have served as a cradle to the little hero whose birth was hailed with such rapture by his expectant grandfather. One would fain believe that this is indeed the identical *berceau de Henri IV.* so much talked of; but it is difficult to reconcile all the improbabilities of its being so: the substitution of another, after the real shell had been burnt in the castle-court, may do credit to those who cherish the hero's name; always provided no less generous motive induced the act; but the tale told to prove its identity is, unfortunately, not convincing.

The shell is suspended in the centre of a chamber, formerly the *salle de réception* of Henry II. d'Albret, and surrounded with trophies, in tawdry taste, which it is the intention to have removed, and the gilt helmet and feathers replaced by some armour really belonging to King Henry.

Those who contend for this being the genuine shell say, that, when on the 1st of May, 1793, the revolutionary mob came howling into the castle-court, with the intention of destroying every relic of royalty, the precious shell was hastily removed, and *another put in its place*, belonging to a loyal subject who had been induced to sacrifice his own to save the public treasure. M. de Beauregard had, it seems, a cabinet of natural history, in which was a tortoise-shell of very similar size and appearance: this he gave up, and, with the assistance of other devoted persons, it was conveyed to the castle, and put into the accustomed place, while the real shell was carefully hidden in a secure retreat. The mob seized upon the substitute, and, with frantic cries, danced round the fire in the court while they saw it burn to ashes, little dreaming how they had been deceived: years after, the truth was revealed, and the cradle of the Béarnais was produced in triumph. Whether, in the midst of the terror attending the proceedings of savages athirst for blood, it was likely that such cool precautions were taken to save a *relic* when *lives* were at stake, is a question which seems easily answered; but there is such a charm about the belief, that, perhaps, *'tis folly to be wise* on the subject.

The fine marble statue of Henry, which is appropriately placed in one of the chambers, was executed soon after the battle of Ivry: it is by Francavilla, and very expressive: it belonged to the Gallery of Orleans, and was presented to the town of Pau by the King.

The room said to be that where Henry was born, and where Jeanne d'Albret sang the famous invocation, "*Notre Dame au bout du Pont*," is on the second story of a tower, from whence, as from all this side of the castle, is a magnificent view of the mountains, and the valley of the Gave. There is nothing now left but bare walls; but on the chimney is sculptured the tortoise-shell cradle, and the arms of Béarn and Navarre; these rooms will be all repaired and restored; at present, the whole *suite* reminded me of the desolation of the castle of Blois, which was desecrated in the same manner by soldiery, who made it a barrack. The room which was Henry's nursery has a few of the original rude rafters of the ceiling remaining, which one would wish should not be removed; but it is said that it is necessary. The thick coating of whitewash cleared away from the chimney-piece will, probably, disclose more sculpture, similar to that in the other rooms.

Queen Jeanne had been unfortunate in losing her other children, one of whom died in a melancholy manner. While she was out hunting with her father and her husband, the nurse and one of her companions, being at a loss to amuse themselves, thought of a game, in which they threw the child from one window to the other, catching it in turns. The poor little prince was made the victim to this cruel folly, for he fell on the balcony which extended along the first-floor, and broke one of his ribs. He suffered much, and survived only a few days. No wonder Queen Jeanne sent her little son, Henry, to a cottage, to be nursed, where there was no upper story!

Nothing can be less imposing, on the interior side of the court, than the castle of Pau: ruined, dilapidated buildings surround the rugged old well which stands in the centre; towers and *tourelles*, of various shapes, lift their grey and green and damp-stained heads in different angles; low door-ways, encumbered with dust and rubbish, open their dark mouths along the side opposite the red square tower of Gaston Phoebus, which frowns at its equally grim brother, whose mysterious history no one knows; other doors and windows are finely-sculptured; and medallions, much defaced, adorn the walls.

On these antique towers, it is said the thunder never fell but once—*that once* was on the 14th of May, 1610, at the very moment when the steel of Ravaillac found the heart of Henry of Navarre. The event is thus recorded:—

"A fearful storm burst over the town of Pau on this day; a thunderbolt fell, and defaced the royal arms over the castle-gateway; and a fine bull, which was called *the King*, from its stately appearance, the chief of a herd called *the royal herd*, terrified by the noise and clamour, precipitated itself over the walls into the ditch of the castle, and was killed. The people, hurrying to the spot, called out The *King* is dead! The news of the fatal event in Paris reached Pau soon after, and they found their loss indeed irreparable."

The shades of Henry and Sully are said sometimes *to walk* along the ramparts even now; and it was formerly believed that near the great reservoir, into which it was said Queen Jeanne used to have her Catholic prisoners thrown, numerous ghosts of injured men might be seen flitting to and fro. One evening I was returning, later than usual, from the promenade in the park, and had paused so often on my way to observe the effect of the purple and rosy-tinted mountains glowing with the last rays of sunset, that it was in quite a dim light that I reached the spot beneath which the ivied head of the old, ruined, red Tour de la Monnaie shows the rents of its *machicoulis*. A double row of young trees is planted here, at the foot of the artificial mound which supports the castle walls, and at the end of the alley is the reservoir, with the square tower of Gaston Phoebus above it. I was startled by a sudden apparition, so vivid that it seemed impossible to mistake its form, passing by the reservoir, as if after descending the steep which leads to it. I *seemed to see* a grey, transparent figure in armour, the head covered with a helmet, with a pointed frontlet, such as I had seen in an old gallery, filled with rusty coats of arms, at the Château of Villebon, near Chartres, where Sully had lived for five-and-twenty years, and where he died. The figure was slight, and moved slowly, waving its head gently: it was in good proportion, but at least eight feet high. I stopped astonished, for the vision was so very plain—and then it was gone. I continued my way, and again I saw it, and it appeared as if several others, less tall, but still in armour, were by its side, by no means so distinct. I paused again, it was growing darker and darker, and I then could distinguish nothing but a row of slender trees, whose delicate leaves were shivering in the evening breeze, and whose stems waved to and fro. I went home—through the chill damp castle court, and across the bridge to the dismal street—impressed with an agreeable, though somewhat tremulous conviction, that I must have seen some of the ghosts which haunt the walks of the old castle.

I expected to hear that the memory of Queen Jeanne was venerated on this spot; but was surprised to find that she holds a place in tradition little more honourable than that occupied by our bloody Queen Mary; for there is scarcely any atrocity in history of which she is not the heroine: whatever might have been her fame with her Protestant subjects, those who succeeded them seemed carefully to have treasured the remembrance of all the cruelties executed by her orders, which, it must be acknowledged, were little in accordance with the religion of peace she professed to have adopted. Her son, whose faith was of so changeable a character that it suited all parties, is the pride and boast of the country; but the object of love appears to be the amiable Princess Catherine, his sister, for whom her mother built, in a secluded spot in the royal park, a residence, called *Castel Beziat*, the last stones of which have now disappeared, as well as the *gardens* originally planted by Gaston XI., in 1460, and said, in the time of Henri II. and Marguerite, *to be the finest in Europe*. It is difficult now to imagine where they were; but they are said to have been on the south side, and probably extended along that part now occupied by the Basse Plante and the baths of Henri Quatre, as far as the present entrance of the park.

Catherine was more sought in marriage, perhaps, than any princess of her time; but her only attachment—which was an unfortunate one—was to the Count de Soissons, who, being her brother's enemy, avowed or concealed, was an unfit match for her, and the alliance was opposed by all her friends. She seemed to possess the accomplishments of her grandmother and mother, and was very popular in Béarn, which she governed, during Henry the Fourth's absence, with great justice and judgment; the Béarnais, however, greatly offended her by their violent opposition to her marriage with the person she had chosen; and she left the Castle of Pau in anger, and never returned. She was forced into a marriage with the Duke de Bar, and her people saw her no more.

There is a romantic story told of an act of the princess's, which shows her kind character, and amiable feeling. There was formerly in the gardens of Castel (or Castet) Beziat, (the *Castle of the beloved*,) a fountain, afterwards called *Des cents Ecus*, which had its name from the following circumstances:

The Princess Catherine of Navarre was one day walking in a musing mood, probably thinking of the many difficulties which opposed her union with him she loved, and almost wishing that her stars had made her one of the careless peasant-girls who tended her flocks in the green meadows beside the murmuring Gave; for happiness was denied her, as she said in after times, when married to a man who was indifferent to her, "Qu'elle n'avait pas son *compte*," mournfully playing on her disappointment. Suddenly she heard voices, and, peeping through the thick foliage, she perceived two young girls seated by the side of the fountain. One was drowned in tears, and the other was leaning over her, with tender words and caresses, endeavouring to console her sorrows. "Alas!" said the fair distressed, "I can see no end to my sorrow, for poverty is the cause; you know, my parents have nothing but what they gain by labour, and though *his* friends are richer, their avarice is extreme; and they say their son's bride must have a dower of a hundred crowns. Ah! my dear friend, what hope then have I! I have heard that there are fairies who have the power to assist true love; if I knew where they were to be found I would consult them, for never was love truer than ours, or more unfortunate."

Her friend did not attempt to combat her affection, but encouraged her with soothing words to have patience, and hope for the best. "Let us meet again here," said she, "every day, and devise some plan; perhaps Heaven will hear our prayers, and take compassion on your sorrow. To-morrow, at this hour, let us meet." "We will so," said the weeping girl, "for if I have no other consolation,—you, at least, give me that of talking of him."

The friends departed, leaving the listening princess full of interest and curiosity: she was resolved to surprise and befriend the lovers whose case was so touching. "There is, then, equal sorrow in a lowly state," she mused, "and love seems always doomed to tears; however, there are some obstacles which fortune permits to be removed—would that I could look forward to relief, as I am resolved these shall!"

The next day saw the two friends again seated on the borders of the fountain; but scarcely had they taken their accustomed place, when they observed, lying on a stone close by, a little bag which seemed to contain something heavy; they opened it, and found a paper, on which these words were written: "Behold what has been sent you by a *fairy*." The delight of this discovery may be imagined, and the pleasure of the princess, by whose command, a few days afterwards, the union of the lovers was accomplished.

It appears that the Castle of Pau was originally built in 1360, or about that time, by the famous prince, Gaston Phoebus, of Foix, who called himself, when addressing the Princess of Wales, *"a poor knight who builds towns and castles."* The great hero of Froissart is even more identified with Pau and its neighbourhood than Henry the Fourth himself, who, though he was born here, lived more at Coarraze and Nerac than in this castle of his ancestors; for he was even nursed in the village of Billières near, where his nurse's house is still shown.

Catherine de Medicis, and her beautiful and dangerous *troupe* of ladies, on the famous progress she made to Bayonne, visited the Castle of Pau, with a deep interest; she there succeeded in detaching the affections of the weak father of Henry from his noble-minded wife, and in laying the foundation of that tragedy which her dauntless and vindictive spirit had conceived. The massacre of St. Bartholomew may be said to have begun on the day that those fatal visitors crossed the drawbridge of the Castle of Pau. Her daughter, Marguerite, the victim of her schemes—an unwilling actor in the drama—suffered much sorrow and privation within these walls, after her marriage with a prince who never could surmount the distaste which circumstances of such peculiar horror as attended their union had given him; and the once cheerful place—the scene of splendour for centuries—lost its glory and its happy character after the beloved family of Queen Jeanne had deserted its towers.

Everything connected with the birth of Henry IV. is in general well-known, and has been so frequently repeated, that it is almost unnecessary to relate any circumstances attending that anxiously looked-for event, — cordially hailed by his grandfather, Henry. The account, however, given by Favyn is so characteristic that it cannot but be read with interest *a-propos* of the château where it occurred:

"The Princess of Navarre, being near her term, took leave of her husband, and set out from Compeign the 15th of November. She crossed all France to the Pyrenees, and directed her steps to Pau, where her father, the King of Navarre, then was. She arrived in the town after eighteen days' journey. King Henry had made his will, which the princess was very anxious to see; because it had been represented to her that it was to her disadvantage, and in favour of *a lady who governed* her father. For this cause, though she had tried every means to get a sight of it, it was a thing impossible; the more so, as, on her arrival, she had found the king ill, and dared not speak to him on the subject. But the coming of his *good girl*, as he called her, so delighted him that it set him on his legs again. The princess was endowed with a fine natural judgment, fostered by the reading of good books, to which she was much addicted; her humour was so lively that it was impossible to be dull where she was; one of the most learned and eloquent princesses of her time, she followed the steps of Marguerite, her mother, and was mistress of all the elegant accomplishments of the age. The king, who was aware of her wish respecting the will, told her she should have it when she had shown him her child; and, taking from his cabinet a great box, shut with a lock, the key of which he wore round his neck by a chain of gold, which encompassed it five-and-twenty or thirty times, he opened the box, and showed her the will. But he only showed it at a little distance; and then locked it up again, saying, 'This box and its contents shall be yours; but, in order that you may not produce me a crying girl or a puny creature, I promise to give you all on condition that, while the infant is being born, you sing a Gascon or Béarnais song; and I will be by.' He had lodged his daughter in a room in the second story of his castle of Pau; and his chamber was immediately beneath: he had given her, to guard her, one of his old *valets de chambre*, Cotin, whom he commanded never to stir from the princess night nor day, to serve her in her chamber, and to come and tell him the instant she was taken ill, and to wake him if he was in ever so deep a sleep. Ten days after the princess's arrival at Pau, between twelve and one o'clock at night, the day of St. Lucie, 13th of December, 1553, the king was called by Cotin, and hurried to her chamber: she heard him coming, and began immediately singing the canticle, which the Béarnais women repeat when lying in:

> "Noustre Dame deou cap deou poun,
> Adjoudat me à d'aqueste hore,"

for at the end of every bridge in Gascony is an oratory, dedicated to the Virgin, called, *Our Lady at the end of the bridge*; and that over the Gave, which passes into Béarn from Jurançon, was famous for its miracles in favour of lying-in women. The King of Navarre went on with the canticle; and had no sooner finished it than the prince was born who now reigns over France. Then the good king, filled with great joy, put the chain of gold round the neck of the princess, and gave her the box containing the will, saying, 'This is your property, and this is mine;' at the same time taking the infant, which he wrapped in a piece of his robe, and carried away to his chamber. The little prince came into the world without crying, and the first nourishment he had was from the hand of his grandfather; for, having taken a clove of garlic, he rubbed his little lips with it; then, in his golden cup, he presented him wine; *at the smell of which, the child having lifted up his head*, he put a drop in his mouth, which he swallowed very well. At which the good king, full of joy, exclaimed, before all the ladies and gentlemen in the room, 'You will be a true Béarnais!' kissing him as he spoke."

Every time I pass through the court-yard of this dilapidated building, I feel that it can never revive from its ruin; the desolation is too complete; the deface-ment too entire. What interest can exist in restorations to effect which so much must be cleared and scraped away that scarcely a trace of what was original can remain? How restore those medallions on the outer walls, which the taste of the first Fair Marguerite, and her Henry, placed in rows at one extremity of the court? how restore those beautifully-carved door-ways, and cornices, and sculptured windows, elaborate to the very roof? or renew the *façade* next the mountains with-out effacing that singular line of *machicoulis* which divides the stages. How replace the terrace—once existing, but long gone—without destroying venerable morsels of antiquity, precious in their ugliness! and how render the whole place sightly without clearing away the rubbish of the old *Tour de la Monnaie*, now built in with shabby tenements? Yet this will probably be done. Considering the state of the town, and the many improvements requisite in it, it would seem more judicious, perhaps, to effect, these, and to abandon the idea of *restoring* the castle. To repave the court, and clear away dirt, might be done with little time and cost; and the old fabric would not suffer by this act. At present the most neglected part is the entrance; and it is sufficiently unsightly. However, I ought to congratulate myself that I did not see it *when it was worse*—as I am constantly told when I complain of the wretched state of the streets.

It is said that part of the royal family are even yet expected to pay a visit to Pau, in the course of next spring, to be present at the inauguration of a new statue of the Great Henry, lately arrived, which is to be erected in the Place Royale.[6]

---

[6] Since this was written, the visit has been paid, and the ceremony gone through.

CHAPTER IV.

Troubadour.

Navarre has not produced many poets in early times; and the only troubadour whom it claims, is the famous lover of Blanche of Castile, the accomplished Thibault of Champagne, who rather belongs to Provins, where he lived so much, and sang so many of his beautiful lays, than to the Pyrenees. All critics, ancient and modern, from Dante to the Abbé Massieu, have agreed in admiring his compositions, in which grace, tenderness, and refinement, shine out in every line, encumbered though his language be with its antique costume. His mother was Blanche, daughter of Sancho the Wise, King of Navarre; his birth took place in 1201, a few months after the death of his father; and it was with difficulty the persecuted widow could retain her government of Champagne and Brie. In 1234, he was called to the throne of Navarre, by the death of his maternal uncle, Sancho le Fort. Soon after this, he left for the Holy Land; therefore, what time he spent in Navarre, does not appear. On his return from *Romanie*, he died at Pampluna, in 1253, and was buried at his beloved Provins, that city of nightingales and roses.

His songs are very numerous, and have much originality. The following will serve as specimens:

CHANSON.

— — — —

"Je n'ose chanter trop tart, ne trop souvent."

— — — —

"I fear to sing too seldom or too long —
I cannot tell if silence be the best,
Or if at all to tune my tender song —
For she denies me pity, hope, and rest.
Yet, in my lay, I might some note awake,
To please her ear more than all lays before;
Though thus, she seems a cruel joy to take,
That I should slowly suffer evermore.

"At once I'd cast my idle lute away,
If I were sure no pleasure could be mine;
But love has made my thoughts so much his prey,
I do not dare to love her, nor resign.
Thus I stand trembling and afraid to fly,
Till I have learnt to *hate* her — lovingly.

"By love and hate's alternate passions torn,
How shall I turn me from my thronging woes?
Ah! if I perish, tortured and forlorn,
But little glory from such triumph flows.
She has no right to keep me her's, in thrall,
Unless she will be mine, my own, my all!

"Well does she know how to delight — inflame,
With soft regards and smiles and words at will,
And none within her magic ever came,
But learnt to hope he was the favour'd still.
She is worth all the conquests she has won:
But I may trust too far — and be undone!

"She keeps me ling'ring thus in endless doubt,
And, as she pleases, holds me in her chain,
Grants she no smiles — I can adore without;
And this she knows, and I reproach in vain!
I am content to wait my chance, even now,
If she will but one ray of hope allow."

— — — —

JEU-PARTIE.

"BALDWIN, tell me frank and true,
What a lover ought to do;
One, who, loving well and long,
Suff'ring and enduring wrong,
At his lady's summons flies,
And presents him to her eyes,
With a welcome, when they meet,
Should he kiss her lips or feet?

"Sire, methinks he would be loth,
Not to kiss her rosy mouth;
For a kiss at once descends
To the heart and makes them friends;
Joy and sweetness, hope and bliss,
Follow in that tender kiss.

"Baldwin, nay, you ought to know,
He who dares such freedom show —
As though a shepherd maid were she,
Would never in her favour be:

I would kneel in humble guise,
For I know her fair and wise,
And humility may gain
Smiles no boldness could obtain.

"Sire, though modest semblance oft
Meet a guerdon, coy and soft,
And timid lovers sometimes find
Reward both merciful and kind:
Yet to the lips prefer the feet
Seems to my mind a care unmeet.

"Baldwin—for worlds I would not lose
Her mouth, her face, her hand—but choose
To kiss her pretty feet, that she
May see how humble truth can be.
But you are bold and daring still;
And know Love's gentle lore but ill.

"Sire, he must be a craven knight,
Who, with her lovely lips in sight,
Is all content and happy found,
To kiss her foot-print on the ground!

"Baldwin, quick gains are quickly o'er,
Got with much ease, and prized no more.
When at her feet, entranced, I lie,
No evil thought can hover night.
And she his love will faithful call,
Who asked no boon, and gave her all."

Luz.

TEMPLAR CHURCH AT LUZ

CHAPTER V.

Road From Pau To Tarbes—Table-Land—The Pics—The Haras Of
Tarbes—Autumn In The Pyrenees—Mont L'héris—Gabrielle D'es-
trées—Chasse Aux Palombes—Penne De L'héris—Pic Du Midi—
Charlet The Guide—Valley Of Campan—La Gatta—Grip—The
Tourmalet—Campana Del Vasse—Barèges-Luz—Cagot Door—
Gavarnie—The Fall Of The Rock—Chaos—Circus—Magnificence
Of Nature—Pont De Neige—Roland—Durendal—Izards—Les
Crânes—Pierefitte—Cauteretz—Cerizet—Pont   D'espagne—Lac
De Gaube—Argelez.

THE road between Pau and Tarbes,[7] like most of the roads south of the Garonne, is an extremely fine one; it is perfectly macadamized, and admirably well
kept; indeed, in this respect, the improvement that appears all over France is quite
remarkable; but if superiority can be claimed anywhere it certainly belongs to
Béarn and Bigorre. It is not, however, the *condition* of the road between the two
towns that forms the attraction; it is the exquisite scenery that meets the eye wher-

[7] For the whole account of the Hautes Pyrénées, I am indebted to my brother, Mr.
Dudley Costello, who made the excursion while I remained at Pau.

ever a break in the woods, or an inequality of the ground reveals the magnificent chain of the Pyrenees. For some distance after leaving Pau the road is nearly level; but about half-way to Tarbes, after passing through a thick wood of oak, and having been rendered impatient by occasional glimpses of the mountains, the traveller climbs a long and winding ascent, and reaches the summit of a fine table-land, from whence an uninterrupted view of this glorious country is obtained. Rich forests of chesnut clothe the steep sides of this table-land, and stretch far away to the southward, mingling with the well-cultivated plains that border the Gave de Pau; beyond these rise, in gradual succession, the lower ranges of the mountains, whose real height is entirely lost in the grandeur of the more stupendous Pyrenean giants, extending as far as the eye can reach, from the Mont Perdu at one extremity, and far beyond the Pic du Midi of the Vallée d'Ossau, at the other. The general colour of these noble mountains is a deep purple, which becomes even more intense, and approaches almost to blackness, until it melts away in the misty valleys beneath. The outline is not only irregular in form, but various in its hue; some of the loftiest heights of the foremost range being patched with snow, while, still more distant and shining in the sun, appear the dazzling peaks of eternal ice, piercing the deep blue sky wherein they dwell.

This table-land is traversed for several miles over a broken common, variegated with heath and fern, and intersected here and there by brawling streams, which take their course to swell the tributaries of the distant Gave. At the eastern extremity of the common, another wide forest of chesnut appears, where the road rapidly descends with many windings to the plain of Bigorre. One of these turns offers the loveliest picture it is possible to imagine. The foreground is formed of steep, rough banks, through which the road winds its sinuous track, the thick yet graceful foliage of the chesnut rises like a frame on either hand, and spreads also in front, while the Pic du Midi de Bigorre, with snow on its summit, and the Pic de Montaigu, with its sharp, dark outline, complete the distance. To give life to the scene, there are the peasants and market-women on their way to the fair of Tarbes,—the former wearing the characteristic brown *berret*, and the latter the black or scarlet-peaked hood, which gives quite a clerical air to their costume. Indeed, to see the women carelessly bestriding their active Bigourdin horses, which they manage with infinite ease, one might readily fancy, at a slight distance, that it was rather a party of monks of the olden time wending to their monastery, than a group of peasants laden with their market-ware. A little further, the road abruptly turns again, and Tarbes lies before us, distant about four or five miles, supported by another range of mountains, amongst which the Pic d'Orbizan is most conspicuous. The plain of Bigorre is now soon gained, and in half an hour we stand in the Place de Maubourguet, in the centre of Tarbes.

Tarbes, as a city, has little to recommend it beyond its situation, in the midst of a fertile plain, watered by the Adour, some of whose tributary streams run through the streets, imparting freshness and securing cleanliness. It has nothing to reveal to the lover of antiquity—no vestige remaining of the architecture of the period when Tarbes was celebrated as the place where the Black Prince held his court.

The cathedral is a modern building, possessing no claim to notice; and, except the royal *Haras*, there is nothing to detain the traveller. Here, however, are some fine horses,—the best amongst them English, except, indeed, a superb black barb, named Youssouf, once the property of an ex-foreign minister more famous in the Tribune than on the Champ de Mars. In consequence, as I was informed by one of the grooms, of the minister's indifferent equitation, his majesty, Louis-Philippe, purchased the barb and sent it hither. The most noticeable steeds besides, are Rowlestone, Sir Peter, Windcliffe, and Skirmisher—the last thirty-seven years' old—whose names bespeak their origin; there is also a fine Arab from Algiers, named Beni. The Haras is beautifully kept, and is surrounded by a fine garden, from whence the view of the distant mountains, beyond Bagnères de Bigorre, is exceedingly grand.

In that direction I decided upon bending my steps, and, returning to my hotel in the Place Maubourguet, my preparations for departure were soon made.

The distance from Tarbes to Bagnères de Bigorre is not more than five leagues, and the road thither would seem to be perfectly level, were it not for the impetuous flow of the Adour, along the left bank of which we travel, reminding us of the gradual ascent. The country is everywhere highly cultivated; and the peasants were busily employed with their second crops of hay, and securing their harvest of Indian corn. One historical site attracts attention on leaving Tarbes;—the old Château of Odos, where died, in 1549, "La Marguérite de Marguérites," Queen of Navarre, the sister of Francis the First, whose name will ever be associated with that of her adopted country. On this spot we lay down our recollections of the past, absorbed, as we approach the mountains, in the thoughts which their magnificence inspires,—which, while they, too, speak of the past, are ever appealing to the present, in their changeless forms and still enduring beauty, their might, their majesty, and their loneliness.

The watering-place of Bagnères has been described by so many tourists, that I spare the description here; and the more readily as it was nearly deserted when I arrived. This was no drawback to one whose desire was to enjoy the last days of autumn amongst the mountains while the weather yet continued fine,—and lovely that autumn weather is, atoning by the richness of its colours for the absence of beauties which belong to an earlier season.

I accordingly made all the necessary arrangements for a guide and horses to cross the Tourmalet on the next day, and devoted the remainder of a lovely afternoon to the ascent of Mont L'Héris—a mountain that supplies the botanist with treasures almost inexhaustible. Crossing the Adour by a rude bridge of only one plank, and traversing some fields, filled with labourers busily employed in getting in their harvest of Indian corn, I reached the pretty little village of Aste, which lies buried in a deep gorge, at the south-eastern base of the mountain. Aste has associations connected with Henri Quatre; for in the castle, now a mere shell, once resided the beautiful Gabrielle d'Estrées, who used here to receive her royal lover. The Seigneur du Village is the Duc de Grammont—a name which appears singularly out of keeping with this romantic and secluded spot.

The ascent of Mont L'Héris is steep but not difficult, for the profusion of flowers and richly-scented plants, scattered over the short elastic turf, beguile the climber's path, and lure him pleasantly upward. The first pause I made was on a bold projection, skirting the forest of Haboura on one side, and on the other hanging over the beautiful valley of Campan. Beneath me lay the town of Bagnères, and, far as the eye could reach, extended the plain of Bigorre, with the clear waters of the Adour marking their track like a silver thread. On the slope of a neighbouring mountain the wild-pigeon hunters were spreading their nets; for the *Chasse aux Palombes* is nowhere so successfully followed as in this part of the Pyrenees. It is a simple sport; but highly productive to those engaged in it. I pursued my route towards the summit of the mountain, the *"Penne de l'Héris,"* as it is still called, retaining its Celtic name. To do so, it was necessary to plunge into the thicket, and for a long time I made my way scrambling over the slippery surface of mossy rocks, as best I might, by the aid of the roots and lower branches of the forest-trees. At length I emerged from the wood, and stood upon the fertile pastures of the mountain; from whence the ascent to the immense block of marble which crowns Mont l'Héris, is tolerably easy. It is a singular mass, on the southern side of which is an enormous excavation; amongst the *débris* of which was a path that led to the top. If the view below was lovely, this was magnificent; my eyes were, however, riveted on one object—the towering height of the *Pic du Midi*, which seemed almost immediately above my head; though the mountain on the other side of the valley of Campan at our feet, showed us how far distant it really was. Directed by the peasant-guide, who had volunteered his services at Aste, I contrived to form a tolerable notion of the track which I was to pursue on the morrow; and it was only the warning shadows which began to creep over the valleys, and the clear tones of the church bells, at Bagnères, marking the hour at which I had promised to join the *table d'hôte* at the Hôtel de France, that expressively told me to loiter no longer on the mountains, lest darkness should entangle my feet before I had cleared its steep declivities. I made haste, therefore, to return to Bagnères, crossing the Adour this time by a bridge no less picturesque than the former, but somewhat more secure.

On the following morning I rose at daylight, and, at the moment fixed upon, Charlet, the guide, whom I had agreed with, rode up to the door of the hotel, leading another small, sturdy, mountain horse, and accompanied by the inseparable companion of his wanderings, a bull-dog named Pluto, which, had sex been considered, should have been called Proserpine, though not for beauty.

We were soon clear of the town, and jogged pleasantly along the road, which lay through the lovely valley of Campan—a scene whose beauty cannot be too highly extolled. On the left hand flowed the rapid waters of the Adour, beneath heights which seemed perpendicular, though Charlet pointed to certain irregular lines which marked the track by which the mountaineers descend on horseback, the very idea of which was enough to make one shudder; on the right hand, the valley spread out into a fertile district, whose gentle slopes gradually blended themselves with the hills which formed the spurs of lofty mountains, and finally shut in the view. In front, was constantly visible the snowy height of the *Pic d' Orbizan*, towering 9,000 feet above the level of the valley.

It was a delicious morning, and the freshness of the air, the beauty of the scenery, and the novelty of the situation, made me fain to linger in this lovely spot; but there was too much before us to admit of delay, and we trotted on merrily, every pause, as the road became steeper, being filled up by the conversation of Charlet.

It is not undeservedly that the Pyrenean guides have acquired the reputation they enjoy for intelligence and civility; and Charlet, of the Hôtel de France, is certainly a most favourable specimen: frugal in his habits, modest in his demeanour, and of great activity of body, he forms the *beau ideal* of a mountain cicerone. I asked him what superstitions were still current in the mountains: he replied, but few; the increasing intercourse with towns and travellers gradually effacing them from popular belief. One, however, he named, which is curious:—Any one who suddenly becomes rich without any visible means to account for it, is said by the peasants to have found *"la gatta;"* in other words, to have made a compact with the evil one, the evidence of which is afforded by the presence of a black cat, whose stay in the dwelling of the contracting party is productive of a gold coin, deposited every night in his bedchamber. When the term has expired, the cat disappears, and ruin invariably falls upon the unwary customer of the fiend. Charlet accounted for the superstition in a very simple way. As smuggling is constant amongst the mountaineers, so near the Spanish frontier, large fortunes, comparatively speaking, are often made; and accident or envy often deprives the possessor of his suddenly-acquired wealth, who may lose his all by an information, or an unsuccessful venture.

Two leagues from Bagnères brought us to Sainte Marie, where the roads separate,—one leading to Luchon, the other, to the right, across the Tourmalet, to Barèges; the latter, which we followed, here makes a very sensible ascent, but continues passable for carriages till we arrive at the little village of Grip—the last cluster of habitations on this side of the chain which divides the valley of Campan from that of the Bartan.

It is a wild and lonely place, and the loneliness of its position is increased by our being able to mark with precision the spot where cultivation ceases and nature asserts her uncontrolled dominion. Here the road ceases altogether, a bridle-path alone conducting across the still-distant ridge, called the Tourmalet, which is crowned by the remoter heights of Neouvièlle and the Pic d'Espade, from whose base flows the Adour—a slender but impetuous stream, whose course becomes visible only as it issues from a dense forest of black fir, which stretches half-way up the mountain.

The ascent to the Tourmalet occupied about two hours; and at high noon we dismounted on the ridge, with the Bastan before us; on every side innumerable peaks, and, winding along the valley, the road which leads to Barèges. Besides those already named, the most conspicuous heights are the Pic de l'Epée, the Pic de Bergons, and, at the further extremity of the valley, the Monné, which overhangs Cauteretz, and is yet visible from this point. The Valley of the Bastan is singularly desolate, presenting nothing to the eye but the rugged flanks of mountains, scored, as it would seem, by the rush of torrents, and massive rocks, whose *débris* lie scattered below, often obstructing the course of the Gave, which finds its source in the melted snows of the Neouvièlle. Some of the peaks near the Tourmalet are of peculiar form: one of them, pointed out to me by Charlet, is called the *Campana de Vasse*—the Bell of the Valley—which the mountaineers believe is to awaken the echoes of the Pyrenees on the day of judgment, and call the dead before the last tribunal.

After resting about an hour on the ridge of the Tourmalet, enjoying the solitude of a scene which was interrupted but once—by a soldier, a convalescent from the waters of Barèges, on his way back to join his garrison at Tarbes,—we remounted, and rode slowly down the Bastan, every turn of the road disclosing some fresh object to excite admiration or surprise. When we reached Barèges, the place was entirely deserted by visitors—even the houses were gone,—for the greater part of those erected for the company who throng the valley in the summer, being merely of wood, are removed to places of greater security than Barèges, where they run the risk of being destroyed by the floods and "moving accidents" of the mountains. We made no stay, therefore; but, like the Lady Baussière, "rode on" at a leisurely pace, the more fully to enjoy the wondrous beauties of the road between Barèges and Luz, where we arrived about four o'clock in the afternoon.

There is only one hotel at Luz; but it is the best in the Pyrenees,—not only for the nature of the accommodation, but the civility and attention of the host, the hostess, and their pretty *protegée*, Marie, who acts as waiter, *femme-de-chambre*, and *factotum* to the establishment. A good dinner was promised, and the promise was faithfully kept,—bear witness the delicate blue trout, which I have nowhere met with so good, except, perhaps, at Berne. But as there yet remained an hour or two of daylight, I employed the interval in visiting the ruins of the old feudal castle of St. Marie, and in sketching the church built by the Templars, which resembles a fortalice, rather than a place of worship. I examined the building carefully, but could not satisfy myself that I had really discovered the walled-up entrance, by which alone, *it is said*, the wretched cagots were formerly permitted to enter the church. The figures which flitted near, pausing, occasionally, to inspect my work, habited, as they were, in the long cloak and *capuchon* of the country, might well have passed for contemporaries of the superstitious fear which excluded the unfortunate victims of disease from an equality of rights with their fellow-men; but the cagot himself is no longer visible. Here I loitered, till it was too dark to draw another line; and then wended back to the *Hôtel des Pyrénées*, to recruit myself after the fatigues of the day, and prepare for those of the morrow.

Long before the day broke, we were again in the saddle, and, as we passed St. Sauveur, its long range of white buildings could only be faintly traced; but, as we advanced, the snowy peak of Bergons, glowing in the rays of the rising sun, seemed to light us on our way, and coily the charms of the valley revealed themselves to my eager gaze. I have wandered in many lands, and seen much mountain-scenery; but I think I never beheld any that approaches the beauty and sublimity of the road to Gavarnie. There is everything here to delight the eye, and fill the mind with wonder,—

"All that expands the spirit, yet appals."

For some miles the road continues to ascend; in many places, a mere horse-track, cut in the mountain side, and fenced by a low wall from an abyss of fearful depth, in whose dark cavity is heard the roar of the torrent which afterwards converts the generic name of Gave into one peculiar to itself. The sides of the mountains are thickly clothed with box, which grows to a great height; and at this season the Autumn tint had given to it the loveliest hues, contrasting well with the dark pines which climb to the verge of vegetation on the far-off slopes. Suddenly, the character of the scene is altered,—the road descends—the foliage disappears, or shows itself only in patches in the ravines, and masses of dark grey rock usurp its place; the noisy waters of the Gave make themselves more distinctly heard, and a few rude cottages appear. This is the village of Gèdre: and here I witnessed one of those mountain-effects which are often so terrible. A week before, two houses stood by the way-side—the homes of the peasants whom we saw at work in a neighbouring meadow. They were then, as now, employed in cutting grass for hay, when a low, rumbling noise was heard in the valley, which soon grew louder; and the affrighted labourers, casting their eyes upwards, saw that an enormous rock had suddenly detached itself from the mountain, and was now thundering down the steep. They fled with precipitation, and succeeded in saving their lives; but when they ventured to return to the spot, they found that an immense block had fallen upon one of the cottages, crushing it into powder, and leaving nothing standing but one of the gable ends. So it still remained,—and so, no doubt, it will continue till the end of time; for the mass is too ponderous to be moved by anything short of a convulsion of nature.

I could have wished to have turned aside at Gèdre to visit the Cascade of Saousa, but Gavarnie beckoned onwards to greater attractions; so again we pursued our route, and I speedily lost all thought for other wonders in the tremendous passes which bear the name of Chaos, and of which the best description can give but a faint and imperfect idea. The huge masses of rock, looking like fallen buildings, which are strewn along the valley in inextricable confusion, defy calculation. There they lie, the consequence of some terrific *déboulement*, which must have shaken the mountains to their centre when the mighty ruin was effected. It is supposed that the accident may have occurred in the sixth century, when a fearful earthquake disturbed the Pyrenees; but no written record remains to attest it. On the first view of this scene of disorder, it seems as if all further progress were stopped; but as we descend amongst the enormous blocks, a path is found winding through them, which the perseverance of the mountaineers has formed. Emerging from this terrific glen, the pastures and fields which surround the village of Gavarnie smile a welcome to the traveller, which is but ill-confirmed when he reaches the gloomy inn—the last and worst in France. Here we abandoned our horses, and after glancing at the cascade of Ossonne, I passed hastily through the village, and, mounting on a flat rock, threw myself down to gaze upon the stupendous Circus of Gavarnie, which, though still a full league distant, appears, at the first glance, to be within a quarter of an hour's walk. I was all impatience to reach the foot of that cascade of which I had so often read, but which I scarcely ever hoped to *see*, and, as soon as Charlet had stabled his steeds, we set out. For the first mile the road lay between narrow meadows, which owe their freshness to the Gave; these then gave place to a stony plain, the dry beds of some ancient lakes; and having traversed their expanse, we crossed the last bridge, constructed by the hands of man, over the river, and then climbing a series of sharp, irregular ascents, which would have passed for very respectable hills elsewhere, but here seemed mole-heaps only, we stood, at length, on the perpetual snow, which forms a solid crust at the foot of the circus of Gavarnie.

It seemed as if I had at length realised one of those dreams which fill the mind when first we read the wondrous tales of old romance: it was, indeed, the very spot described in one of the most celebrated of the earliest cycle; but my thoughts were less of Charlemagne and his paladins—though the Brèche de Roland was now within reach—than of the stupendous grandeur of the scene. It required very little exercise of fancy to imagine that we had arrived at the end of the world—so perfectly impassable appeared the barrier which suddenly rose before us. The frowning walls of granite which form the lowest grade of this vast amphitheatre, rise to a height of twelve hundred feet perpendicularly, and extend to nearly three-quarters of a league, increasing in width as they ascend to the regions of eternal snow; where may be traced a succession of precipices, until they are lost in the bases of the Cylindre and the Tours de Marboré, themselves the outworks of the Mont Perdu, from whose glaciers flow the numerous cascades which, in summer, shoot from the lower ridge of the Circus.

The great waterfall of Gavarnie—the loftiest in Europe—pours its slender stream from a height of upwards of thirteen hundred feet, on the eastern side of the Circus, and in its snow-cold water I dipped my travelling-cup, qualifying with veritable Cognac the draught I drank to the health of distant friends.

My great desire was to make the ascent of the Brèche de Roland; but Charlet had learnt, in the village where he made inquiry, that the snow had fallen heavily on the mountains only the day before, and that, consequently, it would be a matter of extreme difficulty and danger to make the attempt. It was now past mid-day, and the time necessary for accomplishing the ascent with the prospect of returning by daylight, was too limited; so, with reluctance, I gave up the idea. The season at which I visited Gavarnie was, indeed, too late (it was the 9th of October,) to admit of being very excursive, for long days and steady weather are absolutely necessary to enable one to do justice to mountain-scenery. I resolved, however, to remain within the Circus as long as I could, and, after descending to the *Pont de Neige*, from whose blue depths rushes the Gave de Pau, I climbed a rock at the edge of the snow, and sat there lost in admiration of the glorious scene. As I looked in the direction of the Brèche, itself invisible from the spot where I was, I observed an eagle soaring majestically above the cleft where tradition points to the last exploit of the valorous nephew of Charlemagne, whose type the imperial bird might well be deemed. It was here, according to the *veracious* chronicle of Archbishop Turpin, that, after defeating the Saracen king, Marsires, in the pass of Roncesvalles, Roland, grievously wounded, laid himself down to die, the shrill notes of his horn having failed to bring him the succour he expected from his uncle. It is in Roncesvalles that poets have laid the scene of his death, where—

> "On Fontarabian echoes borne
> The dying hero's call"

resounded; and, if truth attaches to the received story of his death, Ronces-valles is, no doubt, the site. But the legend has shed its romance on the immortal heights of the towers of Marboré; and, to account for the fissure in the rock, it must be with these in our recollection, that we read that quaint apostrophe to his sword which the chronicler has preserved:—

After laying himself down beneath a rock, Roland drew his sword, Durendal, and regarding it *"with great pity and compassion,"* he exclaimed, in a loud voice, "plorant et larmoyant:"—

"O très beau cousteau resplendissant, qui tant as duré et qui as ésté si large, si ferme et si forte, en manche de clere yvoire: duquel la croix est faicte d'or et la supface dorée decorée et embellye du pommeau faiet de pierres de beril; escript et engravé du grand nô de Dieu singulier, Alpha et OO. Si bien tranchant en la pointe et environné de la vertu de Dieu. Qui est celluy qui plus et oultre moy usera de ta saincte force, mais qui sera desormais ton possesseur? Certes celluy qui te possédera ne sera vaincu ny estonné, ne ne redoubtera toute la force des ennemys; il n'aura jamais pour d'aucunes illusions et fantasies, car luy de Dieu et de la grace sérôt en profection et sauvegarde. O que tu es eureuse espée digne de mémoire, car par toy sôt Sarrazins destruictz et occis et les gens infidèles mis a mort; dont la foy des Chrestiens est exaltée et la louenge de Dieu et gloire partout le môde uni-versel acquise. O a combien de fois ay je vengé sang de vostre seigneur Jesu-christ par ton puissât moyen, et mis à mort les ennemys de la nouvelle loy de grace en ce nouveau temps acceptable de salut; côbien ay je tranché de Sarrazins; combien de Juifs et aultres mescréant infidèles batus et destruictz, pour exaltation et gloire de la saincte foy Chrestiennie! Par toy noble cousteau tranchant Durendal de longue durée, la chevalerie de Dieu le Créateur est accomplye et les pieds es mainz des larrons acoustuméz qui gastoyent le bien de la chose publicque, gastéz et separéz de leurs corps. J'ay vengé par autant de foys le sang de Jesu-christ respendu sur terre que j'ay mis-à-mort par ton fort moyen aucun Juif et Sarrazin. O, o espée très eureuse de la quelle n'est la semblable n'a esté ne ne sera! Certes celluy qui t'a forgée jamais semblable ne fist devant luy ny après; car tous ceulx qui ont esté de toy blesséz n'ont pu vivre puis après. Si d'aventure aucû chevalier non hardy ou paresseux te possède après ma mort j'en seray grandement dolent. Et si aucun Sarrazin mescréant ou infidèle te touche aucunement j'en suis en grant dueil et angoisse."

Having made this lamentation, the valiant Roland, resolving that his weapon should never pass into other hands, raised his arm, and, with the last effort of ex-piring nature, clove the massy rock in twain, breaking the good sword, Durendal, into a thousand shivers by the force of the blow.

The voice of Charlet roused me from the reverie into which I had fallen, desir-ing me to look in the direction of the great cascade at a troop of izards that were bounding up the rocks. I turned and saw the graceful little creatures scaling, with inconceivable agility, heights which seemed absolutely perpendicular, so slight is the hold which they require for their tiny hoofs. It was but for a minute that I beheld them; in the next they were lost behind a projecting rock, and I saw them no more.

We now turned our faces down the valley, often, however, pausing to look back; and before we again entered the village of Gavarnie we stopped at the little old church to inspect the sculls called "Les crânes des douze Templiers," who are said to have been beheaded by order of Philippe le-Bel. Whether true or false, they are the only antiquities here—the church being comparatively modern. At the unpromising inn we found our horses refreshed by rest; and, without more ado, we remounted and returned by the road we came to Luz, which we reached soon after nightfall.

Quitting Luz the next morning, with much regret at being unable to remain longer to explore the beauties which surround it, we took the road to Pierrefitte, and, after a pleasant ride of about two hours, in the course of which we passed through the most lovely scenery—the most remarkable features of which are the depth and narrowness of the mountain gorges, and the boldness of the bridges which span them, one in particular bearing the characteristic name of the *Pont d'Enfer*—we arrived at the Hôtel de la Poste at Pierrefitte, where my carpet-bag was deposited, to lighten the load of Charlet's horse, for we had many miles that day to travel. We then pushed on towards Cauteretz, ascending by the old road, which, though steep, saves much time to those lightly mounted; from its point of junction with the new one, it is as fine as any in Europe, and the variety which it offers makes the valley as beautiful as any in the Pyrenees, while it retains its own distinctive character, caused by the greater quantity of foliage, thus gaining in softness what it loses in grandeur. After crossing a fine bridge, about half-way up the valley, the road takes a spiral direction, called *Le Limaçon*, the buttresses which support it being remarkable for the solidity and excellence of the masonry; and having made our way to the summit, the peak of the Monné above Cauteretz became visible for the first time since leaving the Tourmalet.

At Cauteretz we merely stopped to breakfast, my object being to visit the Lac de Gaube, at the foot of the Vignemale. It was Sunday morning, and a fair was being held in the market-place, the principal articles for sale being the many-co-loured chaplets manufactured at Betharram: there were many pretty faces in the little stalls, and many sweet voices offered their wares for sale; but I resisted the temptation—the more readily, perhaps, from knowing that the glass beads would have very little chance of remaining unbroken in a scrambling mountain-ride. About half-a-mile from Cauteretz we fell in with a party of dragoons, bringing their horses from the mineral springs, whither they are sent—like other invalids—for cure, from the Haras of Pau and Tarbes. The fine animals looked in excellent condition and spirits, and seemed to have benefited wonderfully by the visit. Passing the baths, we ascended the bridle-road above the Gave de Marcadaou, with dark forests of pine on either hand—a favourite resort for bear-hunters. The great charm of this road consists in the numerous cascades which mark the course of the Gave; they are, without question, the most beautiful in the Pyrenees, where the mountain-falls are, for the most part, deficient in volume. The finest of these, where all are striking, is the cascade of the Cerizet, which bears a greater resemblance to the falls of the Aar, in the canton of Berne, than any I remember. It is not so massive a fall, but it gave me the impression of being more picturesque, from the effect produced by the superb pines which hang over it, whose branches, covered with the spray which rises from the cascade, like vapour,

> "Drop tears as fast as the Arabian trees
> Their medicinal gum — —."

Charlet told me that we saw the Cerizet at the most fortunate hour; for it is at mid-day that the "sun-bow rays," at this season,

> " — — Arch
> The torrent with the many hues of heaven,"

and a lovely iris was settled on it at the moment we descended to a huge rock, on which we stood to watch "the roar of waters."

Beyond the Cerizet are two other fine falls—the *Pas de l'Ours* and the *Coussin*—which we pass on the way to the Pont d'Espagne, where the roads separate; the one in front leading into Spain by the Val de Jarret, and the other—which turns suddenly to the left—crossing the bridge, and conducting to the Lac de Gaube. The Pont d'Espagne is a most picturesque object: two torrents unite a little below it, one of which is the Marcadaou, the other the Gave that issues from the lonely lake; the Marcadaou rushes over a broad, flat rock—foaming and boiling, as if with rage to meet an expected enemy—while the deeper Gave throws itself from its narrow bed, and twists and turns, apparently falling back on itself, as if it sought to avoid the collision: they meet, however, and after the first concussion they flow on, smoothly enough, till a sudden turn hides them from our view, and we hear only their angry voices, caused by some fresh interruption to their course. But to have the finest view of the general effect, the bridge must be seen from below, where a rock stands boldly out, intercepting the heady current. It is constructed of fir-trees, felled on the spot, whose light stems, standing out in relief against the clear blue sky, seem almost too fragile to withstand the concussion caused by the "hell of waters" beneath. Nowhere does the pine appear to so much advantage as beside the Pont d'Espagne; some are the "wrecks of a single winter," others display a profusion of dark foliage, and the branches of all are thickly covered with grey parasitic moss, that hangs to them like hair, and gives to them a most picturesque appearance, like bearded giants guarding the romantic pass.

The narrow pathway through the forest, which leads to the Lac de Gaube, is excessively steep, and turns at least twenty times as it pursues its zigzag course. For the first half-hour nothing was visible but pine-trees, firs, and blocks of granite; and the road was difficult even for the sure-footed beasts which we bestrode; at length, we cleared the wood, and at once the Vignemale rose in awful splendour before us, its glaciers glittering in the sun, ten thousand feet above the bed of the dark blue lake, itself at a vast elevation above the level of the sea. Next to Gavarnie, this view of the Vignemale struck me as the most impressive object I had seen, the presence of the still lake reminding me of similar scenes in Switzerland; none of which, however, imparted the sense of solitude so completely as this. It might possibly arise from the associations belonging to the Lac de Gaube, the mournful evidence of which was before my eyes, in the little tomb raised to the memory of the unfortunate husband and wife who were drowned here in the year 1832. It stands on a small, rocky promontory, enclosed by a light iron rail, and the tablet bears the following inscription in French and English, on opposite sides. I transcribed both, and give the latter:—

"This tablet is dedicated to the memory of William Henry Pattisson, of Lincoln's Inn, London, Esq., barrister at law; and of Susan Frances, his wife, who, in the 31st and 26th years of their age, and within one month of their marriage, to the inexpressible grief of their surviving relations and friends, were accidentally drowned together in this lake, on the 20th day of September, 1832. Their remains wore conveyed to England, and interred there at Witham, in the county of Essex."

The account given me of the manner in which the accident occurred was, that Mr. and Mrs. Pattison visited the lake from Cauteretz in *chaises à porteurs*, and that Mr. Pattison went first of all alone in the boat, having vainly urged his wife to accompany him: after pulling some distance out, he paused, and, by his voice and gestures, intimated how charmed he was with the effect; he then returned to the shore, and overcame Mrs. Pattison's repugnance to enter the boat. She stepped in, and he again rowed about half a mile, when suddenly he was seen by the men on shore to rise in the boat, and in an instant it was overset, and both were plunged in the lake. Mr. Pattison sunk at once, but his wife's clothes buoyed her up for a considerable time; ineffectually, however, for none of the bearers of the *chaises à porteurs* could swim; her cries were in vain, and she, too, perished. How the accident arose, none can tell, and a mystery must for ever hang over the fatal event.

On seeing the wretched apology for a boat, which is still used by the fisherman who keeps a little *auberge* beside the lake, and is the same in which the sad catastrophe occurred, no one can be surprised that an accident should have happened; the only wonder is that it did not founder altogether, for it is little better than the trunk of a tree hollowed out, and turned adrift to take its chance of sinking or floating. Into this crazy contrivance I had no desire to venture, the lake appearing too cold for an impromptu bath.

Reluctantly, from hence, as from every other spot which I visited in the Pyrenees, I turned away, longing to have ascended the Vignemale, but knowing too well how few were the days allotted to my mountain excursion.

We returned by the same route to Pierrefitte, and then bid adieu to the sublimities of the *Hautes Pyrénées*; for, beautiful as the country is at the foot of the mountains, its beauty is tame, and produces, comparatively, little effect on the mind until time has effaced the first impression. It was late that night before we reached Argelez, where the *Hôtel du Commerce* received us.

For fertility, and all the softer charms that render a landscape pleasing, there is, perhaps, no place on earth that exceeds the valley of Lavedan, in which Argelez is situated. It is "a blending of all beauties," tempting the traveller to pause upon the way, and set up his rest in a region where everything seems to speak of peace and happiness. The inhabitants, however, can scarcely be happy, for the disease of *crétinism* is more widely spread here than in any other place in the department. The valley is famous for the breed of Pyrenean dogs, which are to be met with everywhere in the mountains, guarding the flocks and herds. It was my fortune to acquire a very fine specimen, only a fortnight old, which travelled with me in a basket to London, and six months afterwards, the largest kennel could scarcely contain it. These dogs are excessively strong, and are esteemed fierce; but their fierceness belongs rather to the wild life they lead amidst bears and wolves, to whom they prove formidable antagonists.

On one of the hills which skirt the valley of Castelloubon, between Argelez and Lourdes, I once more obtained a view of the Mont Perdu, distant now upwards of forty miles; it was the last glimpse of the wonders of the Hautes Pyrénées that was vouchsafed to me.

The garrisoned fortress of Lourdes,—the picturesque bridge and convent of Betharram, and the smiling plain which borders the Gave de Pau, were all passed in turn, and on the evening of the fifth day from my departure I was again in the streets of Pau.

CASTEL JALOUX

CHAPTER VI.

Vallée D'ossau—Le Hourat—The Rio Verde—Eaux Chaudes Eaux
Bonnes—Bielle—Izeste—Saccaze, The Naturalist.

————

> "Salut Ossau, la montagnarde,
> La Béarnaise, que Dieu garde!
> Avec bonheur je te regarde,
> Douce vallée!—et sur ma foy
> Parmi tes sœurs que je desire,
> De Leucate à Fontarable
> Je te dis que la plus jolie
> Ne peut se comparer à toi."

Ancienne Balade.

————

On rather a cold morning, early in October, we set out from Pau for the Vallée
d'Ossau; the road between the hills covered with vines of Jurançon. Gan and Gelos

are extremely pretty. We passed a house which was pointed out to us as belonging to the Baron Bernadotte, nephew to the King of Sweden, who, being a native of Pau, divides the honours of the town with Henry IV. Formerly, in this spot stood a castle, where a singularly Arcadian custom prevailed; every shepherd of the Vallée d'Ossau who passed by that spot with his flock, was required to place a small branch of leaves in a large ring fixed on the portal. If their lords insisted on no heavier homage than this, their duty was not very severe.

We passed through Gan—a wretched-looking village, once of great importance; one of the *thirteen towns* of Béarn; originally surrounded by walls and towers, of which nothing now remains except a few stones, which have served to build the houses. A *tourelle* is shown in the place as having formed part of the house of Marca, the historian of Béarn: there is an inscription on it, and arms, with the date of 1635.

The further we advanced the more the scenery improved, and as we followed the course of the beautiful, rapid, and noisy river Nès, which went foaming over its shallow, stony bed, making snowy cascades at every step, we were delighted with the gambols of that most beautiful of mountain-torrents, which appears to descend a series of marble stairs of extraordinary extent, rushing and leaping along the solitary gorge like a wild child at play.

The village of Sévignac opens the Vallée d'Ossau; and a host of villages, and a wide spread of pasture-land, with high mountains stretching far away into the distance, were before us. We breakfasted at Louvie, and then continued our route, the road becoming wilder, and having more character, than hitherto; we seemed now to have entered the gorges, and to be really approaching the great mountains, which, in strange and picturesque shapes, rose up in all directions around us. The most striking object here, is an isolated mount, on the summit of which stand the ruins of a feudal tower, called Castel Jaloux, built by Gaston Phoebus, for the convenience of holding the assemblies of Ossau, there to meet the viscounts who were independent of the kingdom of Béarn. The village of Castets is at the base of the rock, concealed amidst thick foliage: this situation is charming, in the midst of gigantic steeps and rich valleys, with the Gave foaming at its foot.

Laruns, the chief town of the canton, is a long, straggling town, almost Swiss in the construction of its houses: it has a small antique church, where there is a *bénitier*, curiously ornamented with figures of *syrens*: this is a favourite ornament in this part of the world, difficult to be explained, unless it is intended to represent some water-nymphs of the different Gaves, for it is too far from the sea to have any allusion to an ocean spirit. The road divides here, one route leading to the Eaux Bonnes, the other to the Eaux Chaudes; we proposed visiting the former on our way back, our intention being, if possible, to attempt the ascent of the Pic du Midi d'Ossau.

We continued to mount by a fine road, having magnificent views before and around, in order the better to enjoy which, we chose to walk for some distance up the height, between walls of rock, of all colours and shapes, covered with purple heath, and changing leaves, and delicate flowers of various hues. When we reached the summit, we found ourselves in a narrow defile, where a party of peasants were endeavouring, by main force, to assist a huge cart, drawn by labouring and straining horses, up the precipitous ascent—a perilous and painful work, which, however, they accomplished very well. We heard beyond a hoarse murmur, which told us we should soon rejoin the Gave, which here runs under the rocks, and reappears in a bed, upwards of four hundred feet deep. The high rocks seemed nearly to meet, and form a way exactly like the approach to a fortified castle: this pass is called *Le Hourat*. A little chapel is built at the other end of the opening, enclosing a figure of the Virgin—an object of great veneration in the neighbourhood. There was formerly here a long inscription in honour of the visit to the baths of the Princess Catherine, sister of Henry the Fourth; but every trace of it has disappeared, though there are many travellers whose eyes are so good as to be able to discern it, notwithstanding the fact of its having been carefully erased at the time of the great Revolution, when no royal *souvenir* was permitted to remain.

From this point, to the village of the Eaux Chaudes, the way is the most savage, wild, and beautiful that can be imagined: the torrent raving along its rocky bed, and foaming cataracts tumbling into its waters from numerous woody heights; at length we saw the little nest where the baths lie concealed; and descended between steep rocks, which shut the valley in so closely, that it appears almost possible to touch the two sides, which incline as if to form a canopy over the houses. We secured rooms for the night at the hotel—a very large one, and, in moderately warm weather, no doubt pleasant enough; but at this period all was as chill and dreary as if it had been in December. With much delay and difficulty we procured horses, and lost no time in setting out for Gabas, though the ominous appearance of the sky promised but little for our attempt; however, for the seven miles we rode along the exquisite valley—unequalled in its kind—nothing could exceed the delight and admiration I felt at the grandeur of the unexpected scenery; piles of naked rocks rose on one side of the road—which is as good as possible—while on the other they were covered with trees of every growth, with, as we advanced higher, a few pines appearing here and there; the torrent met us, rushing down impetuously over large and more encumbering blocks of stone, which, impeding its course, caused the waters to leap and struggle and foam and dash, till clouds of spray filled the valley, and its thundering voice echoed through the hollow caverns on the banks: its rich *green* colour, as clear as crystal, came out brilliantly from its crest of foam, so that the stream looked really a *Rio Verde*.

Long silver lines of shining water came trickling or rushing down from every height amongst the trees and shrubs, sometimes splashing across our path, and joining a little clear course which was hurrying forward to throw itself down the rock into the bosom of the mother Gave, on the other side. We stopped our horses so often to contemplate the beautiful *accidents* of rock and torrent, that by the time we reached the village of Gabas the day was closing in, and we found that it would take us two hours to reach the summit of the great mountain, which we scarcely remembered, in our pleasure at the beauties of the ride, had never been visible to us for a moment; in fact, a heavy mist hung over the snowy peaks, all of which were shrouded. Scarcely regretting the necessity for retracing our steps, we turned back, and had another view of the wonders of the lovely valley. The mountains now wore a more sombre hue, and the deepened shadows gave a severer character to the ravines. An eagle sailed majestically over our heads, much to my delight, as it was the only incident which we seemed to want to render the scene complete in lonely grandeur. That which is unaccustomed has a greater power over the imagination; and to me, who had never seen Switzerland or Italy, and to whom eagles were almost a fable, the solemn flight of one of these monarchs of the air, so peculiar in its movements, sailing along the peaks above the cataracts, was very impressive. It was then, by the shaking I experienced at every step, that I was aware how very steep had been our ascent the whole way from the Eaux Chaudes; our little sturdy mountain-ponies had cantered on so gaily, that I imagined we were on even ground: so far from which, we found on the return the motion so painful, that most of us got off our horses and walked. It was nearly dark when we arrived at the hotel, and we were not sorry to crowd round a blazing fire, and find all prepared for our refreshment.

The night was like winter, and the incessant roaring of the torrent prevented anything approaching sleep; but the sun rose brightly, and the next day was perfectly warm and genial. We took our way to Bonnes, and found the beauty of the journey increased by the fine effects of light and shade which the improved weather allowed; and, as we mounted the steep hill leading to the village, nothing could exceed the splendour of the view; the snowy top of the Pic de Ger, which the day before was not visible, now came out from a canopy of clouds; and huge rocks and verdant mountains, at different heights, descended in steps to the rich and glowing valley beneath, dotted with white cottages and thick groves: the Gave, on one side spanned by a beautiful picturesque bridge, rushes down on the other into a profound ravine, through which its waters run a subterranean course, till they reappear below the Hourah.

The brilliant sun which favoured us exhibited the Eaux Bonnes in its best light, and it seemed a delightful contrast to the chilly gorge we had left at the Eaux Chaudes. The hotels are well furnished, and there appears every convenience for the numerous visitors who crowd here in the summer. We walked to a fine waterfall just behind the inn where we stopped,—formed by the Valentin and the Sonde,—which is grand in the extreme. There are several other fine cascades in the neighbourhood, but this was the only one I saw. A way by a pretty, narrow, winding path to the top of a heathy hill is charming, and here a rustic temple is erected from whence the view is enchanting. Behind rises the majestic Pic de Ger, rugged and hoary, crowned with snow, the first that had shown itself in this region. The rocks and mountains are quite close, pressing in upon the village, and its establishment of baths; but, as the situation is on a height, it has a less confined appearance than the valley of the rival baths, and was, on the day we visited it, like another climate,—warm and genial: it must be extremely hot in the summer, as, indeed, all these gorges cannot fail to be. We talked to a lively young woman at the window of one of the now deserted boarding-houses, who told us she was a native of the Eaux Chaudes, whose merits she considered so superior to those of the Eaux Bonnes, that she had never deigned to cast her eyes, she said, up towards the paltry mountain of Ger, which the people of this gorge had the presumption to compare to that of the Pic du Midi: "One is here buried alive," said she, "with no walks, no mountains, no torrents; it is quite a waste of life, and I am resolved never to go to the top of that mole-hill of Ger, about which they make such a fuss: how disgusted you must be with it after the other!" She had once been to Pau, which she considered another Paris, but not so gay as the Eaux Bonnes; so that we learnt another lesson, which convinced us that every person sees with different eyes from his neighbours, and "proudly proclaims the spot of earth" which has most interest for him, the best.

We were free to differ with this fair Ossalaise; for, much as we admired her beautiful valley, we could not but give its rival nearly as much praise; admiring in particular the stupendous waterfall of the Valentin, where we lingered some time, climbing about the rocks, almost stunned by the roar of the waters, which break from the rock in three divisions; and so rushing over the projecting buttresses till they subside in the broad, cold, pebbly lake below.

The Vallée d'Ossau is said to combine all the beauties of the Pyrenees; and is certainly one of the most enchanting spots in nature: the scenery reminded me, in some degree, of that at the Mont Dore, in Auvergne; but, though superior in some respects, the magnificent *plateaux* of gigantic pines were wanting. It is necessary, in the Pyrenees, to ascend much higher than we did to behold this growth,—a few straggling firs of insignificant size are all that are to be seen in the lower range; but I believe they are very fine in some parts.

We stopped at Bielle to visit the Roman pavement, which has only lately been discovered; it was shown to us by a woman who was surrounded by five little children with black eyes and rosy cheeks; for this region is the Paradise of children; they all look so healthy and handsome. The mother, though still young, looked ten years older than she really was,—worn and tanned, like all I had hitherto seen; her remarkably small feet were bare, and she wore the fringed leggings peculiar to this part, which have a singularly Indian appearance. Beauty is said to be common in this country; but we had not met a single female who deserved to be called so; nor did the costume strike us as otherwise than coarse and ungraceful: in this particular forming a great contrast to the peasantry of Switzerland, with whose mountains there is here a parallel. The *patois* spoken by this family sounded very musical and pretty; and we remarked that the villagers in general seemed gentle and civil: a little boy, who constituted himself our guide, was a strange figure, actually covered with rags and tatters, which hung about him in the most grotesque drapery, as if it had been studied to create laughter: the village looked the very picture of poverty, desolation, dirt, and ruin: the church is a piece of antiquity of great interest. It has evidently been a pagan temple; and, ranged in an outer court, surrounded by circular arches, are placed some stone coffins, which excite wonder and interest; three of them have the lid of the ridged form, called *dos d'âne*: the other is flattened, and all are uninjured. They might seem to belong to the period when Charlemagne's knights required so many tombs in this land. It was in re-constructing a new vestry-room that these treasures were discovered beneath the worn stones which had been removed: no inscriptions give a hint to whom they may have belonged, and there they lie, side by side, mysterious relics of the times of chivalry.

The pillars inside the church are very celebrated for their extreme beauty: they are of white and blue jasper, found in a quarry near Bielle. A story is told of Henry IV., who greatly admired these pillars, having sent to request the town to make him a present of them, as he found nothing in his capital that could compare with their beauty; he received this answer: "Bous quets meste de noustes coos et de noustes beés; mei per co qui es Deus pialars diu temple, aquets que son di Diu, dab eig quep at bejats." "You may dispose of our hearts and our goods at your will; as for the columns, they belong to God; manage the matter with Him."

The Ossalais in this showed no little wit; or, if the tradition is not founded on fact, the story still exhibits their powers of setting a due value on their possessions in a striking light. Bielle was once a place of great importance, and its church belonged to an abbey of Benedictines: there was formerly a stone on the façade, on which was engraved the arms of the Valley — a *Bear and a Bull*, separated by a beech tree, with this device: "*Ussau é Bearn. Vive la Vacca.*" The ancient archives of Ossau are kept in a stone coffer at Bielle; and the dignitaries of the country repair to this spot at certain periods of the year to consult on the affairs of the communes. What habitation they find wherein to meet, suitable to their dignity, it would be difficult to say.

We stopped an hour at Izeste, and strolled along the one street of this wretched bourg while our horses rested: over almost every house we were surprised to see sculptured stones, with half-effaced arms, showing that once persons of condition inhabited these now degraded dwellings. One in particular, in a singular state of preservation, represented the cognizance of the house of Lusignan, and here we did indeed see the effigy which we had failed to find at the castle near Poitiers, of the serpent-tailed Fairy Melusine. We went into the house of the proprietor, who, with his mother and several of his neighbours, hurried out, after peeping from their windows to watch the operation of the sketching of Melusine, and invited us to see another head of a woman which he had found in the garden of his tenement. We passed along several dim, dark passages, and through large, square, dungeon-like rooms, apparently serving as stables, to the garden, where we found numerous remains of ancient Roman wall and bricks and broken columns, and the head of a statue much defaced. Every house seemed capable of exhibiting similar remains, and on many were dates in stone of 1613, 1660, 1673. One tower of defence is tolerably perfect; and walls and remnants of gates here and there prove how strong and how important Izeste once must have been.

We entered a court-yard, where a tailor was sitting working close by a curious door-way, which appeared like the entrance to a church, and was built into a wall, forming part of what was formerly a large mansion. We were so much struck with the extraordinary sculpture round the arch, that we inquired if there was any record of what it had been. The tailor looked up surprised: "Well," said he, "I have lived here all my life, and never took notice of this door-way before: we have plenty of old stones here; but they are worth nothing, and mean nothing, that I know of."

The carving which so excited our curiosity was a series of medallions: some circular, some square, very much mutilated, but still traceable. On one compartment were the figures of a bear *rampant*, and—what might be—a bull: they seemed in the act of combat, and possibly might represent the arms of Béarn and Ossau, though I confess I look upon them as of *very early* date—perhaps the work of the Gauls or Goths, *selon moi*; another enclosed a Sagittarius and a dog; another, an animal like a wolf, holding a club; another, an ape: the rest are too much worn to enable an antiquarian to decide what they were; but the whole offered a very singular and interesting problem, which we found it impossible to solve: the medallions are on stones which have evidently belonged to some other building, and been thus placed over a modern portal.

There is a cavern in the neighbourhood of Izeste, which is said to be worth visiting; but the weather was not propitious to our seeing it.

We stopped on the way from the Eaux Bonnes, on our return, at a place where our driver purchased us some ortolans, and we were almost stunned with the noise and clamour of a crowd of little urchins, with flowers and without, who, in whining accents, insisted on sous; but there was nothing either pretty or romantic about them or their costume; and we were very glad when, having procured the delicate little birds we waited for, we could resume our route. This was just at the season of *La Chasse des Palombes*—a time of much importance in the valley, when hundreds of a peculiar sort of pigeons are sacrificed.

Many of the peaks which had been concealed from us the day before, came forth from their circling mists, at intervals, on our return, and were pointed out to us by their different names; but as we came back in the evening to Pau, the range which was most familiar to us re-appeared in all its splendour, much clearer than when we were nearer to them.

At Beost, in the midst of the valley, lives a man, whose industry and genius have made him an object of curiosity and interest in the country, and whose fame must probably cause considerable interruption to his studies in the season of the baths; for it has become quite the fashion to visit him. He is called Pierrine, or Gaston Saccaze; is a shepherd who has always lived in these mountains, and has made himself so thoroughly acquainted with the botany of the district as to have become a valuable correspondent of the members of the Jardin des Plantes at Paris: he taught himself Latin, by means of an old dictionary which he bought for a few sous, and, by dint of extraordinary perseverance, has made himself master of the whole Flora of the Pyrenees.

GABAS

CHAPTER VII.

Gabas—Popular Songs—Pont Crabe—The Recluse Of The Vallée D'ossau—Marguerite—The Springs.

I made another excursion to the Vallée d'Ossau in the February of 1843, when the weather was singularly mild—infinitely more so than when I was first there in October, and the clearness of the sky enabled me to see all the mountains which were before concealed in clouds. With an adventurous party, all anxious to take advantage of the propitious moment, I undertook a long *walk*—for at this season it is difficult to procure horses—towards Gabas, having this time the Pic du Midi bright and clear and close in view. The carriage was able to advance along the steep road which extends above the foaming Gave de Gabas, nearly half way to the desired spot; for the snow had fallen in very small quantity during the winter, and there had been no interruption to the roads.

From a certain place, however, where two paths diverged, we found that the height we had reached had brought us to the snows, and that it was too slippery for the horses to proceed; accordingly we alighted and performed the rest of the journey on foot. The walk was very exciting and amusing, our feet sinking deep in snow at every step, while a burning sun, *gaümas*, as the guide said, was shining over our heads, glittering on the white peaks above, and sparkling in the deep, clear, green torrent at the foot of the box-covered hills, over which silver streams of water were flowing from the summits into the murmuring wave, which churlishly received their tributary visits, and disputed the place they took, dashing, foaming, and springing over the enormous masses of rock in their course, till all the valley re-echoed with their ceaseless quarrelling.

Every now and then we stopped to look back at the sublime scenery, and to make a hasty sketch of the peaks, which tempted us to pause. Summer and winter seemed combined in our stroll, and it appeared as if we were realizing the fable of *"the man, the sun, and the cloud,"* not knowing whether to yield to the heat or the cold. We met two Spaniards hurrying along, who had crossed the mountains from Saragossa: they were fine, strong-looking men, and sufficiently wild; but too dirty and slovenly to excite much admiration *here*; if we had seen them on the opposite side of the ravine they might have passed for picturesque, in the same manner as the singing of our guide might have delighted our ears had we heard him from a distance: as it was, he indulged our request by intoning some of the pastorals of Despourrins, which, if the spirit of the poet of the Pyrenees is wandering amongst the mountains, must have greatly *perturbed* it.

A long, loud, unmelodious drawl, like a dirge, with many a dying fall, was the vehicle in which the tender expressions of the poet were conveyed to our ears; and I was reproached by my companions for having injudiciously praised the verses of the Swan of Béarn: certainly heard in mutilated fragments, and sung by such a musician—*"La Haüt sus las Mountagnes"* and *"La Plus Charmante Anesquette,"* were not calculated to excite much admiration.

A lady of our party, who was acquainted with the popular songs of Langued-oc, repeated a few verses to our guide, who took up the strain, which was not new to him: it is singular how widely these simple songs are spread from one part of France to the other; indeed, they are scarcely confined to any country, and, like traditions, seem to have wandered up and down into all regions. For instance, I was very much surprised, a short time ago, to see in a work on Persian popular literature, an almost literal version of a song, well-known on the Bourbonnais, which I had met with at Moulins.

I questioned the guide on the subject of the superstitions of the valley, and found that he had himself *seen* the fairies called *Les Blanquettes*: those charming mountain-fairies who roam along the peaks singing mournful songs. "I had often heard of them," said he, "and many of my friends had seen them hovering about the mouths of caverns on the highest points of the mountains. I wished, therefore, to satisfy myself, and went to the spot where others had beheld them, and sure enough there they were, figures in white, like women, in a circle round the entrance of a cavern."

"And were these fairies?" I asked.

He paused a moment, and then said—"As for fairies, that is an old story, which some people believe: these that I saw *were only shadows.*"

It appears to me that superstition is fast wearing out in the Pyrenees, as well as everywhere else.

As we continued our way, we observed, along the snowy path, tracks of the feet of animals—a troop of wild-cats had evidently been before us, and here and there we remarked a print, which could be nothing less than the foot-mark of a wolf. The flight of a large bird, which I believe to have been a vulture, added to the solemnity of the scene; but there were less of these indications of solitude than I hoped to experience, for all was sunshine and gaiety around.

We observed near the Pont Crabe, *i.e.* Pont des Chèvres, on the opposite side of the ravine, a desolate-looking mill, placed in so wild and rugged a position, that one could not but pity those whose fortune might have condemned them to a residence there all the year round: a story attached to the cottage made it still more sad.

It appears that a young girl, the very flower of maidens in the Vallée d'Ossau, had been deceived and deserted by her lover, and on the point of becoming a mother, when she consulted the priest of her parish, confessing to him her weakness, and entreating his aid to enable her to propitiate offended Heaven. The virtuous and holy man, shocked at the infirmity and want of propriety exhibited by the unfortunate girl, was very severe in his censures, and informed her that there was no way left for her but by penance and mortification to endeavour to wipe away her sin. He condemned her, therefore, to take up her abode in that solitary cottage, far away from all human habitation, to spend her life in prayer and lamentation, and to endeavour, by voluntary affliction, to win her way to heaven.

She did so; and she and her child lived for ten years in that secluded spot, where the constant sound of murmuring waters drowned her sighs, and where no intruding foot came to disturb her solitude, except when the good priest, from time to time, visited her, to afford the consolation of his pious prayers. At the end of that time her spirit departed, and her little son was received into the convent, of which he became a member.

THE RECLUSE OF THE VALLÉE D'OSSAU.

"Say, ye waters raging round,
Say, ye mountains, bleak and hoar,
Is there quiet to be found,
Where the world can vex no more?
May I hope that peace can be
Granted to a wretch like me!

"Hark! the vulture's savage shriek—
Hark! the grim wolf scares the night,—
Thunder peals from peak to peak,
Ghastly snows shroud ev'ry height.
Hark! the torrent has a tone,

Dismal—threat'ning—cold—alone!

"Was I form'd for scenes like this,
Flattered, trusting, vain and gay—
In whose smile *he* said was bliss,
Who to hear was to obey?—
Yes! weak idol! 'tis thy doom,
This thy guerdon—this thy tomb!

"When I from my heart have torn
All the mem'ries cherish'd long;
When my early thought at morn,
And my sigh at even-song,
Have not all the self-same theme,
Peace upon my soul may gleam!

"When no more I paint his eyes,
When his smile no more I see,
And his tone's soft melodies
Wake not in each sound to me;
When I can efface the past,
I may look for calm—at last.

"When resentment is at rest,
Scorn and sorrow, rage and shame,
Can be still'd within my breast—
And I start not at his name;
When I weep, nor faint, nor feel,
Then my heart's deep wounds may heal.

"Years, long years, it yet will take,
Spite of pain and solitude,
Ere this heart can cease to ache,
And no restless dreams intrude:
Ere I crush each fond belief,
And oblivion vanquish grief.

"It might be—but in my child
All his father lives the while;
Such his eyes—so bright, so wild—
Such his air, his voice, his smile—
Still I see him o'er and o'er,
Till I dare to gaze no more!

"Is it sin to love him yet?
Was it sin to love at all?
Is my torture, my regret,
For his loss—or for my fall?
Change, oh Heaven!—thou canst, thou wilt—
Thoughts that sink my soul in guilt!

> "Teach me that regret is crime,
> That my past despair is vain,
> And my penance through all time
> Shall be ne'er to hope again, —
> Only in His pardon trust—
> Pitying, merciful, and just."

It is said that La Reine Marguerite, sister of Francis I., wrote the greatest part of her celebrated stories during a sojourn at the Eaux Chaudes: there, surrounded with a brilliant court of ladies and poets, she passed several joyous months, and recruited her health, while she amused her imagination, in wandering amongst the rocks and wild paths of Gabas and La Broussette: in her train were *"joueurs, farceurs, baladins*, and *garnemens de province,"* and nothing but entertainment seemed the business of the lives of those fair and gay invalids, who, so long ago, set an example which has not failed to be well followed since.

The pompous inscription which once appeared in a chapel at La Hourat, in honour of the passage of the Princess Catherine, sister of Henri IV. is now replaced by a modern exhortation to the traveller to implore the aid of the Virgin before he tempts the perils of the pass: and our guides very reverently took off their *berrets*, as they went by the little niche, where stands the image, which is an object of their adoration and hope. Poor Catherine, always disconsolate at her separation from the object of her choice, found but little relief from the waters—they could not minister to a mind diseased—and she had not the joyous, careless mind of her predecessor and grandmother; nor are we told that she attempted to compose amusing histories to distract her thought, nor could exclaim—

> "I write—sad task! that helps to wear away
> The long, long, mournful melancholy day;
> Write what the fervour of my soul inspires,
> And vainly fan love's slow-consuming fires."

All was sad and solitary to her; for the only companion she desired was not there to give her his hand along the rugged paths, to support her amongst the glittering snows, and smooth her way through the pleasing difficulties of the abrupt ascents. Cold ceremony, and, at best, mere duty, attended her whose heart sighed for tenderness and affection which she was never destined to know. At that period, there was neither hotel nor street, and the rudest huts sheltered that simple court; but they might perhaps afford, after all, as much comfort as may at the present day be found, in cold weather, in the irreclaimably smoky rooms of the principal inn at the Eaux Chaudes.

The accommodation is much superior—at least, *out* of the season—at the Eaux Bonnes, the situation of which is, as I before observed, infinitely more cheerful; but in hot weather it must be like an oven, closed in as the valley is with toppling mountains, which one seems almost to touch. Rising up, and barring the way immediately at the top of the valley in which the waters spring, is the isolated mountain called *La butte du Trésor*, on the summit of which is erected a little rustic temple, doubtless the favourite resort of adventurous invalids, during their stay at the waters. I cannot imagine the sojourn agreeable at that period to persons in health, who are led there only by curiosity; for often, while balls and parties are going on in the saloons below, some unfortunate victim of disease is being removed from the sick chambers above to his last home. Nothing but insensibility to human suffering can allow enjoyment to exist in such a spot, under such circumstances. I rejoiced that, at the period of both my visits, we had the scenery all to ourselves, with no drawback of melancholy to spoil the satisfaction we experienced.

These waters were first used, it is said, by Henri II. of Navarre, after his return from the fatal fight of Pavia, where he was wounded by a musketshot. They, from hence, took the name of Eaux des Arquebusades, as they were found efficacious in cases similar to his own.

Michel Montaigne was one of the illustrious visitors to these healing springs, which he calls *Grammontoises*.

Jacques de Thou came to the Eaux Bonnes in 1582; and recounts that, in the week which he passed there, he drank twenty-five glasses of water a day; but in this he was exceeded by a German companion, who took no less them *fifty*.

These springs were forgotten for more than a century after this; and Barèges was preferred to them. The great physician, Bordeu, of whom Béarn is justly proud, restored their reputation in a great measure: but it is rather within the last thirty years that they have reached the celebrity which they now enjoy.

It is generally said that the Vallée d'Ossau combines all the beauties and grandeurs of the Pyrenees; and that the traveller, who has only time to visit this part, has had a specimen of all that is most admirable in this beautiful chain of mountains. For myself, I endeavour to believe this, not having been able to see so much of the Pyrenees as I desired.

CHAPTER VIII.

Peasants Of Ossau—Captivity Of Francis The First—Death Of Joyeuse—Death Of The Duke De Maine—Dances.

A great deal has been said and written about the peasants of the Vallée d'Ossau; and most persons appear to have been guided rather by enthusiasm than truth, exaggerating and embellishing facts as it suited their views or their humour. It is the custom to admire the young girls and children who pester travellers with shabby, faded little bouquets, which they throw into the carriage-windows, and to see something peculiar in the custom; but it does not strike me that there is the slightest difference in this, or any other usage, between the Pyrenees and all parts of France, through which I have passed. On the road from Calais, as well as in the Vallée d'Ossau, ragged dirty groups, eager for sous, place themselves in your way, and endeavour to obtain money: on fête-days they may look better; but on ordinary occasions there is certainly but little to admire, either in their dress or manners.

A lively but sarcastic French writer has observed on the proneness of tourists to exalt the peasants of Ossau into the Arcadian beings of Virgil and Theocritus, representing them as assembling together to sing the verses of Despourrins: that—"it is, perhaps, better to see romance than not to see at all; but those who have discovered these pastoral heroes and heroines, can assuredly never have met with them on the Ger or the Pic du Midi: the only songs that one can hear in that neighbourhood are drawling, monotonous lines, without either rhyme or reason,—a sort of ballad like that of the wandering Jew. As for their occupations, they are commonly employed in knitting coarse woollen stockings, or in preparing, in the dirtiest manner in the world, the poorest and most insipid cheese that ever was made. The youths and maidens are by no means Estelles and Nemourins. I am aware that this account will be considered profane, and the writer of these facts, a morose, disagreeable person; but the truth is, nevertheless, better than false enthusiasm, which causes misrepresentation; and, having always before our eyes so much that is glorious and sublime, it cannot be necessary to inflate the imagination for ever *à propos de rien*.

"Let those who would form an idea of the singing of the Ossalois observe them on a fête-day, in some of their villages, when the young people are returning home. They separate in two bands: some holding each other by the waist, some round the neck. The foremost party go about thirty steps in silence, while those behind sing a couplet in chorus; the first then stop, sing the second verse, and wait till those behind have joined them; and the latter sing the third verse as they arrive at home. This chant is called, in the country, *Passe-carrère*. Every now and then the song is intermingled with sharp, wild cries, called *arénilhets*, peculiar to the mountaineers; which prove the strength of their lungs, if not their ear for melody. All this is performed slowly and heavily, without any appearance of joyousness or gaiety, and seems singularly ill-adapted to a fête."

It must be allowed that, whenever a good voice occurs in this part of the country, it is an exception to the general rule; but this happened not long since, in the case of a young and very handsome girl of Ossau, whose melodious voice and fine execution attracted the notice of an amateur, by whom she was introduced to the theatre at Berlin, and obtained great applause and success. She may be considered as a nightingale who had lost her way amongst a wood of screech-owls; for her talent was quite alone. She used to sing an old historical romance of the valley, composed on the captivity of Francis I., which has seldom since found a voice capable of giving it effect.

There is something in this old ballad very like those of Spain, both in character and rhythm; and there exist several others, on historical subjects, which have the same kind of simple merit:

THE CAPTIVITY OF FRANCIS I.

— — — —

"Quan lou Rey parti de France," &c.

— — — —

When the king, from France departing,
Other lands to conquer sought,
'Twas at Pavia he was taken,
By the wily Spaniard caught.

"Yield thee, yield thee straight, King Francis,
Death or prison is your lot;"
"Wherefore call you me King Francis?
Such a monarch know I not."

Then the Spaniards raised his mantle,
And they saw the fleur-de-lys;—
They have chained him, and, full joyous,
Bore him to captivity.

In a tower, where sun nor moon-light
Came but by a window small;
There he lies, and as he gazes,
Sees a courier pass the wall.

"Courier! who art letters bringing,
Tell me what in France is said?"
"Ah! my news is sad and heavy—
For the king is ta'en, or dead."

"Back with speed, oh, courier, hasten—
Haste to Paris back with speed,

To my wife and little children;
Bid them help me at my need.

"Bid them coin new gold and silver,
All that Paris has to bring,
And send here a heap of treasure,
To redeem the captive king."[8]

— — — —

The following is also a favourite ballad on the battle of Coutras and the death of Joyeuse, the magnificent favourite of Henry III., whose contemptuous remark on his effeminacy was the cause of his exposing himself in the *mêlée*. The episode of the fate of Joyeuse is an affecting one in the life of the valiant and generous Henry of Navarre. The treasure was immense that was taken from the gorgeous army destined to overthrow the harassed Huguenots, but literally cut to pieces by the stern and bold, though ragged warriors. The gold, silver, and jewels that were brought to Henry's tent, after the victory, were heaped on the floor, and the dead body of the beautiful and admired Duke de Joyeuse was brought to him. Henry turned away, sick at heart, and commanded the corpse to be covered with a cloak, and removed carefully; and desired that all the spoil should be divided amongst the soldiers; holding it beneath him to accept any: nor could he restrain his tears at the sight of so much carnage of those whom he looked upon as his subjects.

---

[8] The popularity of this ballad is accounted for by the circumstance of the Prince of Béarn, Henry II. d'Albert, having been made prisoner with Francis; he was, however, more fortunate than the king, for he made his escape. The original runs thus:—

THE CAPTIVITY OF FRANCIS I.

Quan lou Rey parti de France,
Counqueri d'aütes pays,
A l'entrade de Pavi
Lous Espagnols bé l'an pris.

"Renté, renté, Rey de France,
Que si non, qu'en mourt ou pris,"
Quin seri lou Rey de France?
Que jamey you nou l'ey bist."

Queou lheban l'ale deoü mantoü
Troban l'y la flou de lys.
Quoü ne prenen et quoü liguen
Dens la prison que l'an mis.

Dehens üe tour escure,
Jamey sour ni lue s'y a bist;
Si nou per üe frinistote....
U poustillou bet beni.

"Poustillou qué lettres portis
Que si counte tà Paris?"
"La nouvelle que you porti
Lou Rey qu'ere mort ou pris."

"Tourne t'en poustillou en poste,
Tourne t'en entà Paris.
Arrecommandem à ma femme
Tabé mous infants petits.

"Que hassen batte la mounede,
La qui sie dens Paris,
Que men embien üe cargue
Por rachetam aü pays."

The chorus is usually at the end of each verse—"La lyron, la lyré," or "doundoun, doundone."

THE DEATH OF JOYEUSE.

Between La Roche and Coutras
Was heard our battle cry;
And still we called—"To arms! to arms!"
Our voices rent the sky.

Our king was there with all his men,
And all his guards beside,
Within, the Duke de Joyeuse,
And to the king he cried:

"Oh, yield, King Henry, yield to me!"—
"What simple squire art thou,
To bid King Henry yield him,
And to thy bidding bow?"

"I an no simple squire,
But a knight of high degree;
I am the Duke de Joyeuse,
And thou must yield to me."

The king has placed his cannon
In lines against the wall,—
The first fire Joyeuse trembled,
The next saw Joyeuse fall.

Alas! his little children,
How sad will be their fate!—
A nurse both young and pretty,
Shall on them tend and wait:
And they shall be brave warriors,
When they come to man's estate.

———

The next ballad is in the same strain:

THE DEATH OF THE DUKE DE MAINE.

The noble Duke de Maine
Is dead or wounded sore;
Three damsels came to visit him,
And his hard hap deplore.

"Oh! say, fair prince, where is your wound?"
"'Tis in my heart," he said,
"'Twill not be many moments
Ere you will see me dead."

"Oh! call my page, and bid my squire;—
They ink and paper bring;—
For I must write a letter
To my cousin and my king."

And when the king the letter read,
Tears from his eyelids fell;
"Oh! who shall lead my armies now.
Who shall command so well!"

"Oh! who shall guide my valiant bands
To conquest in the fight! —
The Duke de Vendôme[9] must succeed, —
He is a gallant knight."

— — — —

It is seldom now that the tamborine or pipe, celebrated by Despourrins, is heard as an accompaniment to the dances of the peasants. A violin is the usual music; and the antique and pastoral character is at once destroyed.

Sometimes it is possible to see a real mountain-dance, which is certainly picturesque, if not graceful, and belongs peculiarly to the spot, and the objects which inspired it; as, for instance, *"The Dance of the Wild Goat," "The Dance of the Izard," "La Gibaudrie," "La Ronde du Grand Pic."*

The young men are very agile in these exercises; but, in general, the woman's part is very inferior: they, indeed, seldom dance together, and usually are only spectators. This seems to indicate an Eastern origin. There is one exception to this rule in a *ronde*, executed by both sexes, hand-in-hand; but in this the men leap and cut, while the women move their feet slowly and heavily: in fact, they look half asleep, while the young men seem much more occupied with their own feats of agility than with their partners.

As I have not seen any of these dances, nor the peasants in their holiday costumes, I have some difficulty in imagining that there is either beauty or grace amongst them. At the Eaux Bonnes, our female attendant wore her red-peaked *capeline* in the house, which had a singular effect, but was by no means pretty: indeed, the only impression it gives me is, that it is precisely the costume which seems to suit *a daunce o' witches*; and cannot by possibility be softened into anything in the least pleasing to the eye. All the peasants I saw at different periods of the year had a remarkably slovenly, dirty, squalid appearance; and, except in the instance of one little girl of about thirteen, I saw none who had the slightest claim to beauty, or could excite interest for a moment. There is a humble, civil air about the people in the Vallée d'Ossau, which propitiates one: the *berret* is always taken off as a stranger passes, and a kind salutation uniformly given. But, beyond this, there is nothing worthy of remark as respects the common people, who appear to be a simple race, content to work hard and live poorly.

Our guide pointed out to us a village, from the valley, perched up on a height in the midst of snows, where, he said, the inhabitants, who were all shepherds, *were very learned.* "Not one of them," said he, "but can read and write; and, as they are always in the mountains with a book in their hands, and have nothing to interrupt their studies, they know a great deal, and are brave *gens.*" Probably Gaston Saccaze the naturalist belongs to such a fraternity.

[9] Antoine de Bourbon.

CHAPTER IX.

———

"A très lègues de Pau, a cap à las mountagnes
Aprés abé seguit gayhaventes[10] campagnes,
Sus û Pic oûn lou Gabe en gourgouils ba mouri
Lou Castel de Coarraze aüs oueils qu'es bien ouffri."

———

Within a pleasant drive of Pau is the Castle of Coarraze, where the youth of Henry IV. was passed, under the guardianship of Suzanne de Bourbon-Busset, Barronne de Miossens. Of this castle nothing now remains but one tower, on which may still be traced the motto, "*Lo que ha de ser non puede faltar*," from whence is a magnificent view *into* the mountains.

Of the Castle of Coarraze, it will be seen that more marvellous things are told than that Henri Quatre passed much of his childhood there.

Froissart has immortalized it as the scene of one of his romances of Orthez; and this is the tale he tells of its lord:

It seems, Count Gaston Phoebus had such early knowledge of every event, that his household could only account for the fact by supposing that he possessed some familiar spirit, who told him all that had happened in the country, far and near. This was considered by no means unusual; and when Sir John Froissart expressed his surprise on the subject, a squire belonging to the count related to him a circumstance of a similar nature.

"It may be about twenty years ago," said he, "that there reigned, in this country, a baron, who was called Raymond, and who was Lord of Coarraze. Now, Coarraze is a town and castle, about seven leagues from this town of Orthez. The Lord of Coarraze had, at the time of which I speak, a suit before the Pope, at Avignon, respecting the tithes of the church, which were claimed by a certain clerk of Catalonia, who insisted on his right to a revenue from them of a hundred florins a-year. Sentence was given by Pope Urban the Fifth, in a general consistory, against the knight, and in favour of the Churchman; in consequence of which, the

———

[10] Smiling.

latter hastened, with all speed, back to Béarn with his letters and the Pope's bull, by virtue of which he was to enter into possession of the tithes.

"The Lord of Coarraze was much incensed at this; and, in great indignation, went to the clerk, and said, 'Master Peter,' or 'Master Martin,'—it matters not for his name—'do you suppose that I shall be content to lose my inheritance for the sake of those letters of yours? I do not believe you to be so bold as to lay your hands on a thing which belongs to me; for, if you do, it is as much as your life is worth. Go elsewhere, and get what you can; as for my inheritance, you shall have none of it, and I tell you so once for all.'

"The clerk stood much in awe of the knight at these words, for he knew him to be a determined man, and dared not persevere in his demand; he found it safe to retire to Avignon, or, at all events, out of the count's reach; but, before he departed, he said to him, 'Sire, by force, and not by right, you have taken and kept from me the dues of my church, which in conscience is a great wrong. I am not so strong in this country as you are; but I would have you know, and that soon, that I have a champion, whom you will have cause to fear more than you do me.' The Lord of Coarraze, who cared nothing for his menaces, replied: 'Go, in Heaven's name, and do your worst. I value you as little dead as living; and, for all your words, you shall not get my property.'

"Thus they parted: the clerk either to Avignon, or into Catalonia; but he did not forget what he had said to the knight, for soon after there came to his castle of Coarraze, and into the very chamber where he and his lady slept, invisible messengers, who began to riot and overturn everything they found in the castle; so that it seemed as if they would destroy all they came near; so loud were the strokes which they struck against the doors of the bed-rooms, that the lady shook as she lay, and was greatly terrified. The knight heard all; but he took no sort of notice, for he would not seem to be moved by this event, and was bold enough to wait for stranger adventures.

"The noise and uproar continued for a long space in different chambers of the castle, and then ceased. The domestics and squires represented what had happened to their master; but he feigned to have heard nothing, and to believe that they had been dreaming: but his lady one day assured him that she had heard the noise but too clearly.

"That same night, as he was sleeping in his bed, came the uproar again as before, and shook the windows and doors in a wonderful manner. The knight then could not but rouse himself; and, sitting up, cried out, 'Who knocks so loud at my chamber at such an hour?'

"'It is I—it is I!' was the answer.

"'And who sends you?'

"'The clerk of Catalonia, whom you have wronged out of his property; and I will never leave you in peace till you have reckoned with him for it, and he is content.'

"'And what is your name, who are so good a messenger?'

"'I am called Orton.'

"'Orton,' said the knight, 'the service of a clerk is beneath you; you will find it more trouble than profit; leave it, and serve me—you will be glad of the exchange.'

"Now, Orton had *taken a fancy* to the Lord of Coarraze; and, after a pause, he said,

"'Are you in earnest?'

"'Certainly,' replied the knight; 'let us understand each other. You must do evil to no one, and we shall be very good friends.'

"'No, no,' said Orton, 'I have no power to do evil to you or others, except to disturb them when they might sleep.'

"'Well, then, we are agreed,' said the knight; 'in future, you serve me, and quit that wretched clerk.'

"'Be it as you will,' said Orton, 'so will I.'

"From this time, the spirit attached himself with such affection to the lord, that he constantly visited him at night; and when he found him asleep he made a noise at his ear, or at the doors and windows; and the knight used to wake and cry out, 'Orton, let me alone, I entreat!'

"'No, I will not,' was the reply, 'till I have told you some news.'

"Meantime, the lady used to lie frightened to death—her hair on end, and her head covered with the bed-clothes. Her husband would say:

"'Well, what news have you?—from what country do you come?'

"The spirit would answer:

"'Why, from England, or Germany, or Hungary, or other countries. I set out yesterday, and such and such things happened.'

"In this manner was the count informed of all that occurred in every part of the globe for five or six years: and he could not conceal the truth, but imparted it to the Count of Foix, when he came to visit him. The count was greatly surprised at what he told, and expressed a wish that he possessed such a courier.

"'Have you never seen him?' said he.

"'Never,' answered the knight.

"'I would certainly do so,' said the Count de Foix; 'you tell me he speaks Gascon as well as you or I. Pray see him, and tell me what form he bears.'

"'I have never sought to do so,' said the knight; 'but, since you wish it, I will make a point of desiring him to reveal himself.'

"The next time Orton brought his news, his master told him he desired to behold him; and, after a little persuasion, he agreed that he should be gratified. 'The first thing you see to-morrow morning,' said he, 'when you rise from your bed, will be me.'

"The morning came, and when the knight was getting up, the lady was so afraid of seeing Orton that she pretended to be sick, and would not rise. The knight, however, was resolved, and leapt up with the hope of seeing him in a proper form, but nothing appeared. He ran to the windows, and opened the shutters to let the light in, but still there was no appearance in his room.

"At night Orton came, and told him he had appeared in the form of two straws, which, he might have observed, whirled about on the floor.

"The knight was much displeased, and insisted on not being thus played with: 'when I have seen you once,' said he, 'I desire no more.'

"''Tis well,' replied Orton. 'Remark, then, the first object which meets your eye when you leave your chamber, that will be me.'

"The next day the Lord of Coarraze got up, as usual; and when he was ready, he went out of his room into a gallery, which overlooked a court of his castle. The first thing which attracted his notice was a large sow, the most enormous creature he had ever beheld in his life; but she was so thin, that she seemed nothing but skin and bone, and she looked miserable and starved, with a long snout and emaciated limbs.

"The lord was amazed and annoyed at seeing this animal in his court-yard, and cried out to his people to drive it away, and set the hounds upon it. This was accordingly done, without delay; when the sow uttered a loud cry, turned a piteous look upon the knight, and disappeared: nor could any one find her again.

"The Lord of Coarraze returned to his chamber in a pensive mood; and was now convinced, too late, that he had seen his messenger—who never afterwards returned to him: and the very next year he died in his castle."

Beginning almost from the entrance to Pau, extends an immense district of uncultivated land, called the Pont Long. This *lande* is covered with coarse fern and heath, and is intersected with wide marshes; thirty-two communes have a right in this ground; but it chiefly belongs to the Vallée d'Ossau. It was formerly much more extensive than it now is; but, even yet, a very inconsiderable portion has been reclaimed: its extent is about twelve leagues in length, and one and a half in width.

In the centre of this wild country is the ancient town of Morlàas, whose name, tradition says, was derived from the circumstance of a prince—Gaston Centulle—having been there assassinated; from whence it was called *Mort-là*, a derivation, probably, as likely as any other that can be found.

We chose a very bright, warm, and beautiful day—during the continuance of fine weather, in November—to drive to Morlàas. Our carriage was stopped, just as we got out of the town, by a regiment of soldiers who were marching out, and, but for the courtesy of the colonel, we should have been impeded for nearly a league: he, however, kindly ordered the ranks to open, and we were allowed to go on between the two lines. This regiment—the 25th of the line—is a remarkably fine one, and appears to be kept in constant activity by its commanders, going out to great distances to exercise in every weather. It is attended by a pretty troop of young women, whose appearance reminded me of Catherine's *petite bande*, so attractive did it seem. I do not know whether this is a common thing, but I never saw such a troop before in company with a regiment. They wear a costume, half feminine half military; have short dresses of grey cloth—the colour of the men's great coats—sitting close to their shape, very full in the skirt, and with cuffs turned up with red facings, red trowsers, and military boots, a white plaited ruff and habit-shirt, a white—neatly frilled and plaited—cap, surmounted with a small, smart glazed hat, round which is the word *Cantinière*: across their shoulder is slung a canteen, and in this equipment they step along with a military air, and in a dashing style which would be invaluable on the stage. I never saw anything more singular and pretty, and to me so new: almost every one of the women was young and very good-looking, extremely well made, and active and strong; as, indeed, they require to be, for they accompany the soldiers on all their expeditions, and remain out all day. It is something as amusing to behold as the troop of *savans and asses*, taken care of by Napoleon in his Egyptian campaign.

The road to Morlàas is rather monotonous, and that part which crosses the marsh very bleak and desolate: with the gigantic mountains bounding the horizon, it seems as if the marsh-fiend might here well establish his abode; and the salubrity of the air of the neighbourhood I should somewhat doubt. After a considerable distance, the road quits the *Lande*, and mounts a hill, along and from the summit of which is a very agreeable view, which improves at every step. From this point the Lande below appears cultivated, and vines and fields are seen in all directions. You descend the hill, and Morlàas is in sight: that town was once regal, and of old renown, but is now in the very perfection of ruin and desolation.

It was the great market, and our driver was so delighted at the circumstance, that it was with the utmost difficulty we could prevent him from taking us to a plain outside the town, where the horse-fair was going on, as he assured us that there we should see all the *monde*. As we were quite aware of the style of gentry assembled, by the quantity of blue frocks and berrets which we saw from a distance, and by the neighing of steeds which reached our ears, we declined joining the commercial party, and contented ourselves with being jostled and crowded by the assemblage in the streets of Morlàas, whose avenues were blocked up with market-folks, not only from every village and commune round, but from Pau, and Orthez, and Peyrehourade, and Lescar.

We stopped at the once magnificent church of Sainte Foix, before a little low porch, where we had to endure much persecution from beggars, *en attendant* the arrival of the curé who was to show us the interior. We were amused at one of these people, who continued his whining cry of "Charita madama, per l'amor de Déieux!"—half French, half *patois*; till our driver asking him to point out the curé's abode, he answered briskly, in a lively tone; and, having given the required information, resumed the accustomed drawl.

The curé seemed very cross, and little propitiated by our apologies for having disturbed him: he looked sleepy and flushed, and had evidently been enjoying a nap, after a hearty meal and a bottle of Jurançon. He hurried us through the ruined church, from which almost every vestige of its early character has disappeared. On a pillar are still seen some Gothic letters, which may be thus read: "In the year of God 1301, this pillar and this altar were made by Téaza, whom God pardon! in honour of God, St. Orens, and Sainte Foi." A picture of the sixteenth century adorns the choir. It represents the Judgment of our Lord; each of the judges is in the costume of the period; and his opinion is expressed by a label attached to his person.

One little chapel alone remains of all that must have adorned this church: the sculpture of this is very beautiful, and the grimacing heads introduced amongst the foliage sufficiently grotesque. There is a very large antique baptismal font, and near it is a mutilated statue of the Virgin sustaining the Saviour on her knees, which the curé insisted upon was Nicodemus. His scriptural knowledge seemed about equal to his historical; but he evidently had no mean opinion of his own acquirements, which, he almost told us, were of too high a character to be wasted on mere travellers and foreigners, who knew nothing about Notre Dame or the saints. He would not let us see the belfry-tower, which he assured us was unsafe, and was displeased at our stopping him to remark on the extreme antiquity of two of the huge pillars which support the roof, and which, though much daubed with whitewash, have not lost all their fine *contours*. Having got rid of us, the curé hurried back to his siesta, and we strolled round the church. Beautiful circular arches, with zigzag mouldings, almost perfect, adorned several towers, and showed how admirable must once have been the form of the building. We found ourselves carried away by the crowd into the street again, and were obliged to pause and take breath by the side of the clear rivulet, which, as in most of the towns here, runs swiftly through the streets, rendering them much cleaner than they would otherwise be. Here we were accosted, from an open window, by a female who had been watching our proceedings, from the time of our driving into the town, and who seemed quite distressed to see three ladies alone, without a cavalier. "However," she said, "three of you are company, to be sure, and can take care of each other." She was very eloquent on the subject of Morlàas, and had no idea but that we had purposely chosen the market-day for our visit, in order to be *gay*.

We made our way, with some difficulty — through the throng of persons which filled the market-place, and who were busy buying and selling coarse stuffs and mérinos, coloured handkerchiefs, and woollen goods — to the principal façade of the church, against which the ruinous old *halle* is built; and there we contrived to get a sight of the remains of one of the most splendid portals I ever beheld. Of gigantic proportions, circle within circle, each elaborately carved, with figures, foliage, and intersecting lines, the magnificent door-way of the church of Sainte Foi presents a treasure to antiquarians: equal in riches to, but more delicate, and larger and loftier, than that of Malmsbury Abbey, in Wiltshire, it has features in common with that fine structure; but I never saw so wide a span as the arch, or more exquisite ornaments.

It appears that the town of Morlàas, which, ruined as it is, is said to be *rich* (!) is about to restore this fine entrance. A new town-hall and market-place are being built, and, when completed, the miserable huts which disfigure the church will be cleared away, and the façade allowed to appear. Above this door is a fine steeple, crested with figures, which we could scarcely distinguish, but which we found were the *Cows of Béarn* clustered round the summit.

When Morlàas was the residence of the Viscounts of Béarn, it possessed a sovereign court, and a mint of great celebrity, where copper, silver, and even *gold* coins were struck. Money seems to have been coined at Morlàas in the time of the Romans; its pieces were much coveted in the country for their purity, and were considered far superior to any other in Gascony. There was a *livre Morlane* as there was a *livre Tournois*, and it long preserved its celebrity. It was worth triple *the livre Tournois*, and was subdivided into *sols*, *ardits*, and *baquettes*, or *vaquettes*, *i.e. little cows*. A very few of those remarkable coins are still preserved; some exist, in private museums, of the time of the early Centulles and Gastons, of François Phoebus, of Catherine d'Albret, Henry II., Henry IV., and Queen Jeanne. The device they bear is—*"Grâtia Dei sum id quod sum."*

Some Moorish coins, with Arabic inscriptions, have been found in this neighbourhood, which are also preserved in the cabinets of the curious.

The Hôtel or Palace of the Viscounts was formerly called the Hourquie, or Forquie: from whence the money was called *moneta Furcensis*: the town itself was occasionally called Furcas. The *patois* name by which it is known is Morlans. No vestige is left of this magnificent palace; and Morlàas presents, altogether, a most wretched aspect, being literally a heap of stones and ruin. Its situation offers no inducement to its restoration; for, being placed in the midst of marshes, it has no beauty of country which should make it a desirable residence. From time immemorial, prejudice and custom have prevented any attempt being made to cultivate these dismal swamps; or if a few energetic persons have tried to ameliorate their condition, and have taken possession of parts of the waste with such a view, at once the Ossalois have descended from their mountains, with sticks and staves, and driven the invaders from their ground. Even at the present day, as the right remains to the people of Ossau, they have the power, which they are sure to enforce, of preventing any incursions on the *landes* along the valley of Pau; and, if they please, they can pasture their sheep by the banks of the Gave, and pen them in the lower town, beneath the castle, asking "no bold baron's leave." There is no fear, now, of these fierce mountaineers "sweeping like a torrent down upon the vales," as in the days when Lescar, Morlàas, and Pau, were obliged to shut their gates in terror, when they saw their advance.

It is related, that, in 1337, a lord of Serres erected a castle in the midst of the Pont Long, and in a short time nearly two hundred houses were nestling under the protection of his turrets. All was going on well; the ground began to be drained and cultivated, and everything promised a happy result to the undertaking; but a storm of wrath rose in the mountains, the haughty owners of a useless marsh, unwilling that it should serve a good purpose to others, though of no importance to themselves, roused their followers, and, to the number of several hundreds, rushed from their snowy retreats, and, in one night, ravaged and destroyed all they met with. The new settlers fled in consternation, while the Ossalois burnt and threw down their dwellings, leaving a heap of ruins, which may still be traced in the midst of the Pont Long. They took refuge at some distance, where their dangerous neighbours had no right, and built themselves a village, which is that of

Serres-Castel at the present time.

At one period Henry II., the grandfather of Henry IV., was desirous of forming a park for deer, and, taking possession of a track of ground, he surrounded it with walls. The Ossalois consulted together, and discovered that this ground was one of the dependencies on the Pont Long. Without condescending to remonstrance they assembled in bands, and marching down with flags flying, demolished the enclosures and took back their possession.

In the same year, 1543, the sovereign of Béarn was obliged to solicit of these tyrants of the valley permission for his cousin, the Dame d'Artiguelouve, to send her cattle to feed in the Pont Long, to which they consented *"for a consideration"* —*i.e.* by being paid the *baccade*, such as is demanded of the shepherds.

The Princess Magdelaine, governess of Prince François Phoebus, in 1472, obtained, *as a favour*, the permission for her physician, Thomas Geronne, to introduce *seven mares* to feed in the marsh. A letter of the princess entreats, also, at another period, the same grace for the cattle of her treasurer-general.

For more than eight centuries the possession of this *precious* marsh has been the subject of litigation, and it has remained in its barren state.

The Vallée d'Ossau has had to defend its rights sometimes against the viscounts of Béarn, sometimes against the monks of Cluny, and the *Poublans* of Pau. Law or combats have been always necessary to enable them to retain their rights. It was on occasion of a decision in their favour by Gaston IV., that the Ossalois made a gift to that prince of the sum of two thousand four hundred florins, to aid him in finishing the castle of Pau, which was then in the course of erection.

This Pont Long, which has so long been an apple of discord to Béarn, is at the present hour likely to have settled bounds; for, in 1837, the members of the Cour-Royal of Pau occupied themselves on the subject, and a chance exists of something useful being done with the ground: there is a project for encouraging mulberry-trees and silk-worms there, and of making a canal to carry off its waters, and render it fit for cultivation. This is the more necessary, as fever and ague are sufficiently common in its neighbourhood. But, even within a very few years, when an enlightened agriculturist, M. Laclède, endeavoured to clear the ground, and plant and improve, the fury of opposition he experienced was disgracefully extraordinary. Under the pretext that their pastures were invaded, the people came with fire and hatchet, and burnt his trees, and cut away his bridges and aqueducts.

A spot is shown in the Pont Long, called Henri Quatre's marsh; for it is said that this prince being one day out shooting snipes, got so entangled in the mud that it was with the greatest difficulty he was rescued from his unpleasant predicament.

There is an oasis in this desert, the village of Uzein, which is a standing proof of the possibility of effecting all that industry can desire in this condemned place: the people of this flourishing village owe their success to the determined perseverance of their curate, who exhorted and persuaded his parishioners to bring manure for their fields from Serres, and, at the end of a few years, all was brilliant and smiling, and Uzein is considered to produce the best maize in Béarn.

There are a few towers still standing, where castles have been erected on the Pont Long; an old grey tower of Navailles, and one of Montaner, so strong as to have proved indestructible: it was built by Gaston Phoebus, at the same time as that of Pau, and what remains of the walls of its donjon are upwards of ten feet thick!

Lescar was once an important town of Béarn, and in its fine cathedral princes were buried, whose ashes even rest there no longer, and whose tombs have long since been destroyed. Most of its magnificence disappeared at the period when Queen Jeanne declared her adherence to the new doctrine, and gave her sanction to the enemies of Catholic superstition to pull down the *Pagan images*. Angry and fierce was the discussion which took place between the Queen and the Cardinal d'Armagnac, her former friend, on the occasion of the attack on the cathedral of Lescar: the following extracts from their letters, given by Mr. Jameson in his work on "the Reformation in Navarre," are characteristic on both sides.

The cardinal's courier, it seems, waited while Jeanne, without pause or hesitation, wrote her reply to his representation. His letter ran thus:

> "Madam,—The duty of the service in which I was born, and which I have continued faithfully to fulfil, both to the late sovereigns, your father and mother, as well as to the late king your husband, has so complete an influence on my conduct, that I must ever be attentive to the means of sustaining your welfare, and the glory of your illustrious house. Moved by the zeal which attaches me to your interests, I will never conceal from you whatever it is desirable that you should learn, and which I may have previously heard, trusting that you will receive in good part the representations of your long-tried, most attached, and faithful servant, who will never offer to make them for his own private advantage, but solely for the sake of your conscience, and the prosperity of your affairs. I cannot, then, Madam, conceal from you the deep affliction which penetrates me on account of the information I have received of the overthrow of images and altars, and the pillage of ornaments, silver, and jewels, committed in the cathedral of Lescar, by the agents of your authority, as well as the severity of those agents to the chapter and people, by the interdiction of divine service. This proceeding appears to me to be the more monstrous, since it took place in your presence, and resulted from evil counsels which must lead to your ruin. It is in vain for you to conceive that you can transplant the new religion into your dominions at your pleasure. The wishes of the ministers who have assured you of this are at variance with those of your subjects. They will never consent to quit their religion, as they have declared by their protest at the last meeting of the estates of Béarn. * * * And, even supposing that they were reduced to accept your faith, consider what

you would have to fear from the two sovereigns whose territories surround you, and who abhor nothing so much as the new opinions with which you are so delighted. Their policy would lead them to seize your dominions, rather than suffer them to be the prey of strangers. To shelter you from these dangers, you have not, like England, the ocean for a rampart. Your conduct perils the fortunes of your children, and risks the beholding them deprived of a throne. * * * You will thus become worse than an infidel, by neglecting to provide for those of your own house. Such is the fruit of your Evangelism. * * * Has not God, who worked so many miracles through them, (*i.e.* the saints,) manifestly directed us to regard those holy personages rather than Luther, Calvin, Farel, Videl, and so many other presumptuous men, who would desire us to slight those reverend names, and adopt their novelties? Would they have us hold an open council to hear them, or unite in one common opinion against the Catholic Church? * * * Without wasting time in further reflections, let me entreat you to place in their former condition the churches of Lescar, of Pau, and other places, which have been so deplorably desolated by you. This advice is preferable to that given you by your ministers, which it imports you to abandon, &c. &c.—Your loyal and very obedient servant,

"THE CARDINAL D'ARMAGNAC.

"Vielleperite, Aug. 18th, 1563."

To this Queen Jeanne replied in the following terms:—

"My Cousin,—From my earliest years I have been acquainted with the zeal which attached you to the service of my kindred. I am not authorized by ignorance of that zeal to refuse it the praise and esteem it merits, or to be prevented from feeling a gratitude which I should be desirous of continuing towards those who, like you, having partaken of the favour of my family, have preserved good-will and fidelity towards it. I should trust you would still entertain those feelings towards me, as you profess to do, without allowing them to be changed or destroyed by the influence of I know not what religion, or superstition. Thanking you, at the same time, for the advice you give me, and which I receive according to its varied character, the dissimilar and mingled points it touches being divided between heaven and earth, God and man! As to the first point, concerning the reform which I have effected at Pau, and at Lescar, and which I desire to extend throughout my sovereignty, I have learnt it from the Bible, which I read more willingly than the works of your doctors. * * * As to the ruin impending over me through bad counsel, under the colour of religion, I am not so devoid of the gifts of God or of the aid of friends, as to be unable to make choice of persons worthy of my confidence, and capable of acting, not under a vain pretence, but with the true spirit of religion. * * * I clearly perceive that you have been misinformed, both respecting the answer of my estates and the disposition of my subjects. The two estates have professed their obedience to religion. * * * I know who my neighbours are; the one hates my religion as much as I do his, but that does not affect our mutual relations: and besides, I am not so destitute of advice and friends as to have neglected all necessary precautions for the defence of my rights in case of attack. * * * Although you think to intimidate me, I am protected from all apprehension; first, by my confidence in God whom I serve, and who knows how to defend his cause. Secondly, because my tranquillity is not affected by the designs of those whom I can easily oppose, * * * with the grace of Him who encompasses my country as the ocean does England. I do not perceive that I run the risk of sacrificing either my own welfare or that of my son; on the contrary, I trust to strengthen it in the only way a Christian should pursue; and even though the spirit of God might not inspire me with a knowledge of this way, yet human intellect would induce me to act as I do, from the many examples which I recall with regret, especially that of the late king, my husband, of whose history you well know the beginning, the course, and the end. Where are the splendid crowns you held out to him? Did he gain any by combating against true religion and his conscience? * * * I blush with shame when you talk of the many atrocities which you allege to have been committed by those of our faith; cast out the beam out of thine own eye, and then shalt thou see clearly to cast out the moat in thy brother's eye: purify the earth that is stained with the innocent blood which those of your party have shed, a fact you can bear testimony to. * * * You are ignorant of what our ministers are, who teach patience, obedience to sovereigns, and the other virtues of which the apostles and the martyrs have left them an example. * * * You affirm that multitudes draw back from our belief, while I maintain that the number of its adherents increases daily. As to ancient authorities, I hear them every day cited by our ministers. I am not indeed sufficiently learned to have gone through so many works, but neither, I suspect, have you, or are better versed in them than myself, as you were always known to be more acquainted with matters of state than those of the church. * * * I place no reliance on doctors, not even Calvin, Beza, and others, but as they follow Scripture. You would send them to a council. They desire it, provided that it shall be a free one, and that the parties shall not be judges. The motive of the surety they require is founded on the examples of John Huss and Jerome of Prague. Nothing afflicts me more than that you, after having received the truth, should have abandoned it for idolatry, because you then found the advancement of your fortune and worldly honours. * * * Read again the passages of Scripture you quote, before you explain them so unhappily on any other occasion: it might be pardonable in me, a female, but you, a cardinal, to be so old and so ignorant! truly, my cousin, I feel shame for you. * * * If you have no better reasons for combating my undertaking, do not again urge me to follow your worldly prudence. I consider it mere folly before God; it cannot impede my endeavours. *Your* doubts make me tremble, *my* assurance makes me firm. When you desire again to persuade me that the words of your mouth are the voice of your conscience and your faithfulness, be more careful; and let the fruitless letter you have sent me be the last of that kind I shall receive. * * * Receive this from one who knows not how to style herself: not being able to call herself a friend, and doubtful of any affinity till the time of repentance and conversion, when she will be

"Your cousin and friend,
"JEANNE."

We drove to Lescar, which is within a short distance of Pau, anxious to discover some remains of its former grandeur; but, like almost all the towns in this part of France, the glory is indeed departed from it. The situation is remarkably fine; it stands on a high *côteau*, by the side of the road to Bayonne, and from the terrace of the cathedral a magnificent view of the snowy mountains spreads along the horizon. Nothing but dilapidated, ugly stone houses, and slovenly yards, are now to be seen in the town; though it is said the people are by no means poor, as, indeed, the rich gardens and vineyards around testify.

There is not a tomb or monument of any kind left in the cathedral; but it is entirely paved with inscribed stones, few of them earlier than the beginning of the seventeenth century. The church itself has been so much altered as to be scarcely the same; it is still of great extent, and is imposing as to size: a few strange old pillars, with grotesque capitals, remain of its earliest date; but, from these specimens, it is plain that there could never have been much architectural grace displayed in its construction. The organ was playing as we walked through the aisles, and is a very fine one: we could not but regret that, at Pau, there should not be a single church where we could have the advantage of hearing similar music; and that the chief town of Béarn should be denuded of every attraction common to even the most neglected French town. No thanks, however, are due to the arms of Montgomery, that one stone remained on another of the cathedral of Lescar; and that all in Pau should have been destroyed in his time, is not surprising. When one thinks on the former magnificence of this town and cathedral, and the pomp and circumstance of all the royal funerals which took place here; of all the gorgeous tombs and splendid ceremonies; and, looking round, beholds only ruined towns and crumbling walls, the contrast is striking to the mind.

In the ninth century, this part of the country was covered with a thick forest, called Lascurris. The Duke of Gascony, (Guillaume Sance,) about 980, having excited a knight to murder one of his enemies, was seized with qualms of conscience, and, to relieve his mind, rebuilt the church, which was *then* fallen to decay, and founded a monastery in the solitude, which he dedicated to Notre Dame. The assassin, sharing his remorse, became a monk, and afterwards abbot there, and is known as Lopoforti.

The future abbots seem to have been men of valour; for they armed themselves, when occasion called, against the followers of Mahound, who ventured from the passes of Spain into their territories.

The bishops of Lescar had the jurisdiction of 178 parishes, and the diocese comprised two abbeys: it is contended that this was the most ancient bishopric of Béarn; and the town the capital of the country in former days. In the seventeenth century it was certainly a place of importance, and was well defended by walls, gates, and fosses, of which a few picturesque ruins alone remain.

In the choir of the cathedral there are still the sculptured stalls of oak, executed in the time of Louis XIII., which are bold and graceful, and in excellent preservation; some mosaic pavement has lately been discovered, which was laid down by Bishop Guy in very early times; and it is to be expected more discoveries could be made if more zeal were roused in the cause. The chapels are richly adorned, and in better taste than usual, and the church is, on the whole, extremely well kept: the vault-like chill one feels, however, on entering does not say much for its salubrity.

The most important tombs which once adorned this sanctuary, were those of the young Prince of Béarn and King of Navarre, (François Phoebus,) who died in 1483. Jean II. d'Albret in 1516, and his wife, Catherine de Foix. Marguérite de Valois—the Fleur des Marguérites,—in 1548; and Henry II., her husband—the *immortal grandfather* of the great Béarnois. It has been said that the body of their daughter, Jeanne d'Albret, was brought here; but this appears to be incorrect, as her tomb is at Vendôme.

The death of young François Phoebus is one of the most melancholy episodes in the history of the country. It is thus recounted:

He was under the guardianship of his mother, Magdelaine of France, Countess of Foix, a woman of superior mind and qualities, who devoted herself to his interests and those of his kingdom, and spared no pains to foster the noble dispositions which were in her son.

The time *was out of joint*, in consequence of civil dissensions, and the unjust claims on Navarre of the King of Arragon; and her position was very critical; but her wisdom and prudence had greatly calmed the turbulence of those with whom she had to deal, and her subjects looked forward with hope and delight to the majority of her son, who was as amiable as he was transcendently beautiful, and whom, in imitation of the title of their hero, Gaston, they had surnamed Phoebus. Magdelaine was aided in her good intentions by her brother-in-law, the Cardinal de Foix, whose sage advice greatly relieved and guided her, and when she saw her beloved son, then aged fifteen, enter his territories in triumph, apparently received with friendly interest by all contending parties, her heart became joyous, and the future seemed all hope and pleasure to her.

Several marriages were proposed for him; but she was desirous that as much delay as possible should take place before that important step should be decided. Numerous powerful princes came forward, offering their alliances. Amongst others, Don Ferdinand, of Castile, named his second daughter, Doña Juana, who afterwards inherited all his possessions; but the Countess of Foix rejected this, as it would have given umbrage to Louis XI. of France, whose friendship it was necessary to secure; and whose wily mind was working at his own interest, which prompted him to desire that a young nun of Coimbra should be drawn from her sacred retreat, and made the bride of the young king: this was another Doña Juana, for whose claim to the kingdom of Castile the artful monarch of France chose to contend. Louis, therefore, wishing to avoid the vicinity of Spain for his young *protégé*, persuaded his mother to withdraw him from Pampeluna to his castle at Pau, where he went on with his studies, and, by his amiable and conciliating disposition, won the affection of all his subjects, by whom he was quite adored, as well as by his mother, and his sister, the Princess Catherine, to whom he was tenderly attached.

One morning, as they were all three together engaged in their different occupations, a flute was brought to the young prince, who, after a time, took it up with the intention of practising some music; for in this accomplishment he excelled. He had been playing but a short time when his sister observed him turn pale, and the next moment the instrument fell from his hand: he uttered a deep sigh, and dropped senseless on the ground. They lifted him up, used instant means for his recovery, but all was vain; their hope, their joy, their treasure, was gone: François Phoebus—the young, beautiful, and good—was dying. Poison had done its work, and treason was successful: he lived but a few minutes, and his last words were suitable to his pure life. When he saw his distracted mother and sister hanging over him in agony, he whispered, "Do not lament, my reign is not of this world: I leave the things of earth, and go to my father."

What a scene of desolation ensued to the country and the bereaved mother, who had so long struggled with accumulated misfortune! To add to the difficulties of her position, her only support, Louis XI., just then died, and, beset by ambitious ministers and selfish counsellors, betrayed, deceived, and thwarted, the unfortunate Magdelaine sunk under her sorrows, and soon followed her fair son to the grave.

He was buried in great pomp at the cathedral of St. Marie of Lescar, and his young sister, Catherine, was left to reign in his place. Of her Providence made its peculiar care, and her fate, which threatened ill, was happily turned aside.

Olhagaray, the historian of Béarn, gives the affecting answer of the Countess Magdelaine to the ambassador of Spain, who, immediately after her son's death, came to her Court to treat for the hand of the young Queen Catherine. It was thus she spoke, "with an infinity of sobs and tears:"

"Gentlemen,—You find me in poor condition to receive you according to your merits: but you see my desolation and misery, and the ruin which is come upon me. This last torrent of misfortune is as a deluge which overwhelms me—a deep abyss of evil in which I am engulphed. Alas! when I consider the just grief which environs me, I know not where I am! Gaston, the brave Gaston, my lord and my husband, while yet I was in the early joy of his sweet society, and was happy in his precious affection, was torn from me. My woes were softened, and the dark night of my widowhood enlightened by the brightness of my Phoebus. Poor, desolate mother that I am! Heaven envied my content, and has hidden him from my eyes. In this sad spot he expired: here, raising his eyes above, he exclaimed, 'My reign is not of this world!'

"Did we not, nevertheless, expect much of him! would he not, had he lived, have healed the wounds of his country, have applied salutary remedies to all her evils! He saw the difficulties, he prepared himself to thread the intricate mazes belonging to his crown of Navarre; yet, when he held it in his hands, he said, it was not that crown that he expected.

"What means have I now left me in the world that permit me to speak to you of the state of Spain, of the health of the king, the queen, or the court. I have no words but these, no reply but this: go, therefore, and for all answer tell the king of Spain how you found me; say, that my sadness and my tears but ill permitted me to read the letter with which he honoured me; and thank him that he has kept so kind a remembrance of me, praying him to continue me his friendship while I live his humble servant."

CHAPTER X.

The Romances Of The Castle Of Orthez—Tour De Moncade—The Infants—The Son Of Gaston Phoebus—- Legends—The Oath—The Bad King Of Navarre—The Quarrel—The Murder—Death Of Gaston Phoebus—Paradise The Reward Of Hunters—The Captive—The Step-Mother—The Young Countess—The Great Bear—The Return—The Real Cause—The Meeting In The Forest—The Mass.

THE most interesting place on the road to Bayonne is Orthez, once the seat of the counts of Foix. We proposed remaining there a short time, in order to visit its remains on our way to Bayonne, and alighted at the hotel of *La Belle Hôtesse*, which is on the site of *La Lune*, where the historian, Froissart, stopped some centuries before us, and where he heard so many stories and legends which he has immortalized in his charming *romantic* chronicle. The soldiers of Marshal Soult occupied this inn in 1814, when the pale old lady, who is still mistress, then deserved the title which her beauty gave to her house of entertainment.

On approaching Orthez we were struck with the appearance, on a height above the town, of the castle ruins, whose battered walls seem so fragile that a breath of wind might blow them away: the upper part of the great tower is much injured, and its irregular stones project in a manner which threatens their fall: the blue sky shone through the arrow slits and windows, and the whole mass gave us an idea of its hastening to immediate dissolution. It has an imposing and venerable effect, and excited in our minds considerable interest: we therefore hastened up the rugged way to the hill on which it stands, and there found ourselves in the midst of the remains of one of the strongest castles of which this part of Béarn could boast, from the earliest time.

It is called the castle of Moncade, having been, in 734, the abode of a Catalonian knight of that name, who was accustomed to issue forth from this stronghold to combat the Moors of Spain. In after times the fortress was possessed by a warlike lady, called La Grosse Comtesse Garsende de Béarn, who, in 1242, offered her services to Henry III. of England; and, after having fought in his cause with her knights and vassals, and received a large sum of money in requital, she returned home, and expended it on the castle, which she rendered impregnable. It was probably a ruin in the time of Garsende; for the reparations she made in the great tower are very evident; the lower part being more discoloured than the upper story, in which there are windows, at a great height, of trefoil form. The shape of the tower itself is very unlike any I had before seen, and seemed to me extremely curious; it is five-sided, each side presenting an acute angle, and one being flattened at about a quarter of the height by a two-sided projection, which is not a tower but probably a recess within from whence to send arrows; yet there are no openings now visible; nor is there, on any side, a means of entrance, except that a square-headed window opens very high up in the wall towards the part where the rest of the castle joined this donjon. A large hole in the wall, towards the open country, made, perhaps, originally by English cannon in 1814, and enlarged since, allows ingress to the interior. There are arches and recesses, and some ornamental architecture to be traced within, but no doors in any direction; and my idea of the fragility of the building was quickly dispelled when I discovered that the solid walls were at least nine feet thick, the angles sharp as a knife, and the apparently tottering stones as firm in their rocky cement as if just built.

All round, for some extent, are remains of ruined walls, with a few circular and pointed arches here and there; the clear stream flows beneath where once was the moat, in one part, and on the other sides bushes and brambles fill up the defences. A huge, fearful-looking well, of enormous depth, is in the midst of all; where, perhaps, was once the inner court-yard, and here we saw a group of peasants drawing water; for Orthez is so badly supplied that the townspeople have to mount this steep height, and fill their brass-bound pails, from which they dispense the fine clear water to the inhabitants. This must have been long a great inconvenience and trouble; but we discovered afterwards that another fountain has been found in the town, not far from the bridge, where we saw numerous visitors busy in the same occupation.

The view from the castle-height is very fine; the last of the range of snowy mountains seen in such perfection from Pau rises in great majesty, and closes the scene; while the luxuriant plain and hills around are seen to a great distance. The valiant Catalonian, and the fierce countess, must have been dangerous neighbours to their foes, commanding as they did the country, for leagues round.

One of the lords of Moncade was father to a chosen Viscount of Béarn, known in the annals of the country, amongst their numerous Gastons, as Le Bon.

The story told respecting him is as follows: In the year 1170, Marie, Viscountess of Béarn, a young princess of only sixteen, was induced by interested counsellors to do homage for her domains to Alphonso the Second, King of Arragon. This act, which took place at Jaca, required to be confirmed by the barons of Béarn; but the latter, indignant at the infringement of their rights, and attack on the independence of their country, solemnly protested against the transaction, and proclaimed the young viscountess unfit to govern, deprived her of her power, and proceeded to the election of a new ruler.

Their choice fell on a lord of Bigorre, who, not proving himself worthy of his election, but endeavouring to violate the laws, was put to death in open assembly, falling, like Cæsar, by the hand of a patriot. Another took his place, but the Béarnais, it appeared, were particularly unfortunate in their selection, for he turned out no better than the former, and was deposed.

It became necessary to fix on a governor, and the great men of the kingdom, consulting together, came to the following conclusion: The young viscountess, after her banishment, married William de Moncade, one of the richest lords of Catalonia, and the issue of this union was twins, both boys. It was agreed that one of these should fill the vacant seat of sovereignty of Béarn, and two of the *prudhommes* were deputed to visit their father with the proposition. On their arrival at his castle the sages found the children asleep, and observed with attention their infant demeanour. Both were beautiful, strong, and healthy; and it was a difficult matter to make an election between two such attractive and innocent creatures. They were extremely alike, and neither could be pronounced superior to the other; the *prudhommes* were strangely puzzled, for they had been so often deceived that they felt it to be most important that they should not err this time. As they hung in admiration over the sleeping babes, one of them remarked a circumstance that at once decided their preference, and put an end to their vacillation; one of the little heroes held his hand tightly closed; the tiny, mottled palm of the other was wide open as it lay upon his snowy breast. "He will be a liberal and bold knight," said one of the Béarnais, "and will best suit us as a head." This infant was accordingly chosen, given up by his parents to the wise men, and carried off in triumph to be educated amongst his future subjects. The event proved their sagacity, and Gaston le Bon lived to give them good laws and prosperity.

A descendant of this chief was a Gaston, who opposed Edward I., of England, and was thrown into prison by that terrible warrior, who revenged his defeat in Santonge by fearful reprisals, and gave up the town of Orthez to his soldiers, to pillage and destroy as they pleased. Gaston was obliged to agree to a composition with the English prince; and he was released from his dungeon in a castle in Gascony. An appeal to the King of France was agreed on; and, when both were in presence of the suzerain, Gaston threw down his glove of defiance against the King of England, calling him a traitor and felon knight. Edward, starting forward, and commanding his people, who heard the charge with rage, to stand back, picked up the glove himself, and entreated that a single combat might be allowed between them. The King of France, however, opposed this; and the question of their dispute was decided by law — rather an unusual thing in those days.

This tower of Moncade, — rendered, it appears, by Gaston, the father of the little open-handed hero, as like as possible to his château in Catalonia, — is the scene of several tragedies; and every stone could tell some tale of sorrow and oppression. There is something singularly fearful in the aspect of its strong walls and donjon, without an outlet. In this very tower died, by his father's hand, the unfortunate son of Gaston Phoebus, whose touching story is recounted by Froissart. Although well-known, it is impossible to pass it over here, or to forget that equally melancholy history of the young Queen Blanche, poisoned by her sister.

THE SON OF GASTON PHOEBUS.

Froissart, after describing the splendours of the castle of Orthez in glowing terms, continues: "Briefly, and, considering all things, before I came to this court I had visited those of many kings, dukes, princes, counts, and ladies of high quality, but I never was in any which pleased me so well, for feats of arms and gaiety, as that of the Count de Foix. You might see, in the saloons and the chambers and in the courts, knights and squires of honour going and coming; and you might hear them speak of war and of love. All honour might there be found. There I was informed of the greatest part of those feats of arms which took place in Spain, Portugal, Arragon, Navarre, England, Scotland, and the frontiers and limits of Languedoc, &c.; for I met there, on various missions to the count, knights and squires of all these nations.

"Once, on a Christmas Day, I there saw at his table four Bishops, two *Clémentins*, and two *Urbanists* (partisans of the rival popes). There were seated the Count de Foix, and the Viscount de Roquebertin d'Arragon, the Viscount de Bruniquil, the Viscount de Gousserant, and an English knight sent by the Duke of Lancaster, from Lisbon, where he then sojourned. At another table were five abbés and two knights of Arragon; at another, knights and squires of Gascony and Bigorre; and the *sovereign master of the hall* was Messire Espaign de Lyon, and four knights *maîtres d'hôtel*. And the count's two natural brothers, Messire Ernould Guillaume and Messire Pierre de Béarn, served him, together with his two sons, Messire Yvain de l'Escale and Messire Gratien. I must tell you that there was a crowd of minstrels, as well belonging to the count as strangers, who filled up every interval with specimens of their art. And this day the count gave to both minstrels and heralds the sum of five hundred francs; and habits of cloth of gold, furred with *menu vair*, he gave to the minstrels of the Duke of Touraine; the which dresses were valued at two hundred francs. And the dinner lasted till four hours after noon."

One figure is wanting in this brilliant account—the only legitimate son of the magnificent Count of Foix, his child by Agnes of Navarre, whose place, as well as that of her son, is vacant at her husband's table.

What might, even then, be the pangs of remorse that shot along the mind of the mighty chief, as he looked round that brilliant assembly and felt that his honours would end with himself? "No son of his succeeding." Where was the young, blooming, accomplished, and promising heir, so loved by his people, and once the object of his pride and hope? Brilliant and gorgeous as was the present scene, what would have been that which should have welcomed the affianced bride of his son to his court? and many such would have hailed the happy events which might have ensued. His two *natural* sons, Yvain and Gratien, are there, full of beauty, grace, and health; but, as the first approaches, and hands him a cup of wine, he trembles and sets down the goblet, untasted, for an instant. He recovers, however, and quaffs the wine to the health of his friends: the minstrels strike their harps; and one—the chief—bursts forth in a strain of adulation, lauding to the skies the glories and the virtues of the most liberal and magnificent prince of his time. Gaston listens with pride and satisfaction; and, by degrees, the low moaning which had seemed to sound in his ears dies away, and he laughs loud, and dispenses his gracious words around, endeavouring to forget that so great a prince could ever know care, or feel remorse, for what it was his will to do. But it is necessary to tell why Gaston Phoebus felt remorse in the midst of his splendid court.

At the conclusion of a long war between the houses of Foix and Armagnac, it was agreed between the chiefs of the contending parties, that a marriage should take place between Gaston, the young heir of Béarn, and the fair Beatrix d'Armagnac. A temporary house was constructed on the confines of the two territories, between Barcelone and Aire, where now a wooden pillar indicates the division of the departments of Les Landes and Gers; and there everything was settled. The Bishop of Lectoure said mass; and an oath of the most terrible description passed between the two princes, that they would never infringe the treaty. Part of the *formula* ran thus: "And, in case of failing in this promise, they would deny God, *that he might be against them*; and, utterly to damn both their bodies and souls, they would take the devil for their lord, and have their sepulchres in hell, now and for evermore."

The young bride, in consideration of twenty thousand francs of gold, which were given her as a dower, renounced all her rights, both paternal and maternal; and the pope, to stop the effusion of blood caused by the quarrels of the two houses, gave all the necessary dispensations required in consequence of parentage. Then the Bishop of Lescar celebrated the betrothment, that same day, in the Château de Monclar.

Both bride and bridegroom were very young, full of hope, and with every prospect of happiness. *La gaie Armagnoise*, as the young princess was called, lively and happy, and, according to all historians, a lady of the greatest amiability; the Prince of Béarn affectionate, brave, and handsome. With the whole assembly at Monclar,

"All went merry as a marriage bell;"

but they had reckoned without Charles the Bad, King of Navarre!

Like one of those fell enchanters of romance, who appear suddenly in the midst of rejoicings where they have not been invited, and cast a spell upon the guests, changing joy to mourning, Charles of Navarre's influence blighted the

" — —bud of love in summer's ripening breath,"

that

"should prove a beauteous flower — —."

Agnes of Navarre, Countess of Foix, had become the victim of the disputes between her husband and brother: she had been sent from Gaston's court to that of Charles, in order to induce the latter to pay a ransom which he owed the count, and which he treacherously and dishonourably withheld. The unfortunate wife remained at her brother's court, soliciting in vain that he should do justice to the severe husband, to whom she dared not return empty-handed. Her son, attached to his mother, and anxious to receive her blessing on his marriage, entreated permission to visit her in Navarre. He was received there with great demonstrations of honour and affection. Charles the Bad lamented to him the feud between his father and himself, and expressed his regret at the manifest dislike which Count Gaston showed to his wife, and dwelling much on this last cause of sorrow, in which the young prince heartily joined, he gave it as his opinion that the feeling must be occasioned by supernatural means, and could only be combated by a similar power. He had, he said, in his possession a medicine of such virtue that, if it were administered properly, it would counteract any evil influence, and restore the mind of the person to whom it was given to a right tone.

"Take, my beloved nephew," said he, "this bag of powder, and when an opportunity presents itself, pour it into your father's cup, or strew it over the meat he eats: it is a love potion—and no sooner shall he have swallowed it, than all his former affection for your dear mother will return. Think, then, what happy days are in store for us all! Agnes will once more take her place amongst you; will bless you and your fair wife; and I, who am banished from that society I most prize, shall once more embrace my friend and witness his happiness."

This picture was too flattering to the ardent young boy of fifteen: with all the credulity of his time and the simplicity of his age, he caught at such a means of restoring his family to peace and joy, and, gratefully accepting the present of his uncle, he suspended the little bag containing the wondrous drug round his neck by a ribbon, and departed from the Court of Navarre full of hope and expectation.

On his arrival in Béarn he could scarcely refrain, in spite of his uncle's injunctions to the contrary, from communicating his secret to his favourite brother, Jobain (Yvain), his father's natural son, who shared his confidence as well as his couch. Jobain, however, was not long before he observed the ribbon round his brother's neck, and pressed him to explain the meaning of the little bag which he saw suspended there. Young Gaston, confused at finding his secret so nearly discovered, bade him inquire no further,—that there was a mystery attached to it which he dared not tell; "but you will soon see," he added, cheerfully, "a great change in my father: and he and my dear mother will be well together."

A few days after this, the brothers were playing at the *jeu de paume*, and a dispute arose between them which grow more and more violent, till Gaston forgot himself so far as to strike Jobain on the face: it was but a childish quarrel, which the next moment might have healed, but Jobain's passion was so excited, that in his first fury he rushed to his father, and accused Gaston of concealing in his bosom a bag of poison, intended to be administered to the count, in order to cause his death.

Count Gaston, on hearing this accusation, without giving himself time for a moment's reflection, which would have shown him the improbability of the story, burst into so ungovernable a fury that he became almost frantic, and it was with the utmost difficulty his knights prevented his instantly putting his son to death. The states of Foix and Béarn, to whose judgment he was at length induced to refer the sentence of this involuntary parricide, were more moderate. "My lord," said they, "saving your grace, we will not that Gaston should die: he is your heir, and you have no other."

It is even asserted, that those of Foix in particular would not consent to retire until they had received a promise from the count that he would not attempt his son's life. It was, therefore, on the servants of young Gaston that the weight of his fury fell; and he caused no less than fifteen to suffer the utmost extremity of torture, under which they died. As for the unhappy prince, he had already condemned himself. Confined in his tower of Orthez, he had taken to his bed, and there lay, concealing himself in the clothes; and for several days refused all nourishment, giving himself up altogether to despair. Those whose business it was to serve him, finding this, became alarmed, and, hastening to his father, related the fact:

"My Lord," said they, "for the love of God, take heed to your son; for he is starving in the prison, where he lies, and has not eaten since he entered there, for his meat remains untouched as when we first took it into the tower."

Thereupon the count started up, without uttering a word, and, quitting his chamber, hurried to the prison where his son was, says Froissart, and, "by ill fortune, he held in his hand a *small, long knife*, with which he was cleaning and arranging his nails. He commanded the door of the dungeon to be opened, when he went straight to his son, and, still holding the knife in his hand by the blade, *which did not project from it more than half an inch*, he caught him by the throat, calling out, 'Ha! traitor!—why will you not eat?' and by some means the steel entered into a vein. The count, on this, instantly departed, neither saying or doing more, and returned to his chamber. His poor child, terrified at the sight of his father, felt all his blood turn, weak as he was with fasting, and the point of the knife having opened a vein in his throat, *however small it might have been,*—turned him round—and died!

"Thus," continues the chronicler, "it was as I tell you: this was the death of young Gaston de Foix. *His father, in truth, killed him*; but it was the King of Navarre who directed the blow."

The agony of remorse or affection of the inhuman count, it is but just to say, was extreme, on finding how all had ended; "and the body of the child was taken away with cries and tears to the *Frères Mineurs*, at Orthez, and there buried."

What now remained to the brilliant Gaston Phoebus? He had no legitimate child, and he hated the next heir, Mathieu de Castelbon, "because he was not a valiant knight at arms." His intention was to leave his large possessions to his two natural sons; but, before he had made the proper dispositions to secure it to them, he was surprised by death in the hospital of Orion, two leagues from Orthez, as he was washing his hands on his return from his favourite pursuit of hunting the bear, about which he is eloquent in his work on the Chase; and all that Yvain, the betrayer of young Gaston, could do, was to take possession of his father's ring, and his *little long knife*—that fatal instrument!—and by those tokens procured that the gates of the castle of Orthez should be opened to him; hoping to obtain *a part of the treasures* of the count, who had not less than a million of crowns of gold in his coffers.

It was in the month of August, under a hot sun, that Gaston Phoebus had hunted the bear half the day; and on arriving at Orion, about two leagues from Orthez, he appeared delighted at the coolness of the fresh strewn room, where the dinner was prepared: "This verdure," said he, "does me good, for the day has been fearfully hot!" They brought him water to wash, but no sooner did he feel its coldness on his fingers—which were *"fine, long and straight"*—than he was seized with a fit, probably of apoplexy, and was dead almost immediately, to the extreme terror of all with him. Yvain, it seems, was at first full of grief, but listened to the advice of those who recommended him instantly to repair to the castle of Orthez, and secure what treasure he could. Accordingly he rode off, and by showing the count's ring and knife, was admitted; but the coffer, bound with iron and closed with many locks, was opened by a key, which the count always wore round his neck, in a little bag, and that key was found by the chaplain on his master, after Yvain's departure, who was vainly striving to force open the strong chest. The news, in spite of precaution, soon spread in Orthez; and the citizens, who were all greatly attached to their lord, came in crowds to the court of the castle, demanding news of him. Yvain was obliged to speak to them from a window, and declare the truth; appealing to them to protect his right, and not suffer the castle or its contents to be injured. To this they all agreed, as they deplored his being illegitimate, and consequently incapable of succeeding his father.

Then the air rung with lamentations. "Alas!" cried they, "all will go ill with us now! we shall be attacked by all our neighbours: no more peace and safety for us; nothing but misery and subjection, for we have none to defend us now, and none to answer the challenger. Ha, Gaston! unfortunate son! why did you offend your father? We might still have looked to you; for beautiful and great was your beginning, and much comfort were we promised in you. We lost you too young, and your father has left us too soon. Alas! he had seen but sixty-three years—no great age for a knight so powerful and so strong, and one who had all his wishes and desires. Oh, land of Béarn! desolate, and lamenting for thy noble heir, what is to be thy fate? Never shall be seen the peer of the gentle and noble Count of Foix!"

With such cries and tears was the body of Gaston Phoebus, "uncovered on a bier," brought through Orthez to the church of the Cordeliers, and there laid in state; with forty-eight squires to guard it, and four-and-twenty large tapers burning by it, night and day. Then came the burial, where knights and lords and bishops assisted; and the new Count of Castelbon, the heir of all the possessions of the magnificent Gaston, showed becoming honour to his remains. Castelbon then took possession; and his first act was to provide for the two sons, who had no inheritance, and to release the prisoners in the tower of Orthez,—"of which," says Froissart, "there were many; for the Count of Foix, of excellent memory, was *very cruel in this particular*, and never spared man, how high soever, who had offended him: nor was any bold enough to plead for the ransom of a prisoner, for fear of meeting the same fate: *they were put in the fosse, and fed on bread and water*. This very cousin, Castelbon, had been his captive in such a dungeon for eight months, and was ransomed only for forty thousand francs, and he held him in great hatred; and, had he lived two years more, he would never have had the heritage."

The famous work of the count, on Hunting, he dedicated to the King of France; and in it he endeavours to prove the advantages, both to body *and soul*, of the manly exercise of which he was a passionate lover. His own death appears to disprove his arguments, which are curious enough. He thus expresses himself in his Prologue:—"I, Gaston, by the grace of God, surnamed Phoebus, Count of Foys, and Lord of Béarn, have, all my life, been fond of three things—war, love, and hunting; in the two first others may have excelled me, and been more fortunate; but, in the last, I flatter myself, without boasting, that I have no superior. * * * and, besides treating of beasts of chase and their natures, I am convinced that my book is calculated to prove the great good that may arise from the exercise of hunting. A man, by its means, avoids the seven mortal sins; for he has no time to think of the commission of any while he is engaged with his horses and hounds: he is more lively, more ready, more expert, more enterprising, makes himself acquainted with countries, and is quick and active: all good habits and manners follow, and the salvation of his soul as well; for, by avoiding sin, a Christian shall be saved; and this he does; therefore, a hunter must be saved. His life is full of gaiety, pleasure, and amusement, and he has only to guard against two things: one, that he forgets not the knowledge and service of God, *and does not neglect his duty to his liege lord.*

"Now, I will prove this fact. It is well known that idleness is the root of evil; when a man is lazy, negligent, unemployed, he remains in his bed, and in his chamber, and a thousand evil imaginations take possession of him: now a hunter rises at daybreak, and sees the sweet and fresh morning, the clear and serene weather; he hears the song of birds warbling softly and lovingly, each in its language: when the sun is up, he beholds the bright dew glittering with its rays on streams and meadows, and joy is in the heart of the hunter. Then comes the excited delight of the pursuit, the cries, the sound of horns, the cry of dogs, the triumph of success—what time has he to think of evil things! He comes back weary, but satisfied; his early meal was but slight, for he set out so soon; it is late before he seeks a second, and that is seldom otherwise than frugal; he washes, he dresses, and he sups upon his game, and shares it with his friends: then he enjoys the soft air of evening: after his exertions, he lies him down in fine sheets of fresh and fair linen, and sleeps well and healthily, without thinking of evil things. Thus, by frugal living, great exercise, and cheerful occupation, he avoids great maladies, has good health, *and lives long.* And never knew I man, who was attached to hawks and hounds, but was of good disposition and habits; for the love of hunting springs from nobleness and gentleness of heart, whether one be a great lord or a poor man, high or low."

The brother of poor young Gaston, who, perhaps, had a deeper motive than momentary passion when he made the accusation to his father which destroyed him, guilty or innocent, afterwards met a dreadful doom. In that fatal masquerade of savages, when Charles VI. was so nearly burnt to death, Yvain de Foix was one of those, whose dress catching fire, and being sewn on close to his skin, could not be taken off, and he died in extreme torture, after lingering two days. If he had, indeed, intended to effect his brother's death, what must have been his feelings under all the frightful sufferings he endured!

Alas! the glories of the magnificent Gaston Phoebus were fearfully extinguished in blood and flame! Alas! the splendours of the proud castle of Orthez were dimmed with cruelty and suffering! No wonder that spectres are still said to walk and wail around the ruined tower; no wonder that the moans of the feeble prince, fainting beneath the blow of his mail-clad chief, are heard at night echoing through the loop-holes of the battered walls; or that the plaintive cries of another victim startle the shepherd returning late from the hills.

This other victim has also a melancholy story to relate of the injustice and cruelty of near relatives, and the dangers of exalted birth and great possessions.

Charles and Blanche of Navarre, brother and sister, were both "done to death" by those nearest to them; and while the pale shade of Queen Blanche still flits along the ruined battlements of Moncade, the spectre of Prince Charles haunts the streets of Barcelona, where he was poisoned; crying out for ever on his murderess, "Vengeance—Vengeance on Doña Juana!"

STORY OF QUEEN BLANCHE.

THE mother of these two died, leaving the youthful Prince of Vienne heir to her kingdom of Navarre, having just married her eldest daughter, Blanche, to Henry, King of Castile, and her younger daughter, Leonore, to the Count of Foix. She was herself the wife of John, King of Arragon; who, after her death, desired to be himself the sovereign of Navarre, in lieu of his son, Charles, whom he instantly confined in a dungeon in Lerida. The prince was, however, beloved by the people, and the Catalans rose in a body to deliver him: they effected their purpose, and bore off the rescued prisoner in triumph, but not before a cruel step-mother, Doña Juana, who had replaced the first wife of King John, had administered to him a potion, whose effects soon showed themselves, for he died in the hands of his deliverers.

The young Queen Blanche, of Castile, was now the heiress of Navarre; but she succeeded her brother only in his misfortunes and his fate. Married at twelve years old, her husband, when she was sixteen, had already repudiated her, believing himself bewitched, and in danger in her society. Impressed with this imagination, the King of Navarre, in an interview with his wife's brother-in-law, the Count de Foix, agreed that Blanche should be given up to him, and forced to embrace a life of celibacy, in order that her sister, Leonore, Countess of Foix, should enjoy her possessions.

When news was brought to Queen Blanche that she must follow the messengers sent to Olite, to carry her to Orthez, her despair knew no bounds: she felt that her doom was sealed, and her fearful destiny was but too clear to her mind. She even, in her agony, wrote a letter of entreaty to her unnatural husband, to entreat his protection; but he remained deaf and indifferent to her supplications, and the doomed lady was taken away, a prisoner, to the tower of Moncade.

Hero, for two years, languished the ill-fated heiress; her captivity embittered by the sad reflection that her sister was her jailor, and her father and husband her betrayers. A ray of hope suddenly gleamed upon her fortunes; but whether, in her secret dungeon, any pitying friend contrived to let her know that she had yet a chance of escape and triumph, does not appear. Louis XI. came into Béarn. It was not any feeling of compassion for a political victim that influenced him to take part with the captive; for he was just the person to approve of an act, however cruel, which would secure power to a sovereign; but his own interests appeared affected by this arrangement of things; and, in a conference at Pampluna, in which the powerful family of Beaumont offered their services to assist the project, it was agreed that the captive Queen should be demanded at the hands of the Count de Foix, and reinstated in her rights.

Leonora and her husband saw that the time was come when nothing but a further crime could secure them from danger. Blanche, once dead, nothing stood between her sister and the throne of Navarre; and what was her life in comparison with the great advantages they should derive? A deputation from the states of Béarn arrived; the Beaumonts and King Louis sent imperious messages, which were received with the utmost humility by the Count and Countess of Foix: they had no wish to oppose the general desire; there was but one obstacle to the accomplishment of the end in view. They represented that their beloved sister, whose health had long required extreme care, and who had been the object of their solicitude ever since Prince Charles's death, was on a bed of sickness—every hour she grew worse—and, at length, it was their melancholy duty to announce her death.

"Treason had done its worst,"

and Blanche had breathed her last in the Tour de Moncade.

A magnificent funeral was prepared—much lamentation and mourning ensued—and the body of the royal victim was pompously interred with her ancestors, the Princes of Béarn, in the cathedral of Lescar.[11]

Five years after this tragedy, the vengeance of Heaven—still called for by the shades of the brother and sister—overtook Doña Juana, their cruel step-mother. She died in the agonies of a lingering disease, and in her torments betrayed, by her ravings, her crimes to all. Her constant exclamation was, "Hijo! que me caro cuestas!" *Oh, my son! you have cost me dear!* alluding to her own son, for whose sake she had sacrificed the former children of her husband. She died, deserted by all; for that husband, equally guilty, on hearing that her words had betrayed her, thought it policy to feign indignation at her wickedness, and refused to visit her in her dying moments. The memory of the unnatural father is still preserved in a Spanish proverb, which alludes only to his sole good quality—liberality—in which he was extreme: in application to courtiers—who look for presents which are long coming—it is usual to say, "Ya se muriò rey Don Juan."

There is no end to the stories which may be told of the castle of Orthez, and those in its neighbourhood; the knights and squires of Gaston de Foix's court, when not engaged in jousts and tournaments, or in fighting in earnest, seemed never weary of telling histories which their guest, Froissart, listened to with eager attention; amongst them, the following is characteristic of his ready belief, and the credulity of the time:

THE GREAT BEAR OF BÉARN.

Messire Pierre de Béarn, natural brother of Gaston Phoebus, was the victim of a strange malady, which rendered him an object both of fear and pity: there was a mystery attached to his sufferings which no one of the learned or inquisitive attendants who surrounded him could explain; and when Froissart inquired why it was that he was not married, being so handsome and so valiant a knight, his question

[11] Some historians say that Blanche was confined at the castle of Lescar, but there is no foundation for the assertion: no castle but that of Pau or Orthez would have been sufficiently strong to retain a prisoner of so much importance. Moret, and other Spanish authors, relate the event as above.

was met with "the shrug, the hum, the ha," that denoted some secret. At length, as he was not easily to be satisfied when anything romantic was on the *tapis*, he found a person to explain to him how things stood with respect to the brother of the count.

"He is, in fact, married," said the squire who undertook to resolve his doubts; "but neither his wife nor children live with him, and the cause is as follows." He then went on to relate his story:

The young Countess Florence, of Biscay, was left an heiress by her father, who had died suddenly in a somewhat singular manner; his cousin, Don Pedro the Cruel, of Castile, being the only person who could tell the reason of his having been put to death. His daughter, who feared that the friendship of such a relation might be as dangerous to herself, being warned to avoid him, as she had fallen under his displeasure in consequence of having hinted that she knew how his wife, the sister of the Duke of Bourbon, and the Queen of France, met her end, thought it better to escape as quickly as she could from Biscay, leaving her estates in his power; and she came to the Basque country a fugitive, with a small retinue, glad to have saved her life, though all besides was his prey. This distressed damsel, knowing that all honour was shown to ladies at the court of Gaston de Foix, lost no time in directing her steps to the Castle of Orthez, where, throwing herself at the feet of the gallant count, she related her wrongs, and implored his assistance.

Gaston entreated her to be comforted, and assured her that he was ready to do all in his power to assist her: he consigned her to the care of the Lady of Coarraze, his relation, a high baroness of the country. With all his generosity, Gaston Phoebus never seems to have lost sight of his own interest, and it struck him immediately that the heiress was exactly the match he desired for his brother, Pierre de Béarn. Accordingly, he so arranged matters that the young Countess of Biscay and her domains should remain in his family; he married her to Pierre, and re-conquered her lands from the cruel King of Castile.

A son and a daughter were the fruits of this union, which appeared a happy one; but the fates or the fairies did not allow it to remain so. In Béarn, as in other parts of the world, although hunting is a very agreeable amusement, it sometimes brings with it unpleasant consequences, though Count Gaston may say nay. The woods, forests, and mountains, it is well known, belong exclusively to beings who are tenacious of their reign being disturbed, and who generally contrive to revenge themselves on the hardy hunter who ventures to invade their secret retreats. Nevertheless, at all periods, men are found incautious enough to tempt them, and seldom does it happen that they do not suffer for their temerity.

Pierre de Béarn, like his brother, Gaston, was remarkably fond of the chase. The Countess Florence, on the contrary, held the pastime in the utmost abhorrence, and to please her he abstained from the sport he loved during the early period of their union; but at length he became weary of this self-denial, and, in an evil hour, he set forth on an expedition into the forests of Biscay to hunt the bear. He had not been fortunate at first in his search, and had climbed some of the highest parts of the mountain in hopes to meet with game worthy of him, when he suddenly came upon the track of a tremendous animal, such as he had never before beheld in his experience.

He followed it for some time over plains of ice, his gallant hounds in full chase; at length, the mighty beast—apparently, indignant at their perseverance, just as they had arrived at a gorge of the rocks, beneath which a precipice descended on either side—turned round on his pursuers, and presented a front sufficient to daunt the courage of the boldest. The dogs, however, rushed on him, but, with one blow of his enormous paw, he stretched them dead at his feet; four of the finest met the same fate, and several, disabled and wounded, shrunk howling back to their master, who stood firm, his spear poised, waiting the proper moment of attack. Pierre saw that no time was to be lost, for he was alone, having, in his eagerness, outstripped his companions; his dogs were of no further use, and he must trust now to his own strength and skill.

The spear went flying through the air, and struck the monster in the breast; furious with pain, he uttered a hideous howl, and rushed forward, catching, in his long claws, the left arm of the knight, whose right hand was armed with his hunting-knife, which he had hastily drawn from his belt; with this, in spite of the pain he felt, he continued to strike the monster, whose roaring echoed through the caverns of the rock like thunder at every stroke.

At this instant, and just as the knight's strength was nearly exhausted, he beheld, with joy, his friends advancing to his aid; two of them sprang forward and discharged their spears; but still, though desperately wounded, the bear would not release the arm he continued to gripe, and, as he turned upon them, dragged his first foe with him. As, however, his head was directed towards the new comers, Pierre, with a strong effort, made another plunge in his neck, which instantly had the effect of making him release his hold; he then drew his dagger—for his knife remained in the animal's body—and, with the assistance of his friends, the bear was despatched. As the body lay on the ground, a pause of astonishment ensued after the shouts of the victors; for never was so gigantic a beast beheld in the Pyrenees, and it seemed a miracle that Pierre had escaped: his arm was fearfully injured, and he was faint with exertion; but his triumph was so great that he hardly permitted his wound to be bound up. They placed the carcase of the bear on their shoulders, and with great difficulty carried it from the spot where it fell; it was then consigned to their attendants, and the whole train returned in great delight to the castle. As they entered the court, they were met by the Countess Florence and her ladies, who had been uneasy at the long absence of her lord. No sooner had she cast her eyes on the huge beast they were carrying, than she turned deadly pale, uttered a loud shriek, and fainted on the ground.

The lady was borne to her chamber, and for two days and two nights she uttered not a word; but was in great pain and tribulation, sighing and moaning piteously: at the end of that time she said to her husband, "My lord, I shall never be better till I have been on a pilgrimage to St. James; give me leave to go, and to take with me Pierre, my son, and Adriana, my daughter. I beg it as a boon." Messire Pierre, distressed to see her situation, granted her request too readily.

The countess then ordered a great train to be prepared, and set forth on her journey, taking with her treasure and jewels of great value, which was not much remarked at the time; but she knew well that she did not intend to return. Her journey and her pilgrimage accomplished, she announced her intention to pay a visit to her cousins, the King and Queen of Castile; and to their Court she went, and was received with joy. And there the Countess Florence is still, and will not return, nor send back her children. The very night on which he had killed the great bear, Messire Pierre was seized with the malady which has ever since taken possession of him. "He rises," said the squire, "in the night, arms himself, draws his sword, and, with loud and furious cries and gestures, like a man possessed, flies at every one near him, and makes such a terrific noise and confusion that it would seem fiends were in his chamber. His squires and valets awake him, and he is quite unconscious of what has happened, and will not believe those who relate to him what he has done in his sleep. Now, it is said," continued the squire, "that the lady knew well what would happen the moment she saw the great bear; for her father had hunted that very animal, and when he came up to it, he heard a voice which said, 'Why do you persecute me thus? I never did you any ill: you shall die of an untimely death.' And so, indeed, did he, being beheaded by King Pedro the Cruel, without cause. This was the reason she fainted and was in such tribulation; and for this cause she never loved her husband after, for she always feared he would do her a bodily injury; and that harm would happen to her or hers, while she stayed with him."

The squire and the historian's comments on this strange story are more amusing than wise. "We know well," said Froissart, "by ancient writings, that gods and goddesses were in the habit of changing into birds and beasts men and women who offended them. It might well, therefore, happen that this great bear was in his time a knight accustomed to hunt in the forests of Biscay; he probably did something to anger some deity of the woods, and consequently lost his human shape, and got changed into a bear, to do penance for his offence."

Whether Froissart really believed what he was saying, or whether the opinion was merely advanced to afford him an opportunity to display his classical learning, is not clear; but he forthwith inflicts upon his hearer the story of the "*Joli Chevalier Acteon;*" at which the other is marvellously pleased.

They continue to speculate upon the reasons of the Countess Florence for quitting her husband, and conclude that she knew more than she chose to tell. It has been thought that the lady, when very young, was one day in the forest, having strayed from the castle, within whose garden walls she was weary of being kept. She was delighted when she found herself at liberty, and kept wandering on, up one alley and down another, wherever she saw flowers, and the sun streamed through the leaves; till, at last, the evening began to close, and she turned her steps to return; but there was such a labyrinth of trees, and every path was so like another, that she knew not which to choose, and became alarmed lest she should not reach home before night, and her absence would be discovered. She hurried forward in great uncertainty, and her fears increased every moment; for she seemed to be getting further and further in the depths of the forest; suddenly she came upon a great rock in which was a cavern, and at its mouth she paused a moment to look round her, when a sound issued from it which almost paralysed her with terror, and presently forth rushed a huge black bear, who seized her in his paws. She shrieked loudly, for she expected her hour was come, when, to her amazement, she heard a voice from the monster, and these words: "You have intruded on my privacy; I did not seek you; remain and be my companion, or at once I put you to death." She was so amazed that she had scarcely power to answer; but summoning her courage, she replied, "I am a great lady, and the daughter of the lord of Biscay: release me, and it shall be the better for you; kill me, and my father will take a signal revenge." "You shall not quit this forest," replied the monster, "till you promise what I demand. I will then transport you to your father's castle, when you shall make him swear never to hunt in my domains again. If he should do so, he shall die a violent death; and all with whom you shall in future be in connexion shall be under the same promise, or I will cause them to die badly. If any, after this vow, hunt me, and it should happen that I am killed, misfortune shall come on you and your race for my sake."

The lady promised, as indeed she had no choice but to do; and the great bear then ordered her to follow him; she did so, and in a few moments she saw the castle in view. "Now," said he, "give me another promise. If I should be killed by any one belonging to you, swear that you will go to the shrine of St. James, of Compostella, and pray for my soul, for I am not a bear, as I appear, but a knight, transformed for my sins." As he spoke, and while Florence made the vow he required, she saw his skin changing by degrees, and his form taking another appearance, till he stood before her, in the misty light, a fair young knight, the handsomest her eyes had ever beheld; he looked mournfully upon her, and disappeared, and she found herself suddenly in her own turret, in her chamber, on her bed, and no one had perceived her absence. She related this adventure to her father, who, much amazed thereat, refused to credit her tale; nor would he give up his accustomed pastime of hunting for all her entreaties, by which stubborn conduct his fate came upon him as has been related.

The lady, the more she thought of the beauty of the transformed knight, loved him the more; but she had no hope ever again to see him, and her misfortunes having obliged her to quit her country, and take refuge in Béarn, all happened as has been told. She was not more fortunate with her husband than her father, in preventing his hunting in the forests of Biscay; and when she saw the great bear had been killed, she lamented her lover, as well as the ill fate which he had predicted for her lineage. Certain it is, that she never afterwards returned to Messire Pierre, and that she gave great treasure to the church of St. James, of Compostella, that perpetual mass might be said for *a soul in purgatory*.

Bridge of Orthez

BRIDGE OF ORTHEZ

CHAPTER XI.

The Countess Of Comminges—The Charge—The Persecuted Heiress—The Bridge—The Cordelier—Costume—Aspremont—Peyrehorade.

Although Count Gaston Phoebus was a tyrant, who spared none in his anger,
yet he had all the virtues which were admired by the bold spirits of the men of
his time; amongst the chief of which was hospitality. Like a true knight of old, he
afforded protection to distressed ladies and damsels, and his Court was a refuge
sought, and not in vain, by all who had been injured by those stronger than themselves, or who required assistance in any way. Amongst other ladies who came to
throw themselves at the feet of this redoubted righter of wrongs was the Countess
Alienor de Comminges, wife of the Count of Boulogne, and the right heiress of the

county of Comminges, then in the hands of the Lord of Armagnac, who unjustly detained it. This spirited lady one day made her appearance at the Castle of Orthez, with her little girl of three years old in her hand, and demanded protection of Gaston Phoebus. She was received with great honour and respect, and Gaston listened with great benignity to her complaint.

"My lord," said she, "I am on my way to Arragon, to my uncle the Count d'Urgel, and my aunt-in-law, with whom I am resolved to remain; for I have taken a great displeasure against my husband, Messire Jean de Boulogne; for it is his business to recover for me my heritage, kept from me by the Count of Armagnac, who holds my sister in prison; but he will bestir himself in nothing, for he is a craven knight, fond of his ease, and has no care but to eat and drink, and spends his goods upon idle and sensual enjoyment. And he boasts that when he becomes count he will sell his inheritance in order to satisfy his foolish and childish wishes; for this cause I am disgusted, and will live with him no longer; therefore I have brought my little daughter to deliver her into your charge, and to make you her guardian and defender, to keep and educate her according to her station. I know well, that, for the sake of love and relationship, in this my great strait you will not fail me, and I have no safe person with whom to confide my daughter, Jeanne, but you. I have had great difficulty to get her out of the hands of my husband, which I was resolved to do, because I know the danger in which she stands from him, and from those of the house of Armagnac, being, as she is, the heiress of Comminges. I, therefore, beseech you to befriend me, and take charge of her; and when my husband finds she is in your guardianship, he will be himself rejoiced; for he has often said that this child would be a source of great uneasiness to him in the future.

"The Count of Foix heard the lady, his cousin, speak these words with great satisfaction, and instantly imagined within himself, for he is a lord of great fancy," says Froissart, "of how much service the charge of this child might be to him, for she might be the cause of making peace with his enemies, and by marrying her in some high place, he could keep them in check; he, therefore, replied, 'Madam and cousin, willingly will I do what you ask, both from affection and parentage, by which I am bound to assist you. Leave your daughter with me, and rely on it she shall be cared for and treated as if she were my own child.' 'I thank you greatly,' said the lady.

"The young daughter of the Count of Boulogne was therefore left at Orthez with the Count of Foix, and never departed from thence. And her lady mother took her way to Arragon. She came several times afterwards to see her child, but did not request to have her again: for the count, Gaston Phoebus, acquitted himself of his charge as if she had been his own; indeed, it is said that he has a notion of marrying her to the Duke de Berri, who is a widower, and has a great desire to marry again."

Jeanne did in fact become the wife of the Duke de Berri, when she was under thirteen, and he more than sixty; but, after all the care which had been taken of her, and the "coil" that was made for her, she died early, leaving no children. Her mother being dead, the inheritance of Comminges devolved on her aunt, Marguerite, the same who was kept prisoner by the Count of Armagnac. The fate of heiresses in those days was sad enough, and that of this countess particularly so. The Count of Armagnac married her to get her property; after his death she was forced into an alliance with another of the same family, from whom, however, she contrived to get a divorce, and then accepted the hand of a Count de Foix, probably from fear. This latter soon began to ill-treat her, having failed by entreaties to induce her to make over her possessions to him; finding her resolved, he leagued himself with one of her old enemies, Jean d'Armagnac, and they agreed together to share the spoil of her heritage. She was dragged about, from prison to prison, first in one strong castle and then in another, for fear of its being known where she existed; and for many years she languished in this misery. At this time Charles VII. was at the height of his successes, and some friend had contrived to inform her of the changed aspect of affairs in France. In order to induce him to undertake her cause, she, by means of the same friend, let him know that she had named him heir of all her property and estates — knowing, probably, too well, how little weight any consideration but personal interest would have.

The tyrants soon discovered what she had done, and her treatment became still worse. The arrogance and presumption of the Count d'Armagnac, who ventured to put after his name, "By the grace of God," and assumed the airs of a sovereign, added to which, *the unjust manner in which he acted*, at length irritated the king to such a degree that he summoned both lords to appear before him at Toulouse, and commanded that they should bring with them the Countess of Comminges.

Nothing was now to be done but to obey the strongest; and the two tyrants and their victim came to Charles, as he desired; he then took the lady under his protection, and the Estates pronounced *her will valid*; her husband being permitted to enjoy a certain portion during his life. After this the countess remained with the king, and it is to be hoped enjoyed a short period of repose. She died at Poitiers, upwards of eighty years old, and no sooner was she dead than the turbulent and ambitious Armagnacs took possession, in spite of the king, of all her estates, about which, for long years, continual wars and contentions ensued.

Of all the castles in Béarn, perhaps that of Gaston Phoebus at Orthez is the most suggestive of recollections; but I fear I have been led into so many long stories beneath its ruined walls that the actual fortress itself is almost forgotten. We stood upon the irregular mound which its accumulated ruins present, remarking the fine effect of the distant line of snowy mountains, whose outlines varied from those familiar to us at Pau, and enjoyed the sunset from that exalted position, which might have often been admired in the same spot centuries before, by the lords, knights, historians, minstrels, and distressed or contented damsels, who filled the courts of the mightiest chieftain of Béarn.

We descended from the castle, through a long, dilapidated street, which seemed to know no end, and began to despair of ever reaching the bridge, when we were accosted by a good-natured looking woman, who offered to be our guide. After a long walk, through high, narrow, but not ill-paved, streets, at last we came upon the roaring, foaming Gave: one of the most impatient rivers that ever was confined by a bridge, or pent up by crowding houses. On each side rise wild, grey, rugged rocks, some covered with clinging plants, some naked and barren, over and between which the passionate torrent comes dashing and foaming, as if anxious to escape, as fast as possible, from the town which has intruded streets and mills on its original solitude, since the early period when some chivalric baron, or, perhaps, the Grosse Comtesse herself, threw over it the strange old bridge, and placed in its centre the towered arch which no efforts, early or late, have been able to dislodge. To be sure, this is scarcely surprising, if, as tradition says, it was no mortal architect who built this bridge; but a set of workmen whose erections are not easily destroyed, and who, after all, might have laid the first foundations of the fortress on the height, as well as this huge tower, which seems of a-piece with one of the rocks its neighbours. The fact is, the fairies, who inhabited in former days the caverns of the Gave, and used to come out by moon-light in little boats on its waters, got tired of its continual roaring and foaming, and bethought them of a way to cross to the other side, without being either shaken or tossed by its turbulent waves, or wetting their tiny feet by stepping from stone to stone. They resolved, therefore, to throw a bridge over the stream, and, taking a huge hollowed rock for the purpose, by their united efforts they cast it across; and, as the water-spirits were offended on the occasion, and rose up against them, endeavouring to destroy their labours, they found it requisite to build them a tower in the centre, which they defended against all comers. This was effected in a single night; and the shepherds, who beheld in the morning what had been done, would never have been able to account for it, but that, watching when the moon was at the full, they perceived the fairies passing in crowds along the bridge, and directing their way towards the opposite hill, where the castle stands. They have often been seen dancing round the ruined well there; and, it is thought, can plunge into the spring, and reappear far up in the Gave at their pleasure. The shepherds, also, observed that the castle was under their dominion; for they often remark, as they approach Orthez, on returning from the market at Peyrehorade, that the great tower, which is clearly visible on the height at one moment, sinks gradually into the earth, the nearer they come, and, at last, disappears altogether, nor is observed again, till they have mounted the hill, to see if it really "stands where it did;" where they behold it as firm and as frowning as ever, laughing to scorn time and the elements, and refusing to offer any clue to its mystery.

The bridge of Orthez has been the scene of terrible contentions, at different periods. In the tower in its centre is a projecting window, from whence, tradition says, Montgomery, the Protestant leader, by the orders of Queen Jeanne de Navarre,—to whom, in this country, all sorts of horrors are attributed,—caused the priests to be cast into the Gave, who refused to become Calvinists. The window is called *La frineste deüs caperas* (*the priests' window*). In those times of outrage and violence, this might, or might not, be true; but certain it is that three thousand Catholics, men, women, and children, perished in the siege which Montgomery laid to Orthez, and that the sparkling, foaming torrent which we looked at with such pleasure, then rolled along a current of blood.

It is said that, during the assault of the town, a Cordelier was celebrating mass in his convent, and had the courage to finish the ceremony in spite of the tumult around; he then concealed the sacred chalice in his bosom, and cast himself from his convent-window into the Gave. The waters bore him on to the Adour; and his body, tossed and torn by the rocks, was finally deposited on the bank, beneath the walls of a convent of the same order, at Bayonne, where the shuddering monks received and bore his mutilated remains to their chapel, with weeping and lamenting for the misfortunes of their brethren.

The "Château Noble" of Gaston Phoebus had then to endure a terrible siege: the Viscount de Terride had sustained himself there as long as possible; but, wanting provisions, was at length obliged to yield, and was, with all his garrison, carried prisoner to Pau. There those officers who, being Béarnais, had been taken in rebellion against their Queen, were served with a banquet called *le repas libre*, at the conclusion of which they were all put to the sword.

The costume of the female peasants in this neighbourhood is almost invariably a short scarlet petticoat, and brown or black tucked-up gown, with a bright-coloured handkerchief on the head, tied in the usual *gentil* style, with all four ends displayed, so as to show their rich hues,—one being allowed to fall longer than the rest; in dirty weather, the legs and feet are bare, and the sabots carried. Many very large straw hats are worn, lined with smart colours, and tied with ribbon; but it must be confessed that most of these are very old, and have long since lost their early brilliancy.

There is nothing remarkable in the costume of the men,—the customary *berret* being the covering of their heads, and either a blue blouse, or a dark dress, with red sash, and sometimes a red waist-coat, diversifying their appearance. We were not struck with the beauty of any of the peasants we met. Being market-day, the road was crowded for several leagues, and we thought we had a good opportunity of judging: however, a French fellow-traveller told us our idea was erroneous, as the young girls were seldom allowed to come to the market, which was generally attended by matrons only. However this might be, we certainly saw nothing beyond very ordinary faces, and the common defect of mountainous countries—the frightful *goître*—too evident. It is the custom with most persons, when they first arrive in a place, to adopt some received opinion, which not the strongest evidence of their senses is allowed afterwards to shake; and thus it appears heresy, either to disbelieve in the salubrity of Pau, or in the beauty of the inhabitants of all the country round. If beauty were merely comparative, the notion may be true; but, though those who are not affected with *goître*, and who are not hollow-cheeked, and thin, and brown, are prettier than those who are,

> "Yet beautie is beautie in every degree;"

and "pretty Bessies" appeared to me to be very rare in Béarn.

There is a very imposing building situated on the Gave, of which the towns-people are extremely proud: it is a corn-mill, of great power, lately erected, and extremely successful. It appears that the town of Orthez is in a flourishing condition, as to trade. Here are prepared most of the hams so celebrated throughout France, under the name of Bayonne-hams; and here numerous flocks of the fat geese which furnish the markets of the neighbouring towns with *cuisses d'oies*, so prized by gourmands, are to be seen. But the most picturesque *flocks* we observed on this road, were those of the round, pretty sheep, with thick snowy fleeces, just returned from the mountains, where, delicate as they look, they have been accustomed, all the summer, and till late in the autumn, to climb to the highest point of the Pic du Midi itself. They were now being conducted to the valleys and plains for the winter, and the meadows were whitened with them in all directions.

This part of the country was, formerly, thickly-wooded, and occasionally a few oak woods are passed on the road; but the continuous forest which once spread abroad in this direction has disappeared. On approaching the long, desolate-looking bourg of Peyrehorade,—which, however, on market-days, is bustling and crowded enough—a ruin, on a height not unlike that of Orthez, looks proudly over the plain, where two Gaves unite. It is the Château d'Aspremont, once redoubted, and of great force, and belonging to that good and noble governor of Bayonne, who sent back to Charles IX. the answer so often quoted, when commanded to execute all the Protestants in his town of Bayonne—that he had examined the persons under his command, and had found them brave and true soldiers, but no executioners.

The singular-sounding name of *Peyre-Hourade* has the meaning of *Pierced Stone*, and comes from a Druidical monument in the neighbourhood. These remains are rare in the Pyrenees, though so frequently met with in other parts of France. In a meadow, not far removed from the high-road, is a block of granite, nearly flat, of great height, standing upright on the narrowest end: there is no quarry of similar stone in this part of the country; and its isolation and quality render it a subject of surprise—as much so as the unexplained wonders on Salisbury Plain. The fairies, no doubt, if any fortunate individual could make friends with them now, could set the matter at rest;

"But now can no man see none elvés mo!"

CHAPTER XII.

Bayonne—Public Walks—Biaritz—Atalaya—Giant Fernagus—Anne Of Neubourg—The Dancing Mayor.

From Orthez we continued our way to Bayonne, where it was our intention to remain a few days. The entrance to Bayonne, that famous city, whose motto is "Nunquam Polluta"—"*Always pure,*" from the separate town of St. Esprit, which is in the department of the Landes, as well as half of the bridge which connects it with its more important sister, is extremely striking. This bridge is over the fine bold river Adour, which joins the Nive here, and, together, they divide the town between them. Although Bayonne has few public monuments of much consequence, yet the cathedral, the towers of the two castles, and other buildings, rise from the rivers in great majesty; and, as we crossed the immensely long wooden bridge at a slow pace, gave us a good impression, which a closer view did not disappoint. It has a singular aspect, unlike that of any other town, and the air all round it is pure and healthy; and we felt happy for the time to have exchanged the icy chill of the snowy mountains for the freshness of the sea breeze.

There are few old towns in France, which can be called fine in themselves: their advantages lie in situation, and in the modern additions which have succeeded to the ramparts and close-walled enclosures of the ancient time, when to crowd streets together and fence them in was the principal aim; but Bayonne, although still fortified strongly, is less confined than most cities: a thorough air blows through the tolerably well-paved streets; open spaces occur every now and then, narrow and close places have been cleared, and the two fine rivers and their quays prevent its being so crowded as it might otherwise be. The houses are very high, which makes the streets appear narrower than they really are; but they are not very long, and intersect each other in a manner to prevent their being disagreeable.

There are arcades in the old part, as at La Rochelle and Agen, some of which are very dark and narrow, and occasionally strange alleys appear, as sombre and dismal as any in Rouen itself; but this is not the general character of the town. One long, handsomely-paved street, is bordered with fine houses and planted with trees, in the style of Bordeaux, and here are situated most of the hotels; the grand squares of the Theatre and Douane open from this, and the magnificent allées marines extend from this spot.

Everywhere in Bayonne, it is easy to escape from the bustle of the city, and find yourself in a beautiful, shaded walk—an advantage seldom possessed by a commercial town.

Although many are delightful, and there is only the embarrassment of choice, the most beautiful and agreeable, it must be allowed, are the allées marines, which are walks nicely kept, planted with several rows of fine trees, reaching along the banks of the Adour for an immense distance, with meadows on the other hand, and a range of cultivated hills on the opposite shore. The fine broad, sparkling, agitated river, is dotted with vessels of different sizes, some of them moored to the bank; a fresh breeze from the sea comes sweeping along, bringing health on its wings; the citadel crowns the height of St. Esprit; the cathedral rises above the other town; before is the meeting of the bright waters, trees, groves, and meadows everywhere; murmuring streams, spanned by wooden bridges, hurry along to throw themselves into the bosom of the Adour at intervals, and the whole scene is life and brilliancy.

This walk is a kind of shaded jettée, and has, unlike most French promenades, nothing formal or monotonous about it: the trees are allowed to throw their branches out at pleasure, without being clipped into form; they are irregularly planted, so that the favourite straight lines are avoided, and the fine sandy soil does not allow the paths to remain dump half an hour at a time; consequently, it is always a safe lounge, and, assuredly, one of the most charming possessed by any town I ever saw. It is as agreeable, although not resembling it in its features, as the mail which charmed us so much at La Rochelle.

The days were very uncertain, and violent showers overtook us every half hour, while we remained at Bayonne; yet we contrived to escape damp in these pretty alleys, which, one minute swimming with water, were, in an incredibly short space, dry and pleasant again.

The first anxiety on arriving at Bayonne, is always, of course, to get to the sea; even the cathedral, our usual first visit, we neglected, in order to take advantage of a gleam of sun, and hasten to Biaritz, which lies about a league from the town: there is now a fine road to St. Jean de Luz, by which you reach this celebrated bathing-place; and the often-described cacolets, which even now travellers venture to tell of, are dwindled into a tradition. In the season, one or two of these primitive conveyances may still, it is said, be seen, as the English are amused at endeavouring to ride in them; but, except one has a preference for broken limbs to safety, there is no reason why any one should choose such a carriage. They are, in fact, *now*, two panniers, in which two persons sit on each side of a horse, with the legs hanging down: formerly, it was merely a board slung across the animal's back, on which the traveller sat see-saw with his guide; and numerous are the accounts of perils encountered on a bad road in these conveyances twenty years ago. Omnibuses, cabriolets, and coaches of all kinds are now to be had, and there is neither pleasure nor glory in going uncomfortably in the obsolete *cacolet.*

Biaritz has greatly changed its aspect, since Inglis described it as a desolate fishing village: it has grown into a fashionable watering-place, full of fine hotels and handsome houses, with accommodations of all sorts; the sands are, in the bathing-season, covered with pavilions for the bathers, and all the terrors and dangers of the Chambre d'Amour and the Grottos of Biaritz, are over: that is to say, as far as regards persons being carried away by the tide, or surprised by the waves amongst the rocks; for, unless any one was silly enough to place himself in danger, no risk need be run, as it does not *now* come to seek you. The rocks, however, are still terrible to mariners in a tempest; when, in spite of the warning *pharos*, which crowns the height, the vessel is driven into these little bays, bristling with rocks of all sizes and forms, each capable of causing immediate destruction. No winter passes without dreadful disasters on this beautifully dangerous coast, which looks not half so fatal as it really is.

I had so often heard Biaritz described as magnificent, that I had imagined a bold coast of gigantic cliffs and huge blocks of pyramidal stone, piled at distances along the shore, like those at the back of the Isle of Wight, or on the Breton coast. I was, therefore, surprised to find only a pretty series of bays, much lower, but not unlike the land at Hastings, with the addition of small circles of sand, strewn with large masses of rock, over and through which the restless waves drive and foam, and form cascades, and rush into hollows, roaring and beating against the caverned roofs and sides with the noise of cannon, increased in violence according to the state of the elements.

In rough weather the sea is so loud here that the reverberation is distinctly heard at Bayonne, as if artillery was being fired, and its hoarse murmur is generally audible there at all times. A fine light-house has been erected on a height; but this precaution does not altogether prevent accidents, and scarcely a winter passes without sad events occurring on this dangerous coast. A few days only before we visited Biaritz, an English vessel had been lost, with all hands on board, except a poor man, who had seen his wife perish, and his two little children washed on one of the rocks: there they lay like star-fish, and were taken off by the pitying inhabitants. I could not learn the exact particulars, but I believe only one survived, which was immediately received into the house of an English family who reside at Biaritz, and who benevolently took the little stranded stranger under their protection.

There was always, it seems, a look-out house on the hill above the rocks; and formerly it was requisite to watch lest the vessels of those numerous pirates who infested these seas should come down upon the coast. The mount where it stood is called by its old name, *Atalaya*. Whether it has anything to do with the former inhabitant of a ruined tower which still looks over the ocean, as it did in ages past, does not appear; but it may have been connected with the giant Ferragus, or Fernagus, of whose castle this piece of ruin alone remains.

The giant Ferragus was one of those tremendous pagan personages, to conquer whom was the chief aim and end of the Paladins of the time of Charlemagne; and history has recorded the combat of Roland, the great hero of these parts, with this redoubted Paynim.

Biaritz was amongst the places in the Pays Basque, named by the cruel inquisitor, Pierre de Lancre, as *"given up to the worship of the devil;"* he tells us that the devils and malignant spirits, banished *from Japan and the Indies*, took refuge in the mountains of Labourd: "and, indeed," continues this miserable bigot, in whose hands was placed the destiny of hundreds of innocent creatures, "many English, Scotch, and other travellers coming to buy wines in the city of Bordeaux, have assured us that in their journeys they have seen great troops of demons, *in the form of frightful men*, passing into France." Above all, he asserts that the young girls of Biaritz, always celebrated for their beauty, have "in their *left eye a mark impressed by the devil.*"

Bayonne has several new quarters still unfinished, which promise to be very handsome and commodious. There is a sort of imitation of Bordeaux in the style of building, without altogether such good taste: at least, this may be said of the theatre, which, though immensely large, is much less majestic or beautiful; its position is, perhaps, even better than that of Bordeaux, as it stands in a large uninterrupted square, with a fine walk and trees by the quay on one side; and all the streets which extend from it are new and wide.

The street in which the principal hotels are placed is very like one on the *cours* at Bordeaux, and is remarkably striking; but, besides this, there is little to admire in the town, except the singularity of two rivers running through its streets, like another Venice.

The residence of the Queen of Spain, Anne of Neubourg, widow of Charles II., at Bayonne, is still remembered, and anecdotes are told of her during her long stay of thirty-two years. She arrived on the 20th September, 1706, and was received with great honours by all the dignitaries: the town was illuminated, and the streets hung with tapestry, as she passed to the Château-Vieux, where she took up her abode. She seems to have been very much beloved, to have shown great benevolence, and made herself numerous friends. Her generosity and profusion, however, caused her to leave on her departure twelve hundred thousand francs of debt, which Ferdinand VI. had to pay. Scandal was not silent concerning her, and a lover was named in the young chevalier Larrétéguy whose brother was at one time confined in the Château d'If for an impertinent exclamation which he made one day when the Queen's carriage was stopped by the crowd on the Pont Majour—"Room for my sister-in-law." A fine complexion and an air of majesty constituted her beauty; but she grew enormously fat, and was not remarkable for her outward attractions.

She seems to have exhibited some caprice in her rejection of a palace which she had caused to be built at great expense. It was called the Château de Marrac, and had been erected under her orders with infinite care: when it was finished she refused to occupy it in consequence of one of her ladies having presumed to take possession of a suite of chambers previous to her having been regularly installed as mistress. This was the reason assigned; but she had, it may be imagined, a better to give for abandoning a place which had cost her so much money.

She made frequent journeys to St. Jean Pied de Port, Bidache, Cambo, Terciis, &c., for her health, and was always received on her return to Bayonne with sovereign honours. The magistrates of the town went, on one occasion, to meet her with offerings of fruit, flowers, expensive wines, hams, and game, all in silver filigree baskets, beautifully worked.

During a dangerous illness which she had, the shrine containing the relics of St. Léon was lowered, as in a period of general calamity; and, on her recovery, prayers and thanksgivings were commanded, and a solemn procession of all the officers of the town, civil and military, took place.

In 1738 she returned to Spain, greatly regretted by all who had known her at Bayonne; and, it seems, she was so much impressed with sorrow at having left an abode so agreeable to her that she survived only two years, and died at Guadalajara in 1740.

An account of a fête, given by the Queen on occasion of some successes in Spain which greatly rejoiced her, concludes with the following rather amusing sentence: "After the repast was finished, much to the satisfaction of all, a *panperruque* was danced through the town. M. de Gibaudière led the dance, holding the hand of the *Mayor of Bayonne*; the Marquis de Poyanne bringing up the rear: so that this dance rejoiced all the people, who, on their side, gave many demonstrations of joy. It lasted even till the next day amongst the people, and on board the vessels in the river; and the windows of every house were illuminated."

Bayonne has a reputation for being in general extremely healthy; and its position, in reach of the fine fresh sea air, seems to render it probable. To me, after the close atmosphere of Pau, it was peculiarly pleasant; and seemed to give new life, and restore the spirits, depressed by that enervating climate, where, except for invalids, a long residence is anything but desirable.

There seems but little commercial movement at Bayonne, and no bustle on the quays; indeed, except at Nantes, I have always, in France, been struck with the quiet and silent aspect of the seaports; so unlike our own. Just at the time we were there, great complaints were being made, in consequence of the prohibition of Spanish ships from touching at any port of the South of France: commerce was at a stand-still, and all persons in trade seemed vexed and disappointed at the bad prospect before them.

CHAPTER XIII.

Basque Language—Dialects—Words—Poetry—Songs—The Deserter—Character—Drama—Towns.

THE Basque country,—in which the ancient town of Bayonne, or Lapurdum, holds a principal place,—is unequally divided between France and Spain. The one part is composed of La Soule, Basse Navarre, and Labourd, and extends over a surface of about a hundred and forty square leagues; the other portion comprises Haute Navarre, Alava, Guipuscoa, and Biscay, and contains about nine hundred and sixty square leagues: so that the whole country in which the Basque language is spoken, enclosed between the Adour, Béarn, the river Arragon, the Ebro, and the ocean, contains not less than eleven hundred square leagues. Part of this extent is barren, rude, and wooded, and is said to resemble the ancient state of Gaul, as described by historians. Though immense tracts of wood have been cleared away, there is still more in this region than in any other of the Pyrenees; there are three great forests; one of Aldudes, in the valley of Balgorry, where exist the only copper-mines in France; the forest of Irati, near Roncevaux; and that of St. Engrace, which joins the woods of Itseaux.

The habits, manners, and language, of this people have engaged the attention of the curious for a series of years; and the speculations and, surmises to which they have given rise are without end. Although it is generally thought that the Basques are descendants of the ancient Iberians, some learned writers contend that the singular language which they speak, and which has no resemblance to that of any of the nations which surround them, approaches very near the Celtic.

Whether they are *Vascons* or *Cantabrians*, they are called, in their own tongues, *Escualdunac*, and their language *Escuara*. Seventy-two towns, bourgs, and villages, are named, by Du Mège, as appropriated to the people of this denomination,—that is, from the mouth of the Adour to the banks of the Soison and the mountains south of the Pays de Soule. He remarks that no historian of antiquity has made mention of this people, or their language, under the name they at present bear; and it was never advanced till the end of the sixteenth and beginning of the seventeenth centuries, that the inhabitants of Alava, Guipuscoa, and Spanish and French Navarre had preserved the ancient language of the Iberians, and that they were the representatives of that nation; never having been conquered by any foreign invaders, and never having mixed their blood.

Du Mège observes, on these pretensions: "History, studied at its purest sources, and from its most authentic documents, proves that, in the most distant times, several nations,—amongst whom, doubtless, should be included those who first inhabited the coasts of Africa,—came and established themselves in Spain. The Pelasgians, the Greeks of Zacinthus, of Samos, the Messineans, the Dorians, the Phoceans, the Laconians, the Tyrians or Phoenicians, the Carthaginians, the Celts or Gauls, and the Eastern Iberians. Strabo mentions that in the Peninsula were many different languages *and alphabets*; no doubt, as many alphabets as idioms. Great care has been taken to discover the origin of these alphabets, the letters of which *are still to be found in Spain, in several inscriptions engraved on marble*, and in numerous medals."

Nothing satisfactory, however, has been established respecting the language; but a probable one appears to be Velasquez' opinion, that it is formed of dialects of Greek and Hebrew; but this opinion is combated by many learned Spaniards. One author, in particular, was so violent in his enthusiasm, that it led him to discover all the ancient history combined in the Basque language. To him it was of little consequence that the names mentioned by different authors belonged to Spain, Africa, England, or Normandy,—the learned Dr. Zuñiga, curé of Escalonilla, explained them all as *Basque*. Thus, for instance, *Scotland*, called *Escocia* in Spanish, he asserts was so called from *escuocia*, a *cold hand*! Ireland, which is Irlanda in Spanish, means, in Basque, *Ira-Landa*, i.e., *meadow of fern*: and so on to the end of the chapter, in a strain which becomes highly comic. Another writer followed in his steps,—Don Juan de Erro y Aspiroz,—who surpassed him in absurdity; proving to his own satisfaction, not only that the Basque is ancient, but that its alphabet *furnished one to the Greeks*, and that the same nation instructed the Phoenicians in the use of money; added to which, they passed into Italy, and *from them* sprung the Romans—those conquerors of the world.

Certainly, etymologists do fall into strange errors; as when the forgery *pour rire* of Count de Gibelin was taken for the Lord's Prayer in Celtic, and explained as such by the famous Lebrïgant!

Humboldt, in his "Researches" on the origin of the first inhabitants of Spain, falls into errors which are to be lamented; as his great name may afford sanction to the dreams of others. He acknowledges that he is puzzled to find that there is no trace amongst the ancients of the term Escualdunac. He does not go so far as Zuñiga, who discovers in the name of Obulco, engraved on ancient medals, Tri-Gali, i.e. "laughing corn" or Balza-Gala—"black corn:" that Catalonia (evidently a modern name) signifies, "The country of wild cats." Cascantum—"dirty place;" and Hergaones—"good place of the spinners!"

Du Mège observes, that Humboldt has unfortunately followed former writers too much; and though all he writes is worthy of respect, he fails to convince, in this treatise, having begun on false ground. Since then, M. de Montglave has "proved" a fact which is very startling, namely, that there is a great affinity between the Basque language and the dialects of the indigenous nations of South America![12]

This last circumstance, which new observations seem to render more and more probable, would at once put an end, if really proved, to all discussion, and

---

[12] This M. Mazure will by no means allow in his "Histoire du Béarn et du Pays Basque."

open a new field for speculation. It would be somewhat curious to establish the certainty of the South Americans having discovered and colonized Europe many centuries before they were re-discovered by Europeans!—this, once determined, the Druid stones and the round towers of Ireland might all, by degrees, be explained: the obstinate resolve of all learned persons to derive everything in Europe from the Greeks and Romans, or to go to the far East, when fairly driven there, to find out origins, is very hard upon the enormous double continent of the New World, whose wondrous ruined palaces prove the original inhabitants to have been highly civilized and of immense power: and which, by its extent and variety, might cast into insignificance those proud specks which imagine themselves suns, when they are, perhaps, only motes in the sun's beams.

It scarcely appears that the learned and impartial Du Mège has settled the question by his arguments; indeed he seems himself aware that it is yet open, for he rather confutes others than assumes an opinion himself.

He concludes, that the ancient Vascons who overran Aquitaine, in 600, are certainly not the same people as those who now speak the Escuara language, and that these *may have been* "one of those people who invaded the Roman empire in the reign of Probus, or the remains of those tribes to whom, in the time of Honorius, was confided the guardianship of the entrance of the Pyrenees. Thus placed in the defiles of the mountains, *it was easy* for them to extend themselves successively into Aquitaine, Navarre, Guipuscoa, &c., to impose their *language* and their laws on the terrified people, and thus *mix themselves with* the Vascons and Cantabrians of Spain, and the Tarbelli and Sibyllates of Gaul."

Whatever may be their origin, the Basques, as they exist at this moment, are a very singular people, both as to their customs and language: there is not the slightest resemblance between them and their neighbours; they are perfectly foreigners in the next village to that which they inhabit. Some *profane* persons (M. Pierquin, for instance, who goes near to do so, in an article on *la France littéraire,*) have dared to insinuate, that the language of the Basques is nothing more than a mere jargon, *both modern and vulgar;* but this is so cruel an assertion, and one which destroys so many theories, reducing learning to a jest, that no wonder M. Mazure and others are indignant at such boldness.

It must be confessed that, since extremes meet, the same arguments used to prove the classical antiquity of the language would serve to convince that it was merely modern, and made use of, by uneducated persons, to express their wants as readily as possible. There are, in the Basque, terms which represent ideas by sounds, explaining, by a sort of musical imitation, many usual acts, and the appearance of objects; but this is frequently brought forward by its defenders in its favour, and as establishing its antiquity.

M. Mazure, who appears an enthusiast for the Basque language, produces several words to show the sublimity contained in their signification: for instance, he says, "the radical name of *the Moon,* combined with other terms, gives occasion for superb expressions, full of thought, and of a character which no modern language could furnish: thus—*ilarquia,* the moon, signifies *its light,* or its *funereal* light; and *illarguia, ilkulcha, ilobia, ilerria, ileguna,* signify the *coffin,* the *grave,* the *churchyard,* the *day of death.*

"The days of the week are also extremely expressive—as Friday, Saturday, Sunday, which convey the idea of the *remembrance of the death of the Saviour—the last day of work—the great day.* A strictly Christian nation has left, in these words, their stamp." This being the case, how does it agree with the extraordinarily antique origin of the Basques? However, it appears that these are exceptions; other words being sufficiently unintelligible, that is to say, difficult to explain.

M. Mazure considers that the Basque language is, in some respects, the *most perfect* that exists, from the *unity of the verb* which it preserves: its system of conjugation alone were enough, in his opinion, to make it an object worthy of study and admiration to all grammarians. To the uninitiated, the very opposite opinions of M. Mazure and M. Pierquin are somewhat amusing: the former insists that the Basque has nothing to do with Hebrew or Phoenician, but inclines to think it a lost *African* dialect, such as, *perhaps,* might have been spoken by the Moors of Massinissa, who peopled Spain, and probably Aquitaine, at some period unknown.

One singular fact with respect to this mysterious dialect is, that it possesses no written nor printed books older than two centuries since; and no alphabet has been discovered belonging to it; consequently it has no literature; but it has preserved many songs and ballads, some of great delicacy and beauty; and its *improvvisatore,* by profession, are as fruitful as the Italians. One popular song, in the dialect of Labourd, may give an idea of the strange language which occupies so much attention.

BASQUE SONG.

"Tchorittoua, nourat houa
Bi hegaliz, aïrian?
Espagñalat jouaïteko,
Elhurra duk bortian:
Algarreki jouanen gutuk
Elhurra hourtzen denian.

"San Josefen ermitha,
Desertian gorada
Espagñalat jouaïteko
Handa goure palissada.
Guibelerat so-guin eta,
Hasperenak ardura.

Hasperena, babilona,
Maïtiaren borthala
Bihotzian sarakio
Houra eni bezala;
Eta guero eran izok
Nik igorten haïdala.

TRANSLATION.

Borne on thy wings amidst the air,
Sweet bird, where wilt thou go?
For if thou wouldst to Spain repair,
The ports are filled with snow.
Wait, and we will fly together,
When the Spring brings sunny weather.

St. Joseph's hermitage is lone,
Amidst the desert bare,
And when we on our way are gone,
Awhile we'll rest us there;
As we pursue our mountain-track,
Shall we not sigh as we look back?

Go to my love, oh! gentle sigh,
And near her chamber hover nigh;
Glide to her heart, make that thy shrine,
As she is fondly kept in mine.
Then thou may'st tell her it is I
Who sent thee to her, gentle sigh!

— — — —

It appears to me, that there is a very remarkable similarity between the habits of the people of the Basque country and those of Brittany; although they of the South are not rich in beautiful legends, such as M. de Villemarqué has preserved to the world: they have dramas and mysteries just in the same manner: some of which last for days, and are played in the open air by the people. They name their rocks and valleys as the Bretons do: as, for instance, they have the *Vallée du Sang,* the *Col des Ossemens,* the *Forêt du Réfuge,* the *Champ de la Victoire;* and traditions attach to each of these. There is, however, a gayer, livelier character amongst them than that which inspires the pathetic ballads of Brittany. The Basques are very ready to be amused; are more hilarious and less gloomy than the Bretons: yet they have the same love of their country, and regret at leaving it. An author[13] who has written on the subject, says: "To judge properly of the Basque, he should be seen amidst his pleasures and his games; for it is then that he exhibits his brilliant imagination. Often, in the joy of a convivial meeting—when his natural gaiety, excited by wine and good cheer, is arrived at that point of vivacity when man seems united to the chain of existence only by the link of pleasure—one of the guests will feel himself inspired: he rises; the tumult ceases; profound silence is established, and his noisy companions are at once transformed to attentive listeners. He sings: stanzas succeed each other, and poetry flows naturally from his lips. The measure he adopts is grave and quiet; the air seems to come with the words, without being sought for; and rich imagery and new ideas flash forth at every moment, whether he takes for his subject the praise of one of the guests, or the chronicles of the country. He will sing thus for hours together: but some other feels inspired in his turn; a kind of pastoral combat takes place—very like those between the troubadours of old—and the interest of the scene increases. Presently they start into dances,

[13] M. Boucher. "Souvenirs du Pays Basque."

and their steps accompany the words, still more like the custom of the jongleurs. The rivals sing and dance alternately, as the words require it; their movements increase in expression, the most difficult and the prettiest are striven for by the dancers, the time being always well preserved, and the spirit of the poem not lost sight of. When they are obliged to give up, from mere fatigue, a censor pronounces which is the victor: that is, which of the two has given the most gratification to the audience."

The Basque poet has no view in his compositions but the expression of his feelings: he has no idea of gain, or reputation, but sings because he requires to show the emotions which agitate him. It is not a little singular that, in this particular, he resembles the inhabitants of Otaheite; one of whom Bougainville describes as having sung in strophes all that struck him during a voyage.

The Basque language seems very well adapted for light poetry; and, indeed, is peculiarly fitted for rhyme, and has a natural ease which helps the verse along, in a manner which belongs to the Italian. The ideas are always tender and delicate, to a surprising degree, as the following songs may prove:

BASQUE SONG.

— — — —

"Su garretan," &c.

— — — —

I BURN in flames, because my heart
Has loved thee through the dreary past;
And in my eyes the tear-drops start,
To think I lose thee at the last.
My days are pass'd in ceaseless weeping,
And all my nights in vain regret;
No peace awaits me—waking—sleeping,
Until I die, and all forget:
And thou who seest me thus repine,
Hast not a tear for grief like mine!

— — — —

The Basque poet can seldom read or write: he owes nothing to education: nature alone is his instructress, and she inspires him with ideas the most graceful, tender, and, at the same time, correct, for nothing exceptionable is ever heard in his songs. In many of these there is a strain which might parallel some of the sweetest odes of the Persians; from whom, it is not impossible but that they may have derived them; if, indeed, the early troubadours from the East have not left their traces in such lays as this:

BASQUE SONG.

— — — —

"Ezdut uste baden ceruan aingeruric," &c.

— — — —

I CANNOT think in heaven above

Immortal angels there may be,
Whose hearts can show so pure a love
As that which binds my soul to thee:

And when, my ceaseless suff'rings past,
The grave shall make me all forget,
I only ask thee, at the last,
One gentle sigh of fond regret.

Very often these songs take the form of dialogues: the following is one very well known in the country:

BASQUE SONG.

————

"Amodíoac bainarabila choriñoa aircan bezala," &c.

————

The Lover.

Love lifts me gently in the air,
As though I were a bird to fly,
And nights to me, like days, are fair,
Because my gentle love is nigh.

The Mistress.

Thou call'st me dear—ah! seest thou not
Those words have only pow'r to grieve me?
Why is my coldness all forgot?
And why not, at my bidding, leave me?

The Lover.

The love I feel—and canst thou doubt—
I, who would traverse seas for thee!
Who have no power to live without,
And own thy charms are life to me.

The Mistress.

If I have charms, thine eye alone
Behold'st the beauty none can prize;
Oh! in the world exists but one
Who fills my soul and dims my eyes:
That one—ask not who he may be,
But leave me—for thou art not he!

The following may serve as a specimen of their passionate expressions:

BASQUE SONG.

————

"Ene maitcac biloa hori," &c.

— — — —

My fair one, with the golden tresses,
With rosy cheeks and hands of snow,
With hopeless care each heart oppresses,
Around her step such graces glow.

A cloud, upon her brow descending,
Has dimm'd that eye of dazzling ray,
Upon whose glance, the light attending,
Has led my giddy heart astray.

I see thee, like the flow'r of morning,
In sweetness and in beauty shine;
None like to thee the world adorning—
My life, my soul, my life is thine!

The Basques have compositions in various styles—complaints and satires—like the professors of the *gaie science*. War and peace are celebrated by them: there are poems on La Tour d'Auvergne; Napoleon; Wellington, and the Revolution of July: in tragedy and melo-drama they peculiarly succeed; and there exists a modern Basque drama, of singular merit, called Marie de Navarre, the scene of which is laid in the tenth century, in which great power is exhibited, and considerable dramatic effect produced.

There is a saying, well known in the country, *"Ce n'est pas un homme, c'est un Basque;"* which is intended to express the superiority of the native of these regions over all others. It appears that the Basque is, in fact, of much finer form than the rest of the people of the Pyrenees; and the young women are proverbially handsome. I cannot speak from extensive observation; but of this often-named peculiarity of personal appearance I was by no means sensible in the few specimens I have seen—for all the people of this part of the South seemed to me extremely inferior in beauty to those of the North; and, taken in general, it strikes me that the handsomest natives of France I have seen are to be found in Normandy. I speak merely as comparing the people with the same classes in England: and to one accustomed to the sparkling clear eye, fine delicate complexion, tall stature, and finely-developed figures of both our men and women, the inhabitants of the whole of France seem very inferior: there is a monotony in their tanned faces, spare figures, and black eyes and hair, which wearies, and ceases to create interest after the first. Some individuals in the Basque country, however, struck me as handsome and very intelligent.

The Basque is bold and brave, and the French armies never had finer soldiers, as far as regarded spirit, than the natives of these countries: but neither did any region produce so many deserters; for the *maladie du pays* is strong upon them, and they take the first opportunity of returning to their home amongst the mountains. This is not confined to the Basque, but occurs to all the mountaineers of Béarn. One instance will show this feeling; the story was related by a guide to the Brèche de Roland, who knew the circumstances. A young man had been forced by the conscription to join Napoleon's army: he was very young at the time, and went through all the dangers, hardships, and privations like a mountaineer and a man of courage; but, as soon as he saw an opportunity, he deserted, and sought the land where all his wishes tended. He was pursued and traced from place to place; but, generally favoured by his friends and assisted by his own ingenuity, he always eluded search, and, with the precaution of never sleeping two nights in the same village, he managed for several years to continue free. He was in love with a young girl, and on one occasion, at a *fête*, had come far over the mountains to dance with her: he was warned by a companion that emissaries had been seen in the neighbourhood; but he determined nothing should interfere with the pleasure he anticipated in leading out the lass he loved. He had a rival, however, in the company, who gave notice to the officers of justice that the deserter would be at the dance, and, accordingly, in the midst of the revel—as they were executing one of those agile dances, called *Le Saut Basque*—the object of pursuit became aware that, amidst the throng, were several persons whom he had no difficulty in guessing were his pursuers. They kept their station close to the path he must take when he left the spot where they were dancing, and he, with great presence of mind and determined gallantry, finished the measure with his pretty partner: at the last turn, he looked briskly round, and observing that one of his companions was leaning on a thick stick, he suddenly caught it from his grasp, and with a leap and run, dashed past the party who were waiting for him, brandishing the weapon over his head and keeping all off. They were so taken by surprise, that they had no power to detain him; and the villagers closing round and impeding them as much as possible, the young hero got off to the mountains in safety. He was, however, taken some time after this scene, and carried to Bayonne to be tried, when every one expected that he would meet with capital punishment; but it was found impossible to identify him—no one could be induced to appear against him—and the magistrates, wearied out, at length gave him his discharge, and he returned to live quietly in his village, and marry his love, after having been a hunted man in the woods and mountains for nearly ten years.

The Basque is said to be irritable, revengeful, and implacable; but gay and volatile, passionately addicted to dancing and the *jeu de paume*, which he never abandons till compelled by positive infirmity. He is very adventurous, and fond of excitement; it is not, therefore, singular that he should be a hardy smuggler, so cunning and adroit that he contrives to evade the officers of the excise in a surprising manner. If, however, a smuggler falls beneath the shot of one of the guardians of right, all the natives become at once his deadly enemy, and he has no safety but in leaving the country instantly. The women assist their relations in this dangerous traffic, and perform acts of daring, which are quite startling. It is told of one, a young girl of Eshiarce, that, being hard pressed by a party of excise, she ran along a steep ledge of rocks, and, at a fearful height, cast herself into the Nive: no one dared to follow down the ravine; and they saw her swimming for her life, battling with the roaring torrent; she reached the opposite shore, turned with an exulting gesture, although her basket of contraband goods was lost in the stream, and, darting off amongst the valleys, was lost to their view.

The Basques have their comedy, which they call *Tobera-Munstruc*, or *Charivari represented*; and they enter into its jokes with the utmost animation and delight. They generally take for their subject some popular event of a comic nature, and all is carried on extempore. The young men of a village meet to consult respecting it; and then comes the *cérémonie du bâton*. Those who choose to be actors, or simply to subscribe towards the expenses, range themselves on one side; two amongst them hold a stick at each end, and all those chosen pass beneath it; this constitutes an engagement to assist; and it is a disgrace to fail. News is then sent to the villages round of the intention to act a comedy; and preparations are made by the select committee. The representations are positive *fêtes*, and are looked forward to with great pleasure; crowds attend them; and their supporters are usually picked men, who have a reputation for talent and wit. Crimes never come under their consideration: it is always something extremely ridiculous, or some ludicrous failing, that is turned into contempt and held up to risibility. It is quite amazing to what an extent the genius of the improvvisatores go at times; they display consummate art and knowledge of human nature, quick *répartie*, subtle arguments, absurd conjunctions, startling metaphors, and are never at a loss to meet the assertions of their adversary on the other side; for it is always in the form of law-pleadings, for and against, that the comedy is conducted.

It is usually carried on in the manner following:

The crowd assembled, a man on horseback opens the *cortège*: he is dressed in white trowsers, a purple sash, a white coat, and a fine cap, ornamented with tinsel and ribbons; flutes, violins, tamborines, and drums, succeed; then come about forty dancers, in two files, who advance in a cadenced step; this is the celebrated dance called the *Morisco*, which is reserved for great occasions. This troop is in the same costume as the man on horseback; each dancer holding in his right hand a wand, adorned with ribbons, and surmounted by a bouquet of artificial flowers. Then come the poet and a guard, a judge and two pleaders, in robes; and a guard on foot, bearing carbines, close the procession.

The judge and advocates take their places on the stage, seating themselves before three tables, the poet being in front on the left.

A carnival scene now takes place, in which are all sorts of strange costumes, harlequins, clowns, and jokers; in this a party of blacksmiths are conspicuous, whose zeal in shœing and unshœing a mule, on which a *huissier* sits, with his face to the tail, creates great merriment. When all this tumult is quieted by proclamation, music sounds; the poet advances and improvises an address, in which he announces the subject of the piece; his manner is partly serious, partly jesting. He points out the advocate who is to plead the cause of morals and propriety: this one rises, and, in the course of his exordium, takes care to throw out all the sarcasm he can against his rival, who rouses himself, and the battle of tongues begins, and is carried on in a sort of rhyming prose, in which nothing is spared to give force to jest or argument against the reigning vices or follies of the day. As the orators proceed and become more and more animated on the subject, they are frequently interrupted by loud applause. Sometimes, in these intervals, the poet gives a signal, which puts an end to the discussions before the public are fatigued; and, the music sounding, the performers of the national dance appear, and take the place of the two advocates for a time. These combatants soon re-commence their struggle; and, at length, the judge is called upon to pronounce between them. A farcical kind of consultation ensues between the judge and the ministers around, who are supposed to send messengers even to the king himself by their mounted courier in attendance.

The judge at last rises, and, with mock solemnity, delivers his fiat. Then follow quadrilles; and the famous *Sauts Basques*, so well-known and so remarkable, close the entertainments.

These *fêtes* last several days, as in Brittany, and are very similar in their style. I am told, however, that, though very witty, these representations are not fit for *la bonne compagnie*.

"If to what we have been able to collect on what are called Basques," says Du Mège, "we add the remarks of General Serviez, *chargé d'administration* of the department of the Basses Pyrénées, a complete picture is presented of the manners and habits of the descendants of the Escualdunacs, who may be subdivided into three tribes, or families: the *Labourdins*, the *Navarrais*, and the *Souletins*."

"They have rather the appearance of a foreign colony transplanted into the midst of the French, than a people forming a portion of the country, and living under the same laws and government. They are extremely brave, and are always the terror of the Spaniards in all wars with them; but their aversion to leaving their homes is very great, and their attachment to their personal liberty is remarkable. They are much wedded to their own habits and customs, and are almost universally *unacquainted* with the French language. They are said to be the *cleanest people in the world*; in which particular they singularly differ from the Bretons, whom, in some respects, they resemble.

"Mildness and persuasion does much with them, severity nothing: they are choleric in temper, but soon appeased; nevertheless, they are implacable in their hatred, and resolute in their revenge. Ready to oblige, if flattered; restless and active, hard-working; *habitually sober and well-conducted*, and violently attached to their religion and their priests. They seem rarely to know fatigue, for, after a hard day's work, they think little of going five or six leagues to a *fête*, and to be deprived of this amusement is a great trial to them.

"They are tenacious of the purity of their blood, and avoid, as much as possible, contracting alliances with neighbouring nations; they are impatient of strangers acquiring possessions in their country. They are apt to quarrel amongst each other at home; but there is a great *esprit du corps* amongst them when they meet abroad. There are shades of difference in their characters, according to their province. In general, the *Souletins* are more cunning and crafty than the rest, resembling their neighbours of Béarn in their moral qualities. The *Navarrais* is said to be more fickle. The *Labourdins* are fonder of luxuries, and less diligent than the others; and it is thought, consequently, less honest; the latter are generally sailors, and are known as good whalers."

There seems a desire amongst *improvers* in France to do away amongst the common people with the original language, or *patois*, which exists in so many of the provinces; and in many of the schools nothing is taught but French. This would seem to be a benefit, as far as regards civilization; but it shocks the feelings of the people, who are naturally fond of the language of their fathers. The Bretons, like the Welsh with us, are very tenacious of this attempt: the people of Languedoc, with Jasmin, their poet, at their head, have made a stand for their tongue; and the Basques, at the present moment, are in great distress that measures are now being taken to teach their children French, and do away altogether with the language of which they are so proud, and which is so prized by the learned. In a late *Feuilleton* of the Mémorial des Pyrénées, I observed a very eloquent letter on the subject of instruction in French in the rural schools, from which the Basque language is banished. The children learn catechism and science in French, and can answer any question put to them in that language by the master, like parrots, being quite unable to translate it back into the tongue they talk at home, where nothing but Basque meets their ears.

It is, of course, quite necessary that they should understand French for their future good; but there does not appear a sufficient reason that they should neglect their own language, or, at any rate, that they should not be instructed in it, and have the same advantage as the Welsh subjects of Great Britain, who did not, however, obtain all they claimed for their primitive language without a struggle.

The writer in the Mémorial contends that the children should be taught their prayers in Basque, and should know the grammar of that dialect in order to be able to write to their friends when abroad—for many of them are soldiers and sailors,—in a familiar tongue, since those at home by their fire-sides know nothing of French, and could not understand the best French letter that was ever penned. The question is, could they read *at all*, and if the epistle were read for them by a more learned neighbour, would not French be as easy as Basque? for the friend must have been at school to be of use.

Be this as it may, the "coil" made for the beloved tongue shows the feeling which still exists in Navarre for the *"beau dialecte Euskarien."*

"Do you know what you would destroy?" exclaims M. de Belsunce, in somewhat wild enthusiasm; "the sacred relic of ages—the aboriginal idiom, as ancient as the mountains which shelter and serve for its asylum!

"The Basque language is our glory, our pride, the theme of all our memories, the golden book of our traditions. Proud and free in its accent, noble and learned in its picturesque and sonorous expressions, its formation and grammatical form are both simple and sublime; add to which, the people preserve it with a religious devotion.

"It is the language spoken by our illustrious ancestors—those who carried the terror of their arms from the heights of the Pyrenees to Bordeaux and Toulouse. It is the language of the conquerors of Theodobert, Dagobert, and Carebert; and of the fair and ill-fated wife of the latter—the unfortunate Giselle. Were not the sacred cries of liberty and independence uttered amongst our mountains in that tongue, and the songs of triumph which were sent to heaven after the victory of the Gorges of the Soule? It is the dialect named by Tacitus, as that of those who were never conquered — *Cantaber invictus*: immortalized as that of the *Lions of War*: spoken by the most *ancient people in the world* — a race of shepherds with patriarchal manners, proverbial hospitality, and right-mindedness; light-hearted, friendly and true, though implacable in vengeance and terrible in anger as undaunted in courage.

"Our chronicles live in our national songs, and our language proves an ancient civilization. To the philosopher and the learned who study it, it presents, from its grandeur, its nobility, and the rich harmony of its expressions, a subject of grave meditation; it may serve as the key of the history of nations, and solve many doubts on the origin of lost or faded languages."

Perhaps M. de Belsunce takes a rather pompous view of the subject; but he has, nevertheless, much reason in his appeal.

As specimens of this extraordinary language, some of the names of the Basque towns may amuse and surprise the reader; perhaps, in the Marquesas islands, lately taken possession of by the French, they may find some sounds which to Basque sailors, of which a ship's crew is almost certain to have many, may be familiar.

Iratsodoqui.
Urruxordoqui.
Mentchola.
Orgambidecosorhona.
} Places in the district of Forest of Saint Eugrace.

Furunchordoqui, near the Port d'Anie.
The Pic d'Anie is properly called Ahuguamendi.

In Basse Burie occur the following names; —

Iturourdineta.
Iparbarracoitcha.
Aspildoya.
Lehintchgarratia.

In the arrondissement of Bayonne may be met with: — Urkheta, Hiriburu, Itsasu, Beraskhoitce, Zubernua, and others equally singular in sound.

CHAPTER XIV.

Cagots—Cacous Of Brittany.

ONE of the most puzzling and, at the same time, interesting subjects, which re-curs to the explorer in the Pyrenees, is the question respecting that mysterious race of people called Cagots, whose origin has never yet been satisfactorily accounted for. All travellers speak of the Cagots, and make allusion to them, but nothing very positive is told. When I arrived in the Pyrenees, my first demand was respecting them; but those of my countrymen who had ever heard of their existence assured me that their denomination was only another word for *Crétin* or *Goîtreux*: others insisted that no trace of the ancient *parias* of these countries remained, and some treated the legends of their strange life as mere fables.

I applied to the French inhabitants; from whom I heard much the same, though all agreed that Cagots were to be found in different parts of the mountains, and that they were still shunned as a race apart, though the prejudice against them was certainly wearing away.

I inquired of our Béarnaise servant whether she could tell me anything about the Cagots, upon which she burst into a fit of laughter, which lasted some time, on her recovery from which she informed me that they were accustomed to use the word as a term of derision. "Any one," said she, "*whose ears are short—cut off at the tip*, we call Cagot; but it is only *pour rire*, it is not a polite word."

I hoped, from her information, and the manner in which she treated the subject, that the Cagots were indeed extinct, and known only as a by-word, which had now no meaning; but I found, by conversing with intelligent persons who had been a great deal in the mountains, and given their attention to such discoveries, that the unfortunate people, once the objects of scorn and oppression to all their fellow-men, are still to be found, and still lead an isolated life, though no longer proscribed or hunted like wild beasts as formerly.

I examined, with the aid of a friend in Pau, the archives of the town, and found several times mention made of these people up to a late period, in which they were classed as persons out of the pale of the law; a price is put on their heads, as if they were wolves; they are forbidden to appear in the towns, and orders are issued to the police to *shoot them* if found infringing the rules laid down; punishments are named as awaiting them if they ventured to ally themselves, in any way, with any out of their own caste, and they are spoken of together with brigands and male-factors, and all other persons whose crimes have placed them out of the protection of their country.

In Gascony, Béarn, and the Pays Basque, it is well known that for centuries this proscribed race has existed, entirely separated from the rest of their species, marrying with each other, and thus perpetuating their misfortune, avoided, persecuted, and contemned: their origin unknown, and their existence looked upon as a blot on the face of nature. At one period the Cagots were objects of hatred, from the belief that they were afflicted with the leprosy, which notion does not appear to be founded on fact; in later times, they have been supposed to suffer more especially from *goître*; but physicians have established that they are not more subject to this hideous disease than their neighbours of the valleys and mountains. Nevertheless, a belief even now prevails that this wretched people, and the race of Crétins, are the same, and that they owe their origin to the Visigoths, who subdued a part of Gaul.

Ramond, in his "Observations on the Pyrenees," has the following curious passage: "My observations on the Crétins had thrown little light on the subject; and learned persons whom I had consulted had not placed it in a clearer point of view: I found myself obliged to add another proof to the many that exist, to demonstrate that the resemblance of effects is not always a sure indication of the identity of causes; when my habitual intercourse with the people entirely changed the nature of the question, by showing that it was amongst the unfortunate race of Cagots that I should find the Crétins of the Valley of Luchon.

"It was with a shyness which I found much difficulty in overcoming, that the inhabitants of this country avowed to me that their valley contained a certain number of families which, from time immemorial, were regarded as forming part of an infamous and cursed race; that those who composed them were never counted as citizens; that everywhere they were forbidden to carry arms; that they were looked upon as slaves, and obliged to perform the most degrading offices for the community at large; that misery and disease was their constant portion; that the scourge of *goître* generally belonged to them; that they were peculiarly afflicted with the complaint in the valleys of Luchon, all those of the Pays de Comminges, of Bigorre, Béarn, and the two Navarres; that their miserable abodes are ordinarily in remote places, and that whatever amelioration of prejudice has arisen in the progress of time, and the improvement of manners, a marked aversion is always shown towards that set of people, who are forced still to keep themselves entirely distinct from the free natives of the villages in their neighbourhood."

There hare, however, many parts of Béarn, Soule, and Navarre, for instance, in following the course of the Gave of Oloron, inhabited by Cagots who are by no means subject to the infirmity of *goître*, by which it appears that it is merely an accidental complaint with them as with others.

The prejudice which has peculiarly attributed to them this horrible affliction is therefore erroneous: and equally so is the idea that they carry in their appearance any indication of a difference of species: for, instead of the sallow, weak, sickly hue which it was believed belonged to them, it is known that they differ in nowise from the other natives in complexion, strength, or health. Instances of great age occur amongst them; and they are subject to no more nor less infirmities than others. Beauty or ugliness, weakness or strength, deformity or straightness, are common to the Cagots as to the rest of the human race. This, however, is certain, that in some villages the richest persons are of the proscribed order; but they, nevertheless, are held in a certain degree of odium, and their alliance is avoided: the state of misery and destitution in which they were represented to M. Ramond exists but partially at present; for, being in general more active and industrious than the other inhabitants, they very frequently become rich, although they never are able to assume the position in society which wealth in any other class allows.

The following is a fearful picture, which it is to be hoped is exaggerated at the present day. It exhibits the Cagots according to the opinion a few years ago prevalent, and denies to this people the health for which others who defend them contend:

"Health," says the French author of "Travels in the French Pyrenees," "that treasure of the indigent, flies from the miserable huts of Agos, Bidalos, and Vieuzac: three villages, so close together, that they constitute one whole: they are situated in the valley called Extremère de Sales. The numerous sources which spring beside the torrent of Bergons, the freshness and solitude of these charming retreats, the rich shade of the thick chesnuts, which in summer form delicious groves—all is obscured by the miserable state of the inhabitants: diseases of the most loathsome kind prevail for ever in this smiling valley: Crétins abound, those unhappy beings *supposed to be the descendants of the Alains*, a part of whom established themselves in the Pyrenees and the Valais. Whether this connexion really exists or not, a stupid indifference, which prevents them from feeling their position, exists in common with the Crétins amongst those people known as Goths, or Cagots, *chiens de Gots*, and *Capots*, who are a fearful example of the duration of popular hatred. They are condemned to the sole occupation permitted to them, that of hewing of wood; are banished from society, their dwellings placed at a distance from towns and villages, and are in fact excommunicated beggars; forced, besides, in consequence of the profession of Arianism, adopted by their Gothic ancestors, to wear on their habits a mark of obloquy in the form of a goose's foot, which is sewn on their clothes; exposed to insult and every species of severity; condemned to the fear of having their feet pierced with hot irons, if they appear bare-footed in towns, and pursued with the most bitter rigour that bigotry and animosity can indulge in."

The words, *Stupides, Idiots, Crétins*, and *Cagots* have been considered synonymous; but this is an error: the last wretched class being separated in their misery, and distinct from the rest. The beautiful valleys of the Pyrenees are frightfully infested with the disease of *goitre*, and few of them are free; but the Cagots merely share the affliction, as has been said before (following the learned and benevolent Palassou) with the rest of the inhabitants.

The notion which, at first sight, would seem better founded, is, that the Cagots are descendants of those numerous *lepers* who formed a fearful community at one period, and were excluded from society to prevent infection; but the more the subject is investigated the less does this appear likely: though banished, from prudential motives, and even held in abhorrence, from the belief that their malady was a judgment of Heaven, those afflicted with leprosy, when healed, had the power of returning to the communion of their fellows: they were not excommunicated, nor placed beyond the mercy of the laws: they were avoided, but not hated; and they had some hope for the future, which was denied to the Cagots.

In the Basque country they are called *Agots*, and it is ascertained that, though held in the same aversion as in Bigorre, Navarre, and Béarn, they have no physical defects, nor any difference of manners or appearance to the rest of the natives: they are there also vulgarly said to descend from the Goths.

The popular notion of the shortness of the lobe of the ear, which is supposed to be a characteristic of a Cagot, seems to be only worthy of the laughter which accompanied its first announcement to me; yet it is an old tradition, and has long obtained credence.

The learned Marca, who has treated this subject, remarks: "These unfortunate beings are held as infected and leprous; and by an express article in the *Coutumes de Béarn* and the provinces adjacent, familiar conversation with the rest of the people is severely interdicted to them. So that, even in the churches, they have a door set apart by which to enter, with a *bénitier* and seats for them solely: they are obliged to live in villages apart from other dwellings: they are usually carpenters, and are permitted to use no arms or tools but those expressly required in their trade: they are looked upon as infamous, although they have, according to the ancient *Fors de Béarn*, a right to be heard as witnesses; seven of them being required to make the testimony of *one uninfected* man."

Though previous to the time of Louis VI. called Le Gros, in 1108, the Cagots were sold as slaves *with* estates, it does not appear that their fate, in this respect, was different from that of other serfs, who were all transferred from one master to another, without reserve. A denomination given to a Cagot, however, in the record of a deed of gift, mentioned by Marca, gives rise to other conjectures, involving still more interesting inquiries. It is there stated, that with a *"nasse"* was given a *Chrétien*, named Auriot Donat; that is to say, the *house* of a Cagot and himself with it.

In the cartulary of the *ci-devant* Abbey of Luc, in the year 1000, and in the *Fors de Béarn*, they are designated as *Chrestiàs*, and the term *Cagot*, we are informed by Marca, was first employed in acts relative to them in the year 1551. They are called *gaffos* in an ancient *Fors* of Navarre, in 1074; and the term *Chrestiàas* even now is used to denote the villages where the Cagots reside.

It appears that the Cagots of the present day are ordinarily denominated *Agotacs* and *Cascarotacs*, by the peasants of Béarn and the Basque country: that of *Chrétiens* seemed affixed to them formerly, but was equally so to the lepers who were obliged to live isolated, and their abodes were called *chrestianeries*.

As the serfs became emancipated, the Cagots, who had been slaves peculiarly appropriated by the Church, and called by them, it seems, *Chrestiàs*, were allowed similar privileges: added to which, from having belonged to the ecclesiastics, and from not enjoying the rights of citizens, they were exempt from taxes. In later times, this led to innovations by these very Cagots, who, becoming rich, endeavoured to usurp the prerogatives of nobility. The Etats of Béarn, issued a command to the *"Cagot d'Oloron,"* —who appears to have been a powerful person—to prevent him from building a *dovecote*, and to another to forbid him the use of arms and the costume of a gentleman.

At the church of St. Croix at Oloron is still to be seen a *bénitier*, set apart for the use of this race; and at the old fortified church of Luz, was a little door, now closed up, by which they entered to perform their devotions.

The prohibition to carry arms, which never extended to *lepers*, would seem to indicate that the Cagots, always separately mentioned in all the public acts, were persons who might be dangerous to public tranquillity. And this, together with the appellation of *Christians*, may give colour to another opinion, entertained by those who reject the idea of their being descendants of those Goths who took refuge in the mountains after the defeat of Alaric by Clovis.

The opinion to which I allude, and which is adopted by Palassou, is that they come from those Saracens who fled from Charles Martel in the eighth century, after the defeat of their chief, Abderraman, near Tours: these Saracens are supposed to have sheltered themselves from pursuit in the mountains, where, being prevented by the snows from going further, they remained hemmed in, and by degrees established themselves here, and conformed to Christianity; but does this account for the contempt and hatred which they had to endure for so many centuries after? for no race of people, once converted, were any longer held accursed in the country where they lived. If, indeed, they remained pagan, this severity might naturally have visited them; but the Cagots were certainly Christians from early times, as the accommodations prepared for them in churches proves.

There seems little doubt that the armies of Abderraman spread themselves over the Pyrenees, where they long kept the French and Gascons in fear: traditions of them still exist, and the name of a plain near the village of Ossun, in Bigorre, called Lane-Mourine, seems to tell its own tale, as well as the relics found in its earth of the skulls of men, pronounced by competent judges to be those of the natives of a warm climate: in other words, of Saracens, or Moors. But still there seems nothing to prove that the Cagots are the children of these identical Moors, who are said to have been infected with leprosy, and consequently shunned by the people amongst whom they had intruded themselves.

Lepers, at all times, were ordered to be kept apart from the rest of the people, and were placed under the care of the Church to prevent their wandering and carrying infection with them; and the miserable condition in which the proscribed race of Cagots existed, probably made them more liable to take the hideous disease which would have separated them from their kind, even if not already in that predicament: but there must have been something more than mere disease which kept the line for ever drawn between these poor wretches and the rest of the world.

It is expressly defined in the speeches of ministers from the altar to those afflicted with leprosy:—"*As long as you are ill* you shall not enter into any house out of the prescribed bounds." This applied to *all* afflicted with leprosy; but the embargo was never taken off the Cagot.

At one period, the priests made a difficulty of confessing those who were Cagots, and Pope Leo X. was obliged to issue orders to all ecclesiastics to administer the sacraments to them as well as to others of the faithful.

They were during some time called *gezitains,* or descendants of Gehazi, the servant of Elisha, leprous and accursed; but by what authority does not appear. The leprosy was called the *Arab evil,* and supposed to have been brought into Europe by the Saracens: the *suspicion* of *infection* which attached to this race might have caused them to be so shunned; and, whether afflicted or not, they never got the better of this suspicion.

The greatest number of Cagots are to be found in those parts of the Pyrenees which lead directly to Spain, which may strengthen the supposition that the Moors are really their ancestors. A sad falling off to the glory and grandeur of this magnificent people is the notion that all that remains of them should be a race of outcasts, loathsome and abhorred! I cannot induce myself to adopt this idea till more proof is offered to support it, and better reason given to account for the contempt and hatred shown to a people, who, though once followers of Mahomed had become *Chretiàas.*

Amongst other names given them are those of *gahets* and *velus,* for which there seems no explanation; but every new fact involves the question in still deeper obscurity.

It was always enacted that *catechumens,* during the two or three years of probation which they passed previous to being received as children of the Church, should live apart from professed Christians, being neither allowed to eat or frequent the baptized, or give them the kiss of peace: and the Saracens of course were subjected to the same trials, from whence might first have arisen the habit of their living apart, and being looked upon with suspicion, both on account of their former faith and their supposed leprosy. This is, however, I think, scarcely sufficient to warrant the long continuance of the enmity which has pursued them.

One of the acts of the parliament of Bordeaux shows with how much harshness they were treated, and what pains were taken to keep them from mixing with the people, long after the panic of leprosy must have disappeared. In 1596 it was ordained that, "conformable to preceding decrees, the *Cagots* AND *gahets* residing in the parishes and places circumjacent, shall in future wear upon their vestments and on their breasts a red mark, *in the form of a goose's or duck's foot,* in order to be separated from the rest of the people; they are prohibited from touching the viands which are sold in the markets, under the pain of *being whipped,* except those which the sellers have delivered to them; otherwise, they will be banished from the parish they inhabit: also, it is forbidden to the said *cagots* to touch the holy water in the churches, which the other inhabitants take." The same decree was issued to put in force ancient ordinances concerning them, in Soule, in the year 1604.

Still further animosity was shown to these miserable people in 1606. The three states of the said country of Soule, in a general assembly, passed an order by which it was forbidden "to the Cagots, under pain of whipping, to exercise the trade of a miller, or to touch the flour of the common people; and not to mingle in the dances of the rest of the people, under pain of corporal punishment."

Severe as these laws were, those against *lepers* were still more cautious: for whereas Cagots were allowed to enter the churches by a private way, the lepers were not permitted to attend divine worship at all; and had churches appropriated to them alone, which was never the case with the Cagots, who were merely placed apart in the lowest seats.

Much the same arrangements were made respecting the *Cacous* of Brittany, who were allowed to occupy a distant part of the churches, but not to approach the altar, or touch any of the vestments or vases, under a fine of a hundred sous; but chapels, or *fréries*, were permitted them at the gates of several towns—an indulgence apparently never permitted to the *Cagots*.

Lobineau derives their name from Latin and Greek words signifying *"malady,"* a denomination which strengthens the opinion of those who imagine the crusaders brought the leprosy back from Palestine on their return from their pilgrimage.

That the Cagots were exempt from leprosy, appears from a circumstance which took place in 1460, when "the States of Béarn demanded of Gaston de Béarn, Prince of Navarre, that he would command the rule to be enforced that the Cagots should not walk bare-footed in the streets, for fear of communicating the leprosy, and that it should be permitted, in case of their refusing to comply with the enactment, that their feet should be pierced with a hot iron, and also that they should be obliged, in order to distinguish them, to wear on their clothes the ancient mark of a goose's foot, which they had long abandoned: *which proposition was not attended to,* thereby proving that the council of the Prince did not approve of the animosity of the States, and did not consider the Cagots infected with leprosy."

The law was more severe in Brittany, about the same period; for, in 1477, the Duke François II., in order to prevent the *cacous, caqueux, or caquins,* from being under the necessity of begging, and mingling with persons in health, granted them permission to use, as farmers, the produce of the land near their dwellings, under certain restrictions; and at the same time insisted on their renewing the red mark which they were condemned to wear. He also ordered that all commerce should be interdicted to them except that of *hemp,* from whence it comes that the trade of a cordwainer is considered vile in some cantons of Bretagne, as those of swineherd and boatman were in Egypt.

In some places in Brittany, the trade of cooper was looked upon with contempt, and the opprobrious name of *caqueux* was given to them because they were thought to belong to a *race of Jews* dispersed after the ruin of Jerusalem, and who were considered *leprous from father to son.*

It was *only as late as* 1723, that the parliament of Bordeaux—which had long shown such tyranny towards this unhappy class—issued an order that opprobrious names should no longer be applied to them, and that they should be admitted into the general and private assemblies of communities, allowed to hold municipal charges, and be granted the honours of the church. They were to be permitted in future to enter the galleries of churches like any other person; their children received in schools and colleges in all towns and villages, and christian instruction withheld from them no more than from another. Yet, in spite of this ordinance, hatred and prejudice followed this people still; though, protected by the laws, they fell on them less heavily.

At Auch, a quarter was set apart for the *Cagots*, or *capots*, and *another* for *the lepers*. The *gakets* of Guizeris, in the diocese of Auch, had a door appropriated to them in the church, which the rest of the inhabitants carefully avoided approaching.

"This prejudice," says Brugèles,[14] "lasted till the visit paid to the church by M. Louis d'Aignan du Sendat, archdeacon of Magnoac, who, in order to abolish this distinction, passed out of the church by the *porte des Cagots*, followed by the *curé*, and all the ecclesiastics of the parish, and those of his own *suite*; the people, seeing this, followed also, and since that time the doors have been used indifferently by all classes."

Although my idea may be laughed at by the learned, it has occurred to me, that this race might be the descendants of those Goths who were driven from Spain by the Moors, introduced by Count Julian in consequence of the conduct of Don Roderick.

There seems scarcely a good reason why the Goths under Alaric should stop in the Pyrenees on their way to a safer retreat, when pursued by the troops of Clovis, the Christian; Spain was open to them, and to remain amongst the enemy's mountains seemed bad policy. Again, why should Abdelrahman, after his defeat, when his discomfited people fled before the *hammer* of the great Charles, have paused in the Pyrenees? Spain was their's, and surely the remnant would have sought their own land, even if detained awhile by the snows, and not have remained a mark of contempt and hatred in the country of their conquerors.

But when Roderick and his Goths fled from the Moors, after the fatal battle of Guadalete, and they remained monarchs of Spain, there was no safety for the ruined remnant but in close concealment; and the Pyrenees offered a safe retreat. The Christians of France, however, would not have received them as friends, and they could not return to their own country; therefore, they might have sheltered themselves in the gorges, and when they appeared have been looked upon with the same horror as the Arians of the time of Alaric, or even have been confounded by the people with those very Moors who drove them out of Spain.

The difficulty, which is the greatest by far, is to account for the unceasing contempt which clung to them *after* they became *Chrestiàas*.

An ingenious person of Pau, who has considered the subject in all its bearings, has a theory that the Cagots are, after all, the *earliest Christians*, persecuted by the Romans, compelled, in the first instance, to take shelter in rocks and caves; and, even after the whole country became converted to Christianity, retaining their bad name from habit, and in consequence of their own ignorance, which had cast them back into a benighted state, and made them appear different from their better-instructed neighbours. Their name of *Christians* appears to have given rise to this notion.

I am looking forward very anxiously to a work of M. Francisque Michel, on the subject, of the Cagots, which I hear is now in the press. His unwearied enthu-

---

[14] "Chroniques Eccl. du Dioc. D'Auch."

siasm and industry, and the enormous researches he has made both in France and Spain, will, doubtless, enable him to throw some valuable light on the curious question,[15] if not set it at rest for ever.

---

[15] M. Francisque Michel's announced work bears the following title: "Recherches sur les Races maudites de la France et de l'Espagne. (Cagots des Pyrénées. Capots du Langue-doc. Gahets da la Guienne. Colliberts du Bas Poitou. Caqueux de la Bretagne. Cacous du Mans. Marrons de l'Auvergne. Chreetas de Mayorque. Vacqueros des Asturies.)"

URDOS

CHAPTER XV.

The Cagot—Vallée D'aspe—Superstitions—Forests—Despourrins—
The Two Gaves—Bedous—High-Road To Saragossa—Cascade
Of Lescun—Urdos—A Picture Of Murillo—La Vache.

THE subject of the Cagots has occupied the attention of learned and unlearned persons both formerly, and at the present time; and the interest it excites is rather on the increase than otherwise; like the mysterious question of the race and language of the Basques, it can never fail to excite speculation and conjecture. A gentleman, who is a professor at the college of Pau, has devoted much of his time to the investigation of this curious secret, and has thrown his observations together in the form of a romance, in a manner so pleasing, and so well calculated to place the persons he wishes to describe immediately before the mind's eye of his reader, that I think a few extracts from his story of THE CAGOT, yet unpublished, will give the best idea of the state of degradation and oppression in which the Cagots were forced to exist; and exhibit in lively colours the tyranny and bigoted prejudice to which they were victims. I avail myself, therefore, of the permission of M. Badé, to introduce his *Cagot* to the English reader.[16] The story thus opens:

[16] Most of the scenes of the story in the Vallée d'Aspe have become familiar to me,

THE CAGOT.

A BÉARNAIS TALE.

"ON a fine night in the month of June, 1386, a mounted party, accompanied by archers and attendants on foot, were proceeding, at a quiet pace, along the left bank of a rivulet called Lauronce, on the way between Oloron and Aubertin. A fresh breeze had succeeded the burning vapours which, in the scorching days of summer, sometimes transform the valleys of Béarn into furnaces. Myriads of stars glittered, bright and clear, like sparkles of silver, in the deep blue sky, and their glimmering light rendered the thin veil still more transparent which the twilight of the solstice had spread over the face of the country; while through this shadowy haze might be seen, from point to point, on the hills, the ruddy flame of half-extinguished fires.

"From time to time, those who composed the cavalcade paused as it reached higher ground, in order to contemplate the magnificent spectacle before them and the effect produced by the doubtful and fleeting shadows which rested on the fields, on the dark woods, and on the broken and uncertain line in the southern horizon which indicated the summits of the Pyrenees. The air was full of the perfume of newly-cut hay; the leaves sent forth a trembling murmur; the cricket uttered his sharp chirrup in the meadows; the quail's short, flute-like cry was heard, and all in nature harmonized with the beauty of the summer night."

The party, who are travelling at this hour in order to avoid the heats of the day, are then introduced by the narrator as the Baron de Lescun and his niece, Marie, an orphan confided to his care: they are on their way to the Court of Gaston Phoebus, Count of Foix, at Orthez, who is about to give a series of *fêtes* and tournaments: they have been joined by a lady and her son—the Dame d'Artiguelouve (a name of old standing in Béarn, and still existing,)—and the young *domenger*, (the Bérnais title of *Damoiseau*,) Odon, escorted by their pages and valets. Conversation ensues between them, in which the young lady expresses some doubts as to their prudence in choosing so witching an hour, however beautiful the time, for their journey; when it is known that evil spirits and sorcerers are abroad on their foul errands.

They presently arrive on the territory of Faget, when they are startled to observe, as if flitting near them, human forms, which glide noiselessly along, like shades in the darkness. Some of these mysterious beings placed themselves in a stooping position on the margin of the streams, with their faces bent close to the water. Others, divesting themselves of their garments, entered, with hurried and noiseless stops, a neighbouring field of oats, and there concealed themselves. Some of the strangers were astonished at what they saw, and could not resolve in their own minds whether or not these were, indeed, phantoms that appeared in their path.

"'Midnight must be near, and the *fête* of St. Jean is about to begin,' said the Sire de Lescun; 'for these are the poor people who are on the watch for the unattainable moment, when, it is thought, the water changes into wine, and has the power

---

and I can vouch for the truth of the descriptions.

of healing all their infirmities: the dew of this night, received on the body in the fields, is also said to be endowed with the same marvellous virtue.'"

A confused noise now met their ears as they entered the forest of Lorincq, and a singular spectacle was presented to them:

"The forest, all resplendent with illuminations, seemed full of bustle and animation. Numerous torches sparkled amongst the trees to which they were suspended or attached; others were borne along, whirled from place to place, their black smoke sending its long wreaths into the air, and their red flame flashing through the gloom. A thousand voices burst forth, as if simultaneously, from height and valley, above, around, and underneath; an immense crowd hurried along — some mounting, some descending — amongst the crackling branches, until the intricate alleys and close retreats of this labyrinth of verdure were filled with human beings.

"The lame and wounded, the infirm and paralytic grouped themselves around the fountains, to be ready at the right moment to plunge their afflicted limbs in the cold waters, and then to cast in their offering of a piece of money: some, providing for the future, busied themselves in filling, from the beneficent source, their vases and pitchers to overflowing; for it was firmly believed, that, in memory of the holy baptism administered by the patron of the *fête*, Heaven had endowed the waters with peculiar powers during that favoured night; allowing the virtue to take effect from midnight to the rising of the sun.

"In the humid fern might be seen cattle sent to graze at will, in the hope of being cured of some malady, their tinkling bells indicating where they wandered. Parties of old men, women, and children, dispersed here and there, were eating cakes prepared for the occasion; while young men and girls danced in circles beneath the ash and elm trees, to the sound of the *flute of three notes*, accompanied by the nasal cadence of the lute of six strings.

"After halting for a considerable time, and taking their part in the religious advantages of the *fête*, the cavalcade resumed its route; and soon descended into the valley of the Bayse, as the sky began to be tinged with the hue of dawn. When they arrived at the hospital of Aubertin, the first rays of the sun were casting a golden light on the Roman transepts of the church."

At the moment that the Dame d'Artiguelouve and her son are alighting from their horses, they are arrested, and impressed with a superstitious feeling of terror, by observing a fine white courser at the door of the church, held by a page. This was, at the period, a bad omen for the stranger who first saw it, and boded no good to any one.

"'I would not', said Joan Bordenabe — a peasant standing by, — 'for the castle of Artiguelouve, have met with so bad an omen, as the Ena[17] Garsende and her noble son, who have come at once, face to face, with that animal, covered, as it would seem by his colour, with the snows of the Pyrenees: by our Lady of Sarrance, their <u>future years will</u> be as black as he is white!'

[17] En and Ena are titles of Béarnaise nobility, answering to the Spanish Don and Doña.

"'But,' replied his companion, 'if I were the knight to whom the charger belongs, I would part with him instantly, even if, at the same time as I drowned him, I must throw into the Gave my sword and golden spurs: don't you see that spiteful-looking magpie, which has just started up before him, after having chattered in his very face? What awful signs of evil are these! and on such a morning, at the rising of the sun! * * * May the *bon Dieu*, the Holy Virgin, and the white fairies of the subterranean caves, who are always combing their hair at the first glimpse of dawn, and looking into the clear mirror of the fountains, protect that beautiful young lady, who is at this moment entering the church. It is to be hoped she has made an ample provision of fennel to lay under her bed's head, and in her oratory, to counteract the evil influence of the *Brouches!*'"[18]

While the young lady, Marie de Lignac, enters the church to perform her devotions, the rest of the party leave her, to join the chase of the wild boar, which the Lord of Artiguelouve, the father of Odon, is following, as his horns announce, in the adjacent forest.

The Hospital of Aubertin, which still exists, is a building of the twelfth century, and was one of many establishments depending on the order of monks hospitalers of Sainte Christine: it served as an asylum to the pilgrims of St. James, and as a resting-place to travellers going and coming to and from Spain, Marie found the church filled with persons of different professions: merchants from Arragon and Catalonia; pilgrims adorned with palms and cockle-shells, emblems of their wandering; shepherds in their red dresses and brown berret-caps; and wayfarers of many sorts, waiting only for the morning to continue their journey in various directions, and offering up their prayers previously to setting out. Among others, she noticed particularly a young knight (un beau caver[19]) devoutly kneeling at the foot of the altar of the Virgin, while his archers and men-at-arms were engaged in prayer close behind him: she judged that to him must belong the white charger at the church-door, which had inspired the peasants with so much superstitious terror. Nothing appeared to disturb the devotion of the knight; neither the neighing of steeds without, nor the clatter of the hoofs of mules in the court, as the different groups prepared to depart; nor the coming and going of the merely curious, who were busied observing the beauty of the edifice, the materials of which, according to popular belief, were furnished by the Holy Virgin herself, who directed the elaborate and beautiful ornaments of the pillars and cornices still to be seen there.

The knight's costume was half civil, half military; of one sombre colour, without blazon or distinction—a circumstance unusual at the period: the expression of his face was grave and melancholy: he was somewhat bronzed with the sun, otherwise his complexion was fair, and his blue eyes were full of character and softness.

Even the appearance of the lady does not cause the knight to cease his prayers, and she remains looking upon him, half-divided between her duty and a sudden feeling of admiration and involuntary esteem for which she is unable to account, except by considering him as an apparition sent from heaven,—when a violent

---

[18] Witches or Sorcerers of Béarn.
[19] *Caver.* Chevalier, knight.

noise without, accompanied by the cries of hunters and their horns, effectually put a stop to the religious occupation of all within the church. All hurry out, and, amongst the rest—her orisons over—is the young lady, attended by her page. She had scarcely left the door, and was hastening to the neighbouring hostelry, when she saw before her, at a very short distance, surrounded by a furious pack of hounds, who, bleeding and wounded, were yet attacking their enemy boldly, an enormous wild boar, evidently rendered savage by his sufferings. The beast rushed along, his white tusks gleaming fearfully, and his hot breath already reaching the terrified girl and her feeble protector. Marie turned back, and darted towards the open door of the church, and in another moment might have been out of the reach of the infuriated animal; but a stone imprudently aimed at the boar by a peasant from the wood, sent him, foaming, exactly in the direction she had taken. She saw there was no escape—made a bound, and fell senseless on the threshold of the church: the boar had just reached the spot, and one stroke of his terrible tusk had sufficed to crush the fragile being, who lay extended before him, when a young peasant, with a swiftness almost supernatural, interposed between her and her fate; and, with an axe with which he was armed, discharged so well-directed a blow on the head of the brute, that he extended him dead at his feet.

Certainly, never had succour arrived at a time of more need; and it was impossible to deny that the young man's intrepidity had saved the lady's life: nevertheless, when the crowd collected around them, as Marie, assisted by her terrified page, began to recover consciousness, and her deliverer stood, his axe yet reeking with the blood of the animal from whom he had saved her, and whose carcase lay recking, the skull cleft in two,—it was with anything but applause or commendation that this act of self-devotion was hailed by all present.

As they cast their eyes on the coarse and ragged garb of the young man, those nearest observed on the breast a certain piece of red cloth, cut in the form of *a goose's foot*: a cry of horror and contempt, mingled with surprise, accompanied this discovery, and the words—"It is a Cagot! it is a Cagot!" rang through the assembly, and was repeated by a hundred voices in different intonations of horror. * * *

The object of this popular disgust was a tall, handsome, powerfully-built youth, fair, and of fine complexion: he stood in an easy attitude, in which the majesty of recent action was conspicuous: his colour was heightened, and his bright eyes flashed with satisfaction at the deed he had performed; but when he heard the rage of the people rising, and the fatal and detested name of *Cagot* sounded in his ears, a far different feeling—the consciousness of his utter degradation, which he had for a moment forgotten, returned to him with added force. Suddenly recalled from his illusion, his head sunk mournfully on his bosom, and he seemed at once to retire within himself, gathering all the courage and patience of which he was capable to enable him to endure the outrages and violence which he knew but too well awaited him.

"'Accursed Cagot![20]—down with the accursed Cagot!' repeated a host of confused voices.

[20] At the period at which this story is laid, the Cagots were called *Chrestiaàs*, but the term *Cagot*, adopted later is more generally known in Béarn.

"'Death to the leprous wretch!—to the river with him!—drag him to the river!—he has infected our fields—the holy dew is on him yet!'

"'He has laid his infected hands on our master's goods—he has dared to touch the game!' cried one of the huntsmen, coming up.

"'Hound of ill omen!' thundered Odon d'Artiguelouve, dashing through all the crowd, with his lady-mother and all his mounted attendants—'has he dared to place his devilish claw on that which belongs to us?'

"'He has bewitched our woods, and blighted our harvests!' exclaimed a peasant, giving him a blow, and spitting in his face.

"'To the flames with the sorcerer!—to the fire with the broomstick-rider!—to the fire with the comrade of the infernal spirits!' cried others; and one threw at him a half-burnt log of the St. John's fire, which, striking him on the forehead, sent the unfortunate Cagot reeling to the foot of a tree, against which he leaned for support.

This, and much more insult was lumped upon the unfortunate young man, accompanied by furious howlings and execrations, which became every moment louder: hisses, laughter, and showers of mud and stones were sent towards him as he stood, motionless and calm; his eyes half-closed; without uttering a groan or a word; but, apparently, resolved to endure without shrinking the undeserved fate which pursued him.

Every moment the crowd increased, and with it the fury of popular hatred, until, at length, fatigued with the patience of their victim, the people proposed at once to drag the Cagot to the river. He was, therefore, seized, bound, and, in spite of his resistance and his strength, they prepared to carry their threats into execution; at the same time uttering those savage cries, known in the country as *les cris Basques*, and imitating, in derision of the wretched creature they were injuring, the sharp voice of the goose, and the nasal call of the duck. The young Ena Marie, for whose sake her deliverer was thus suffering, wept, entreated, and appealed to the senseless multitude in vain, and implored the mercy of Odon and Dame Garsende, who treated her prayers with indifference, and appeared to think the conduct of the mob perfectly justifiable. But, at the moment when all hope seemed lost, the interference of the young knight of the church prevented the execution of the crime about to be perpetrated.

Followed by his archers and men-at-arms, he rushed forward, and commanded that the prisoner should be released, in a tone and with gestures so commanding, that the astonished crowd was, for a time, arrested in their project, and a general silence ensued, presently broken by a voice at a distance, which exclaimed—"Noble and generous child! the blessing of Heaven be on thee!" All eyes were directed towards the speaker—an old man with silver hair, clothed in a dark mantle, with the hood drawn over his head: he stood on an elevated mound above the scene of action, and on finding himself observed hurried away from the spot.

Meantime, taking advantage of the awe his appearance had excited in the public mind, the knight hastened to the poor Cagot, cut with his sword the cords which bound him, and set him at liberty. Amazement was painted on the victim's countenance, as he observed the relief which approached him: to be the object of care to a noble knight—to be defended, treated like a human creature was indeed a prodigy to him! The being, but an instant before stupified and inert, from whom insult and injury had drawn no cry nor tear, this evidence of humanity touched to the quick: he cast a long look of tenderness and gratitude on his deliverer; and large tears rolled down his bleeding cheeks. But the panic of the instant soon passed away; hoarse murmurs arose, and threatening words, and the tumult recommenced, Odon d'Artiguelouve advanced to the knight, and demanded, in a haughty tone, by what right he interfered with the execution of the laws.

"'I am not a stranger to this country,' replied he, calmly, 'though it is some time since I quitted it; and I know its *fors* and *customs* probably as well as you can do, Messire.'

"'Then,' answered Odon, 'you should know that a Cagot is forbidden to appear in an assembly of citizens, and that all commerce with them is expressly denied him; that he has no right to touch any article intended for their use; and yet you defend this wretch, who has defiled, by the contact of his accursed hand, the game which belongs to a gentleman.'

"'It appears, then,' answered the knight, with bitter irony, 'that a gentleman singularly loves his game, since he attaches more value to a boar's head than to the life of a noble lady, which this poor Cagot preserved at the risk of injuring one of these precious animals.'

"'Was it for high deeds of this nature,' interposed the Lady of Artiguelouve, seeing that her son's countenance fell, 'that the knight took his vows, when he received the honour of the accolade?'

"'I swore, madam,' answered the *caver*, 'to consecrate my arms to the service of religion, and the defence of the widow, the orphan, and the *unprotected*.'

"'And by what enchantment,' rejoined Dame Garsende, 'does your knight-errantship behold in us giants or monsters?'

"'A loyal and christian knight ever sees a monster in oppression, madam. No man can be punished before he is judged, and I see here neither jury, court of knights, or *cour majour*.'

"'If that is all,' cried Odon, 'every formality shall be gone through. Seize this miserable wretch, my friends, and drag him to the justice-seat; we will follow.'"

An immediate movement was made to obey this order; but the knight again interfered.

"'It is well,' said he; 'but if you have a right to take him before a court, he has that of claiming sanctuary. From whence come you, friend?' he added, turning to the Cagot.

"'From the Vallée d'Aspe, sir knight,' was the answer.

"'Then, it would suffice to reach the Pène d'Escot, at the entrance of this valley, to be in an inviolable security, and we would, if it were necessary, escort you as far; but closer still a refuge attends you; you have only to reach the *circle of sanctu-*

ary which yon church of Aubertin offers.'"[21]

A great struggle now ensues, the Béarnais resolving to oppose the Cagot's entrance to the sanctuary, and the knight and his followers maintaining his attempt. The young Marie of Lignac at length forces her way through the crowd, and laying her hand on the Cagot, demands, by virtue of the *fors et coutumes*, that he be given up to the protection of a noble lady who claims her right to shelter the guilty.

This appeal was not to be treated with contempt; and the mob, perhaps tired of the conflict, gave way with a sudden feeling of respect; while Marie led the persecuted Cagot, surrounded by the knight's men-at-arms, to the door of the church, where he entered, and was in safety.

The next scene of the story introduces the reader to the old knight of Artiguelouve, and the interior of his castle,[22] where the late events are recounted to him by his wife and son, with great bitterness; and envy and offended pride excite the mother and son to resolutions of vengeance, which the father, a man apparently soured with misfortune, and saddened by some concealed sin, can only oppose by expressions of contempt, which irritate the more.

The demoiselle de Lignac, meantime, is arrived at the Castle of Orthez, and received, as well as her uncle, with great honour by Gaston de Foix, who proposes instituting his beautiful guest the queen of the approaching tournament.

The unknown knight, having left the Cagot with the monks of Aubertin, and acted the part of the good Samaritan by his charge, is next seen pursuing his way southward; where, in the mountains, an interview takes place between him and his father, who is, it seems, a proscribed man. They meet after many years of absence, during which the young knight has won all kinds of honour, having gone to the wars under the care and adoption of a brave champion, Messire Augerot de Domezain; who, dying of his wounds, had recommended his young friend to the King of Castile, from whom he receives knighthood. He learns from his father that the holy hermit, brother of Augerot, under whoso care he was brought up, is dead; and he further learns, that the time is nearly come when the secret of his father's misfortunes will be revealed to him. All that the knight, in fact, knows about himself is, that a cloud hangs over the noble family to which he belongs, and that his father is obliged to conceal himself to escape persecution.

The father and son separate: the one retiring to his retreat in the Vallée d'Aspe, the other journeying onwards to the court of Gaston Phoebus.

He has arrived at Orthez, and has just reached the famous *Hôtel de la Lune*, described by Froissart, when he falls into an ambush, and is carried off by unknown enemies, and thrown into a dungeon in the ruins of an abandoned castle, situated on a hill to the south of the Valley of Geu, between Lagor and Sauvelade—a spot which may still be seen. Here the unfortunate knight is left to lament and mourn, that all his hopes of distinguishing himself in the tournament, and of again seeing

[21] By a charter of 1103, churches allowed an asylum within a space of thirty paces in circumference. *Ecclesiæ salvitatem habeant triginta passuum circumcirca.—Marca.*

[22] The castle of Artiguelouve is still standing—a curious monument of ancient grandeur; it is situated near Sauveterre.

the beautiful Marie, are destroyed at once.

The *fêtes* go on, and every thing at Orthez breathes of gaiety and splendour; the people have their games; the Pyrrhic dances, called *sauts Basques*, are in full force, performed by the Escualdunacs in their parti-coloured dresses, and red sashes; the Béarnais execute their spiral dances,[23] and sing their mountain-songs and ballads; some cast great stones and iron bars, in which exercises is distinguished Ernauton d'Espagne, the strong knight mentioned in Froissart as being able to bring into the hall of Gaston an ass fully laden with fuel, and to throw the whole on the hearth, to the great delight of all present. These scenes give occasion to the author to introduce many of the proverbial sayings of the people, which are curious and characteristic. Their strictures on the dress and appearance of the knights and nobles, are in keeping with the freedom of the habits of the day, when the commonalty, however oppressed in some particulars, were allowed a singular latitude of speech.

Amongst their homely sayings, occur the following: —

"Habillat ù bastou qu', aüra l'air d'ù baron."
Dress up a stick, and you can give it the air of a baron.

————

"Nout basquès mey gran hech que non pouchques lheba:"
Do not make a larger fagot than you can lift.

————

"Quabaü mey eslurras dap l'esclop que dap la lengue."
It is better to slide with *sabots* than with the tongue.

————

"Yamey nou fondes maysou auprès d'aigue ni de seignou."
Never build a house near a torrent nor a great lord.

————

"Las sourciéros et lous loup-garous
Aus curés han minya capons."

————

Witches and loup-garoux make priests eat fat capons, *i.e. are to their advantage*—an adage which would seem to infer that the search for sorcery was known to be a *job* in all ages.

The tournament goes on: and, to the great disappointment of the lady of the lists, no stranger-knight appears; and her admirer, Odon, is the victor over all others; when, just at the last moment, the trumpet of the Unknown sounds, and he comes into the arena, and challenges the envious knight, after defeating all the others, Dame Garsende has recourse to a stratagem to overcome him, which fails in regard to him, but overwhelms her son in confusion, and causes his defeat: she cuts the cord of a canopy under which the knight has to pass, in the hope that it

————

[23] *i.e.* lifting their partners into the air.

will fall in his way, and encumber his advance; but he adroitly catches it on the end of his spear, and Odon, in falling from his horse after the knight's attack, gets entangled in the garlands and drapery, and makes a very ridiculous figure. Of course the stranger-knight is made happy in the chaplet placed on his brow by Marie, and the kiss of custom by which the gift is accompanied. His rival retires, vowing vengeance.

A grand feast then takes place; and as the guests arrive they are severally recognised by the people. The stranger-knight, whose device is *a branch of vine clinging to an aged tree*, is hailed with acclamation, and a tumult of enthusiasm, consequent on his successes and his honourable reception by Gaston Phoebus; to whom, when questioned as to his name and family, he replies that he is called Raymond, the adopted son of Messire Augerot de Domezain. Gaston instantly recognises in him a knight whose valorous deeds are on record, and who saved the life of Marie de Lignac's father, at the battle of Aljubarotta.

Raymond produces a chain of gold, which the dying knight had charged him to deliver to Gaston, to be sent to his daughter; and the tears and thanks of the young lady are the reward of his accomplished mission.

The stranger-knight is now at the height of favour: adopted by Ernauton d'Espagne as his brother-in-arms; welcomed by the gorgeous Gaston Phoebus; hailed by the people; and, above all, loved by Marie. He is, of course, exposed to the evil designs of Garsende and her son, from which he twice escapes; but they are obliged to conceal their enmity, and he is ignorant from whence he is attacked. During a grand banquet, a minstrel, whose verses had warned him to avoid a poisoned cup, unable to approach him near enough to deliver a billet, gives it in charge to one of his favourite men-at-arms, who places it in the sheath of his sword till he can transmit it to his master. This action is observed by Garsende; who, afterwards, taking advantage of the soldier's fondness for the fine vintage of Jurançon, contrives to get possession of the letter, and excites the jealousy of Marie, who imagines it written by a woman, deceived by the expressions, "My beloved Raymond," and the signature of "The Being dearest to your Heart," and the mysterious rendezvous appointed, all of which is, in fact, written by his exiled father. This plot, however, fails, through the candour and devotion of Marie; and the knight keeps the tryst which his father had appointed at a ruined hermitage, formerly tenanted by the preceptor of Raymond, on a lonely hill above the Vallée d'Aspe. Here they meet; and a scene of tenderness on the part of the son, and mystery on that of the father, ensues; in which the latter entreats yet a little time before he discloses certain secrets of moment, concerning the young knight, whose successes appear to produce a strange effect on his mind, almost amounting to regret, for which the other cannot account. When they part, he agrees that, when he has once seen him the husband of Marie,—who, though aware of the mystery which envelopes him, has generously granted him her hand,—and when he knows him to be *removed from all danger*, he will no longer withhold the information he has to give.

They separate; but enemies have been on their track; and the father is watched to his concealed retreat, while Raymond remains sleeping at the foot of the altar, in the hermitage. The intention of Odon d'Artiguelouve, who is on the spot, had been to murder him as he slept; but the information brought him by his spies, who have watched the old man, entirely changes his intentions. A more secure revenge is in his power, and he returns to his castle with extraordinary satisfaction; leaving the happy lover of Marie, and the successful victor of the lists, to his dreams of future bliss.

The great day arrives on which Gaston de Foix has announced a solemn festival, to be held in honour of the Knight of the Vine-branch, and his affianced bride, Marie de Lignac. All the nobles of the country assemble; and, amongst them, the old "grim baron," Loup Bergund d'Artiguelouve, and his family. Minstrels sing, music sounds, and honours and compliments pour upon the favoured knight; and even his rivals, to judge by their joyous countenances, have only pleasure in their hearts. The Prince of Béarn, and his brilliant court, enter their decorated pavilion amidst the shouts of the assembled guests; the people are admitted to view the jousts; and Raymond advances to the foot of the throne, and receives a paternal embrace from the courteous Gaston Phoebus. The signal is given for the amusements to begin, when a loud voice is heard above the trumpets and the clash of instruments: the herald-at-arms pauses; and Odon d'Artiguelouve, who had cried, "Hold!" stands up in his seat, and thunders forth these ominous words:

"'Suspend the solemnities; for I behold here, on this spot, in presence of our august assembly, one of those impure beings on whom the sun shines with disgust,—who excite horror in heaven and on earth,—whose breath poisons the air we breathe,—whose hand pollutes all it touches. Hold! for, I tell you, there is a Cagot amongst us!'"

As he spoke, he pointed with a frantic gesture of malevolence towards an aged man, wrapped in a large, dark, woollen cloak, who was vainly endeavouring to conceal himself in the crowd.

A cry of horror and indignation burst from all sides: all shrunk back from the profane object indicated; leaving a space around him. A deadly paleness, the effect of amazement and consternation, passed over the face of Raymond; for, in the person of the accused, he recognised—his father!

Raymond almost instantly, however, recovers from the effect of this terrific announcement; and springing forward, and placing himself before the old man, cried out, in a loud and firm voice:

"'He who dares make such an assertion has lied!'

"'How! exclaimed Odon d'Artignelouve; 'dost thou give me the lie? Here is my gage of battle: let him take it up who will.' And, throwing his glove into the midst of the assembly, he continued:

"'I, Odon d'Artiguelouve, to all gentlemen present and to come—knights and nobles—offer to maintain my words, with sword, or battle-axe, or lance, against all who shall have the boldness to deny that yonder old man, wrapped in a dark mantle, now before us, has dared to trample under foot our laws and ordinances, and sully by his impure presence our noble assembly; for he is no other than a vile

Cagot, leprous and infected, belonging to the Cagoterie of Lurbe, hid, like a nest of snakes, amongst the rocks of Mount Binet, at the entrance of the Vallée d'Aspe.'"

A shudder of horror ran through the crowd as these words were uttered.

"'And I,' cried the knight, in a voice of furious indignation—'I, Raymond, the adopted son of Augerot de Domezain,—whose real name will, I trust, one day appear,—in virtue of my privileges, my title, and my oath, protest, in defiance of thy rank, thy strength, and thy youth; in despite of thy sword, thy lance, and thy battle-axe,—I protest, in the face of God and the men who hear me, that, from the crown of thy head to the sole of thy foot, thou art an infamous and perjured impostor,—a traitor as black as hell can make thee,—and that thou hast lied in thy throat. My arm and my sword are ready to engrave upon thy body, in characters of blood, the truth of my words!'"

The tone of energetic conviction with which Raymond spoke, his bold and martial bearing, the flash of his eye, and the indignant rage of his manner, impressed his hearers as they listened, and a murmur of applause followed his exclamation. Marie, pale as death, sat like a statue of marble; her hands clasped, her breath suspended, and her eyes fixed wildly on the trembling old man,—the object of all attention.

Odon was about to reply, when Count Gaston, with a heightened colour and an excited air, rose and spoke:

"We are," he said, "deeply displeased that such a discussion should have disturbed the peace of our assembly. You are not ignorant, Sir Raymond, that our laws accord to all men of Béarn the right of combat against the aggressor who has outraged him by the injurious epithets of false and traitor. And you, Sir Odon, remember that here, as in the *Cour Majour*, we owe justice to all,—to the weak as well as the strong; and that, before judgment, proof is necessary."

The old man is now required by Odon to stand forth and answer in full assembly whether he is not called Guilhem, whether he is not a Cagot, and whether he is not a member of the Cagoterie of Lurbe.

A profound silence ensues in the assembly; all, in breathless anxiety, await the answer of the accused, who stands hesitating and apparently unable to utter a word; at length, with an effort, and in a hoarse and trembling voice, he falters from beneath the thick hood which he had drawn over his face, "Heaven has so decreed it—Alas! it is a fatal truth!" Now comes the triumph of the rival of the unfortunate knight; he starts up, wild and fierce, exultation trembling on his envenomed tongue:

"Béarnais!" cried he; "listen to me! If this man, who has dared to call me false and traitor, were a knight, as he calls himself, or a noble, like me, he would, by our laws, be entitled to claim the right of duel, to which he had provoked me, on foot or on horseback, armed at all points; or, were he a man belonging to the people, I being a gentleman, he could oppose me with a shield and a club; or were we both equally peasants, we could fight, each armed according to our rank. But, were I ten times the aggressor, and he the offended party, all combat between him and me is impossible, for he is beneath the knight, the noble, the citizen, the serf, the labourer; beneath the lowest degree in the scale of humanity—beneath the beasts themselves; he is a vile Gesitain, a dog of a leper, an infamous and degraded Cagot, and yonder stands his father!"

Horror takes possession of all—knight, lady, prince, and people. In vain the unfortunate Guilhem, throwing back his cowl and imploring to be heard, proclaims aloud that he is not the father of the noble knight; that Raymond does not belong to their unhappy race, and calls the Redeemer to witness that he speaks the truth; he is treated with scorn and contempt, and the popular fury rises at the disavowal.

Gaston Phoebus commands silence, and calls upon the knight to disprove the fact alleged, and confirm the hope he entertains; but Raymond has no words but these:

"No, noble Prince; I have no power to speak other than the truth; and were the torments I endure ten times heavier, I have only to confess—this is, indeed, my father."

Marie, as he spoke, uttered a wild shriek, and fell senseless to the ground; a yell burst from the crowd, joy and triumph glowed on the countenances of Odon and his mother, and Gaston Phoebus cast himself back in his seat, and covered his face with his robe.

"'Go, Cagot!' roared the pitiless Odon; 'who now is a false traitor, who now has lied, and proved himself a vile impostor? Away with thy helmet, thy sword, and thy spurs; away with all the armour of the craven! Let the herald at arms degrade thee before the world! Where is now thy name, thy titles, thy prerogatives? where are thy fiefs and thy domains? Thy name is *Cagot*, thy possessions leprosy, and every foul disease—every impurity of soul and body; thy castle is a mud hut in the Cagoterie of Lurbe, and this is thy blazon!'"

As he spoke he raised his arm in the air, and, with the frantic force of hate, dashed in the face of the distracted Raymond a piece of red cloth cut into the form of a *goose's foot*.

At the sight of this emblem the populace rose with fury, and rushed in a body, with savage cries, on the unfortunate pair.

A scene of horror now takes place; Raymond is deserted by all his people but one, his favourite man-at-arms, and the generous Arnauton, who will not quit his adopted brother even in such degradation; together they stand against the mob, whose rage the Prince himself is unable to restrain. Odon leads them on; the poor old man is with difficulty rescued from their grasp by the determined valour of his defenders, who are, however, too few to contend against their foes, and Odon is on the point of attaining the object of his wishes, and beholding the heart's blood of his rival—when assistance comes in the shape of the young Cagot who had saved the life of Ena Marie. At the moment when the blow is falling, and Raymond has no chance of escape, he darts forward, and, seizing Odon in his powerful grasp, drags him to the bridge of the Gave, which is thrown over the torrent, where a mill-wheel is working. There a fearful struggle goes on, which is closed by both combatants being precipitated into the stream, to reappear crushed and mangled by the mighty engine under which they fell.

The bravo young Cagot casts one dying look, full of tenderness and gratitude, towards those who watch his end with pity and despair, and all is over.

On the evening of that fatal day, Guilhem and Raymond, both exhausted and overcome with grief and fatigue, rest themselves in a miserable hut, far away amongst the rocks, in one of the steepest and wildest gorges of Mont Binet. It was one of the accursed and abhorred dwellings of the Cagot village of Lurbe.

The night was black and fearful: a tempest raged in all its terrors without, and occasional gusts of wind and rain penetrated the wretched retreat where the unfortunate fugitives sat, their vestments torn, and their bodies as severely wounded as their minds. Several Cagots, both male and female, from other cabins near, hovered round them, tenderly administering to their wants, and preparing such balms to heal their wounds as their simple knowledge afforded. They accompanied these friendly offices with tears and passionate gesticulations, accompanied by half inarticulate exclamations, such as savages, unused to speech, might do in a strange unvisited land.

CAGOT VILLAGE

"'It is, then, true, my father,' said Raymond, as he looked round on these beings, ill-clothed, poor, degraded by oppression and contempt, scarcely endowed with common intelligence, and miserable to regard—'It is, then, true, that you are a Cagot, and that these are my brothers and my equals? Ah! why did you let me wander into a world which I ought never to have known? Why did you not let me live and die a Cagot as I was born? These, then, are Cagots!'

"'Yes,' cried Guilhem, weeping bitterly; 'Yes, we are Cagots, and all men are our persecutors; and yet, when one of *their* children falls into our hands, we do not ill-use it, we do not torture it, we do not crush it beneath the wheels of a mill; we do good for evil, and they repay us by evil alone! Ah! I am as if bound on a flaming pile, my tears are like molten lead on my cheeks. I!—a wretched, vile Cagot!—I should die with pity if I saw one of my executioners in the state to which they have reduced me!'

"'My father, my dear father, calm yourself,' said Raymond, with tender affection; 'your son, at least, is left you.'

"'No, no,' cried the old man, passionately;'my son is not left me; my son is dead; he was torn in pieces by the mill-wheel of Orthez. I am not your father; you are not—you never were, you never can be—my son; this is the first word of the secret I have to tell you.'

"'What do you tell me!' cried Raymond, in amazement! 'Your disavowal was not, then, a deception, prompted by paternal affection! What! are you not my father? and was that generous creature, sacrificed for my sake, indeed your son!'

"'He was my child, my only child! the only living being attached to me by the ties of blood—the only creature who would have listened to my last agonized sigh at my hour of death. And see what was his fate, for me! I allowed him to venture for my sake amongst the ferocious people; see to what an end his devotion and gratitude to you had led him!' So saying, the unfortunate old man uncovered the mutilated remains of his unfortunate son, rescued from the stream, and transported to the spot by the compassionate care of Arnauton d'Espaigne. The body lay on a rustic couch, enveloped in a white shroud, which is always, according to the usage of the country, prepared long before death, a taper of yellow wax shed its feeble rays on the corpse'."

The grief and lamentations of Guilhem are interrupted by the rites which then take place; the men wringing their hands, and gesticulating, and cursing the cruelty of the world: the women weeping and wailing; and one of those endowed with poetical powers, improvising a lament over the body, uttering her words in a melancholy cadence, deeply expressive of the grief of all.

"'Alas, Gratien!' she moaned; 'thou hast then left us! thou hast deserted thy aged father—gone without a pressure of the hand! Gratien, may God receive thy soul! To live is to suffer. Life is like the wheel by which thou wert torn. Thou wert in the right to fly it. Happy child! thou art gone to a place where there are no Cagots, no men to persecute thee; thou wilt know now who were the ancestors from whom we descend. Thou hast no more use for the pruning-knife and the infamous axe. No more toil nor suffering await thee; no more contempt nor outrage! Accursed be the wheel, oh, Gratien, which crushed thee! never may the torrent wash out thy blood which stains it; let it turn for ever red and bloody! No bell tolled for thy soul; but the thunder and the wind, oh, Gratien! Toll louder still—no bell for the Cagot! But Heaven weeps with us, the trees groan with us. Old man! thou dost not weep alone. Adieu, dear Gratien, thy body is returned to thy cabin; but thy soul, escaped the demon, is fled on a beam of the moon to the great house of heaven! Yes, he cries—I am in heaven; I am telling the Cagots, our ancestors, that their children are still in suffering!'"

Guilhem, comforted by the tenderness of Raymond, recovers in some degree his self-possession, and proceeds to relate to the young knight the manner of his falling, when an infant, into his charge. The narrative is as follows:—

"'In 1360, twenty-six years ago, when I was myself thirty-nine years of age, the event happened which I have now to tell you. I was a Cagot from my birth, by my parents and my ancestors—a proscribed outcast of unkind nature, like these you see around—poor, ignorant, timid, and a mark for insult and contempt. I had already suffered much; for God, alas! had given me a heart formed to feel and to love; yet long habits of endurance had, in great measure, rendered it callous and insensible, unaided as I was by intellectual culture.

"'I married a woman of my race; but, after a year, she died, leaving me in lonely widowed sorrow, with one child. Alas! he has just rejoined his mother, and rude is the journey which has conducted him to her!

"'At this period, as you know, and as I afterwards learnt from the mouth of your venerable preceptor, the holy hermit, all France was overrun with bands of marauders and robbers of every nation, called the *late-comers*.[24] Béarn was no more free from them than other parts of the kingdom. One day, I was returning from Oloron, my heart more sad than usual,—cursing men and life, for I had been the object of new injuries,—when a chief of one of these predatory bands suddenly presented himself before me; and, addressing me, said: 'Good man, will you do a kind action? Take this infant, abandoned to my men-at-arms by an unfaithful servant. I have saved it from their inhumanity: it has that about it which will pay your trouble.' I saw that he held in his arms a child, who was weeping bitterly; when I looked on its lovely face—round, innocent, and rosy—my heart was touched, and I accepted the charge.

"'Alas! the sweet creature knew not that it had fallen into the hands of a Cagot; for no sooner had I received it on my bosom, than it ceased crying; and, so far from showing repugnance to one about to become its father, its hands were stretched towards me, and it smiled in my face. My dear Raymond, thou wert this infant sent by Providence to my care.'"

The old man then relates his bringing home the child; employing a goat to nourish it; and at length confiding it to the charge and instruction of the hermit of Eysus, the only being whose religion or charity allowed him to listen to the confession of the Cagot. While Raymond, however, was yet an infant, and but a short time after Guilhem had received him, the latter was, one day, returning from an expedition to the town, where the wants of his family obliged him to resort, and passed by the ruins of the old tower (the very place in which Raymond afterwards became a prisoner, and was rescued, by the fortunate familiarity of Guilhem with the spot, in time to appear at the tournament).

[24] Tard-venus.

"'I had,' said he, 'taken from my dress the ignominious mark of my degradation; and, in full security, was gathering at my leisure some herbs destined for your use, when it so happened that some shepherds of the Vallée d'Aspe observed and at once recognised me; and their usual superstition acting on them at the supposed ill-omen of meeting a Cagot picking herbs, they attacked me with one accord, and commenced pelting me with stones, and using every epithet of opprobrium. I was struck to the earth; then they dragged me to the entrance of a sort of inclined cavern, called in the country 'The Den of the Witches'[25]. With coarse jests they thrust me through the opening, exclaiming that, as the evil spirits raised tempests when stones were thrown in there, perhaps they would be appeased by receiving the body of a Cagot.

"'I fell to some distance, rolling along the declivity; and my body stopped at the bottom on the damp earth. When I had a little recovered, I prepared to attempt an escape, as I heard that my tormentors had departed; but, on reaching the opening, I found a barrier which I had not looked for: these wretched men had lighted a fire of weeds and brushwood at the mouth of the cave. The flames raged violently, excited by the current of air from within, and I soon felt the effect; sparks and pieces of burning timber fell in; and my wounded body was soon a prey to a scorching shower which poured down upon me.

"'A greater fire rose within my soul,—my injuries had driven me to despair; my brain reeled, and the torments of hell seemed within me and around. Hatred and bitter vengeance rose boiling from my heart; and I cursed all human nature,— invoking ruin and destruction on mankind, from whom I had never known pity, I raved in my burning prison, and gave myself up to fury and despair, when Heaven took compassion on my misery. A lighted brand which fell from above disclosed, by the vivid flash it cast through the gloom, an opening at the other end; and I clearly distinguished a covered way, evidently made by human hands, which seemed to run along to some distance before me. I retreated into its shelter, and my heart revived once more.

"'I advanced some little way and reposed myself, when, suddenly, I thought I could distinguish in the distance vague and interrupted sounds. A shudder came over me; and at first I dreaded to move; but, at length, I forced myself to do so; and, gathering up one of the lighted brands, I yielded to my curiosity, and proceeded forward.

"'Presently the sounds became more distinct; and I could not mistake the voice of wailing and lamentation, which found an echo in my own heart and awakened its sympathies. I continued my way cautiously; and, after a few minutes, found myself at an opening, formed in a shelving position, in the manner of a loop-hole, closed with two flagstones, not so near but that a space was left wide enough for me to see into a vaulted chamber beyond, which at the moment was lighted by a torch.

"'A young and beautiful woman was seated on the ground, in an attitude of profound grief, leaning against the wall opposite. A man of high stature, and who

---

[25] Tutte de las bronchos.

might be about my own age, stood at a little distance, and looked towards her with a ferocious and menacing air, in which there was, nevertheless, an appearance of what might be thought shame, for the glance was oblique, as if he avoided meeting her eye. The light fell full upon his face, which was so remarkable in its expression, that I could not detach my regard from him, and his features remain deeply graven on my memory.

"'You are, then, obstinately resolved to drive me to extremity,' said he, 'and will not consent to my demand?'

"'What?' answered the lady, in a voice of grief, but full of energy, 'shall I despoil my son of his rights and his inheritance without knowing that he is dead, and that in favour of my most cruel enemies? No! he may yet live—Providence may yet watch over him—restore him one day to the world, when he will come to claim his own and revenge his mother's wrongs!'

"'You have no alternative but a fearful death, remember!' said the man, in hoarse accents.

"'Rather any death than abandon my child!' was the answer.

"'Then, madam,' returned her companion, 'your will shall be done—impute your fate to your own conduct.'

"As he pronounced these words, he approached the door of the dungeon, where stood another female in the shade, who contemplated the scene in silence, with an unmoved and chilling aspect. They then left the place together, fastening the heavy door carefully, while the sound of their keys and chains sent a fearful echo through the vaulted apartment. Their victim fell back in a state of desolation, pitiable to behold, and burst into passionate tears, praying fervently to Heaven, and uttering exclamations which might melt the stoutest heart.'

"'I was deeply moved to behold her; and, in a low voice, ventured to exclaim: 'Madam, be of good cheer! Heaven hears you; and has sent one to your aid who is ready to exert every effort, for your relief.'

"'What voice is that?' cried she, starting.

"'Be not terrified!' I answered; 'it is that of a mortal, guided hither by the hand of God!'

"'At the same time I applied myself to loosen the stones at the loop-hole, and with much difficulty succeeded in doing so; but, in spite of all my precautions, the unfortunate lady, bewildered with fear and grief, was so astonished when I appeared through the opening, that she uttered a cry and fainted on the ground.

"'Without losing a moment, I took her in my arms, and carried her through to the subterranean way. I then replaced the stones as closely as I could, and hastened to bear her to the mouth of the cave, which I now found without obstacle, the fire extinct, and nothing to impede our progress.

"'Oh, Raymond! the ways of Providence are inscrutable! This dungeon, from whence I had rescued that innocent victim, is the same where, a few days since, you were thrown by the hands of enemies; and the lady who had nearly perished there was—your mother!'

"'Great Heaven!' exclaimed Raymond, 'my mother! condemned to such horrors—buried in the earth alive;—oh! to find the author of her injuries!'

"'I saw that person this very day,' replied Guilhem; 'I recognised him in the old man who was seated on the right of your rival.'

"'That was his father, the lord of Artiguelouve,' cried Raymond.

"'Then it was no other than the lord of Artiguelouve who was your mother's persecutor.'"

The Cagot now goes on to relate, that, on bringing the unfortunate lady to this village, she recognised, in the infant he had adopted, her own son. She recounted, that those persons whom he had seen in her dungeon had plotted to remove both her and the infant, as their existence interfered with certain plans of their own. One of her servants had been bribed, who, under pretence of bearing the child to a place of safety, and the better to deceive her, having taken with it jewels of value, had feigned to be set upon by robbers, and had her son forcibly torn from him. Three months afterwards, the man, overcome with remorse and wretchedness for his crime, fell sick, and, on his death-bed, desired secretly to see the mother, who wept for her infant as dead; to whom he related the truth. This information was fatal to herself; for her enemies now threw off the mask, and insisted on her renouncing for her son all claim to the estates and titles of which he was the heir; which she having refused to do, they treated her in the manner that has been related.

A mystery still hung over the revelations of the lady, who named no persons in her story, and who appeared to dread to make further disclosures; and, above all, she desired that no vengeance should be taken on the authors of her grief.

"'There are crimes,' she said, 'which recoil on those who perpetrate them: he who sows vengeance, reaps not peace: and I would that my son should feel that mercy is the highest attribute of humanity. Keep, therefore, the secret of his birth from him, and let him know only tranquillity and joy.'"

The Cagot promised to comply with her christian desire, and, together with the pious hermit of Eysus, to bring up her son in piety, and ignorance of his station, until he should be one day safe from the danger of his enemies. The unfortunate mother left a letter, addressed to the Sire de Lescun—a friend on whom she could rely—which, on some future occasion, was to be delivered to him; but the long absence of the Knight of Lescun, in the wars, had hitherto prevented its being done.

Whether the mother of Raymond would have continued in the same intentions, cannot be known; for grief and sickness soon brought her to the close of her sad career. When she was dying, the poor man who had succoured her and her child, conceiving that he was not acting according to his conscience, in withholding from her the exact situation in which he was himself placed, threw himself on his knees at her bed-side, and with tears entreated her forgiveness, for that he had the misfortune to be *a Cagot*.

"'Have pity upon me,' said he, 'that I thus add to the weight of sorrow which you carry with you to the tomb.'"

Instead of the start of abhorrent contempt which the persecuted man dreaded, she turned upon him a look of the most ineffable benevolence; and, placing her cold hand upon his head, uttered these words:—

"'It is well;—Cagot since thou art, I bless thee; for thy heart is more noble than the proudest blazon could make it.'

"No human description can convey an idea of the impression made on the heart of the good man by these few words,—the first of pity and consolation he had ever heard addressed to one of his own fated race. A new life, a new being seemed given him as he heard them; and, from that instant, he vowed to exist only for the salvation of the being left behind by the angel who had shed her benediction upon him. She died, and he kept his word."

The supreme tribunal of Béarn, the *Cour Majour*, was assembled at Orthez, in one of the grand saloons of the castle of Moncade, to dispense to the people, by its irrevocable decrees, the national justice of its celebrated *Fors*. Great excitement prevailed; for it was known that the Knight-Cagot, or Cagot-Knight, as Raymond was called, was about to appear, to defend himself from his accusers.

"The Lord and Lady of Artiguelouve were present in the great assembly, summoned to appear for their deceased son, to support the charge he had made. The fair Marie de Lignac sat pale and agitated, supported by her uncle, the Knight of Lescun. The Bishops of Lescar and Oloron, the eleven judges,[26] and all the nobles of the country attended, and were seated on elevated benches, in due order, near Prince Gaston de Foix."

After a consultation of some length, these *equitable* magistrates had decided that justice should be allowed to the complainant, and punishment awarded to those who had injured him, provided that he could prove that he was *a man* and not *a Cagot*.

Nothing now remains for Raymond but the presentation of his mother's letter, and all the proofs which establish his birth. On opening the paper, and on examining the embroidery on the mantles which wrapped the rescued infant; on looking at the initials of the chain of gold, the Knight of Lescun recognised the son of his cousin, Marguerite d'Amendaritz, first wife of Messire Loup Bergund, who, when he hears the truth, is seized with sudden remorse and amazement, and, being now without an heir, is not sorry to recover him whom he had before abandoned to destruction. In spite, therefore, of the indignation of his wife—and her endeavours to repress his agitation throughout the scene—he starts up, and proclaims himself the father of Raymond: who, he declares aloud, is his long-lost son,—stolen from him by *routiers*—whose loss had cost him the life of a beloved wife, whom he deplored.

The result is, however, far different to his expectations, or that of all present. The young knight, on finding that he is the son of a man so laden with crime as

---

[26] The number of twelve was reduced to eleven since the period that the village of Bidous was removed from the territorial jurisdiction of Béarn.

Loup Bergund, is seized with a frenzy of contempt and disgust.

"His open and expansive forehead became contracted with horror—he stood silent a few seconds, petrified and overwhelmed with his emotions—his body shrinking back in an attitude of repulsion and dislike, as if a venomous reptile were before his sight. His regard then fell full on Loup Bergund, and the terrible severity of its expression made the unworthy tyrant shrink beneath his glance of fire.

"*You* my father!"—exclaimed he, at length, in a terrible voice—"do *you* open your arms to me as to your son? Hence!—back! there is nothing in common between us—we can be nothing to each other! I know you not. Go—say to your captive of yonder dungeon that her son is dead; that the *routiers* have stolen him: you my father! no; you have no son—it is a falsehood—you are a great lord, and I a wretched foundling—a being without a name—one disdained by wolves and robbers. No; you are not my father. I have no other but he who stands beside me; I am the son of no other than the poor Cagot."

As he spoke, Raymond dashed the chain of gold on the ground, and trampled it under his feet—he seized his mother's letter from the hands of the Knight of Lescun, and thrusting it into the flame of a torch hard by, burnt it to ashes; then, throwing himself into the arms of Guilhem, he burst into a passion of tears. Recovering himself, however, in a few moments—while all looked on silent and aghast—he cried aloud—

"'And now I am, indeed, a Cagot—irrevocably so—and it is my glory and my joy! But hear me all! while I proclaim what you are worth, and those whom you dare to despise, and for whom the Redeemer died, as well as for us all: You are decked in gold and gorgeous raiment, and they are in rags; but they have hearts which beat beneath, and you have souls of ice: you are their executioners, and they are martyrs. You cast your wives and children into the dungeons of your castles, from whence the poor Cagots save them: you are great upon the earth, but they will be great in Heaven!"

These last words fell, like thunder, upon the ears of all, but most on those of Gaston Phoebus—who thought of his murdered son—and writhed with agony. Raymond continued:

"'God will yet do justice, in his time, to the oppressors of the innocent. Your names, in future ages, will be execrated. Meantime, keep your pomp, your pleasures, your grandeur, and your luxury; while our possessions are opprobrium and contempt, shame, banishment, and suffering—days without sun, and nights without repose or shelter. Yes, drive us from you—you know that we are infectious, that we shall contaminate your purity—Away! Room, room for the Cagots!'"

And Raymond and Guilhem retired through the crowd, which shrunk back, appalled, to let them pass.

The next day Marie de Lignac received a letter, the contents of which were never seen but by her tear-dimmed eyes; nor ever re-read by her after she entered the convent of Marciniac.

The Lord of Artiguelouve, on his death-bed, was a prey to the most bitter repentance: he implored that some priest of more than common sanctity should hear his last confession; and one was discovered in a holy hermit, who, when he was summoned from his retreat, was found kneeling beside a humble tomb, where he passed all his days in prayer, with rigorous fasting and unwearied penance. He obeyed the call of the expiring sinner, and received his last sigh. Thus did the repentant Lord of Artiguelouve meet the forgiveness of his son, Raymond: for it was he that closed his eyes with a blessing, and then returned to his hermitage to weep by the tomb of his father, the Cagot.

I am indebted to M. Baron du Taya's (of Rennes) learned researches and obliging kindness for a few particulars respecting the Cacous of Brittany.

It is thought there that this proscribed race are the descendants of *leprous Jews*, which would at once account for the detestation in which they continued to be held, but for the term *"Chrestaàs"* applied to them, which destroys that supposition: again, it is said that they are descended from original *lepers*, and that diseases are inherent in their blood—though not leprosy, it may be epilepsy: for this reason, the *rope-makers* of Ploermel were held in abhorrence, and are even now shunned: they are irritated when the term *caqueux* is applied to them, but it is common to call them *Malandrins*—a word of opprobrium, only less shocking to their ears. They had always their separate burial-ground and chapel; and, till the revolution of 1789, the prejudice existed against them: even now it is not entirely extinct.

Rope-makers, coopers, and *tailors* are still held in a certain degree of contempt in Brittany, as those of these trades were formerly all looked upon as Cacous.

The Cacous of St. Malo met with some compassion from Duke Francis II., the father of Anne of Brittany; and also in the time of Francis I., King of France, ordinances were made in their favour; but they were not so fortunate as their brethren of Rome, who, in the sixteenth century, are said to have sold, in one Holy week, rope to the amount of two thousand crowns, to make *disciplines*.

In 1681, a law was passed to this effect; "Seeing that there are no longer any Leprous, *Ladres*, or *Caquins* at Kerroch, parish of St. Caradec d'Hennebon, there is in future to be no distinction made in the inhabitants of this village—who formerly had their burial-ground and chapel apart—and all shall be admitted to the benefit of parish assistance during their lives, and buried in the church after their death. For it is considered that it *was ill and abusively* ordained by the Bishop of Vannes, in 1633, that the wives of the said inhabitants should not be purified, except in their own chapels; for it is well ascertained that no native of the said village of Kerroch has ever been afflicted with leprosy."

Notwithstanding this sensible and humane act, the people of Kerroch are not free from the absurd suspicion even yet.

"It would appear," observes M. Baron du Taya, "that the Cacous were first a subdivision of lepers, and afterwards, by hereditary *remembrance* of them, the latter were always the objects of commiseration amongst the professors of religion and chivalry. Thus the first Grand Master of St. Lazare was himself a leper. Several great names occur amongst these Grand Masters: such as Jean de Paris, in 1300; a

Bourbon in 1521; and, under Henri IV., a Philibert de Nerestang."

In 1436 a prohibition was issued against the *Cacosi* receiving the kiss of peace, and the kiss of the monks, *before men who were whole*; it was not denied them, but they were to be *the last*.

In many places in Brittany the rope-makers work out of the towns near those places where lazar-houses were once established. They were not authorized to place their benches in the lower part of the church at Pontivy till after the revolution in 1789! The villagers still look upon certain rope-makers, tailors, and coopers, as possessing *an evil eye*, and are in the habit of concealing their *thumbs* under the rest of their fingers,[27] and pronouncing the word *argaret* as a counter-spell: this word is unintelligible even to the Bas-Bretons themselves. The prejudice still exists in Finisterre against the Cacous: the village of Lannistin is one of their abodes. The Cagot girls of Béarn are said never to be able to draw water from a brook or well without spilling half of it: so that their houses are always dirty, and themselves thirsty. Probably the same misfortune exists in Brittany, for there is little cleanliness to be found there.

Perhaps, after all, the most probable conjecture as to the origin of these unhappy Cagots is, that they were persons *suspected of witchcraft*, and banished in the first instance from society, to which traditional prejudice prevented their return; and, though the cause of their banishment was no longer remembered, the abhorrence they had once inspired did not wear out with ages. The supposition of their having been *the first Christians*, persecuted and contemned, and never regaining the world's good opinion, seems a notion difficult to adopt, except that the first Christians were suspected of sorcery and communication with evil spirits. "He casteth out devils through Beelzebub, the chief of the devils." If such were, indeed, the case, what a lesson for prejudice and superstition, that the descendants of the earliest converts should be persecuted by their Christian brethren!

The Vallée d'Aspe, where the scene of the preceding story is laid, is one of the most picturesque of Béarn, and the customs of its people remarkable.

The Pic d'Anie, whose solemn height rises above the village of Lescun, is regarded by the Aspois as the sojourn of a malignant deity. From thence come the fearful storms which desolate the country, and no inhabitant of the village will dare to climb the ascent: it is looked upon as a piece of presumption to attempt it; for it is believed that the Jin of the mountain, called the Yona Gorri, or flame-coloured spirit, has there fixed his solitary abode, and has his garden on the summit, which he will not allow to be visited by strangers. Certain evil spirits have occasionally been seen in his company, each holding a lighted torch and dressed in shining scarlet habiliments: they thus surround the chief, and dance round him to the music of an unearthly instrument, like a drum. Loups-garoux, and sorcerers mounted on dragons and other animals, may be seen in the air, wending their way towards Anic, as far as from Jurançon, Gan, and St. Faust.

At Escout is a fairy oak, beneath which, whoever places an empty vase, having

---

[27] This practice is similar to that of the Neapolitans, who wear a little hand in coral (*gettatura*) as a preservative against the evil eye.

belief, will find it, after a short period, when he returns, full of gold and silver: there are known to exist persons in the Vallée d'Aspe whose fortune had no other source.

There is a famous rock at the entrance of the valley, the object of attraction to all females who desire to become mothers. Many of the superstitions are similar to those in the Landes where the belief in the power of the demon is generally received. The *Homme Noir*—a fearful spirit with large black wings—may frequently be seen perched on the summit of the highest peaks, shaking from his pinions showers of hail, which break the early flowers and crush the rising corn.

There are persons, even now—though they are rarer than in the time of that acute discoverer, De Lancre—who are believed to deserve the name of *Poudoueros, Hantaumos, Brouchos, Mahoumos,* for they are votaries of the evil one, and many spells are requisite to avoid their "witch knots," and "combs of care," &c.

Presages can be drawn from the croak of a magpie, from the rush of waters, and the howling of dogs. If a flower is seen to expand on a barren rock, or in a place where there is no other vegetation, it is looked upon as an augury of an abundant harvest throughout the country. But if a tree spreads its branches over the roof of a house it announces all sorts of misfortunes: the sons of that house will perish in a foreign land: the lovers of those daughters will be faithless: the parents will be abandoned by their children, and die in aged destitution.

If a single rose is left

> "——Blooming alone,
> Its lovely companions all faded and gone;"

and if it grows with its beautiful head inclined towards a cottage, woe to the inhabitant; he has but a brief space of existence left him! Let every one beware of insulting the fountains; for if a stone or any rubbish is thrown into their waters, the person doing so will perish by thunder!

At the entrance of the Vallée d'Aspe, on the Spanish side, is St. Christine, where formerly stood one of those *hôpitaux des ports,* erected by benevolence for the safety of pilgrims and travellers. This was called, in a bull of Innocent III., *one of the three hospitals of the world;* but it has been long since destroyed.

The forests of Itseaux, Gabas, Benou, and Irati, were formerly the most considerable in this part of the Pyrenees: that of St. Engrace is still very extensive. About a century ago the forest of Itseaux was so thick, and so little known in its vast extent, that more than one person was lost in its depths. A singular circumstance occurred at that period, which may give an idea of the perfection of its solitude. A young girl of about sixteen or seventeen was found there in a savage state: she had been a denizen of the shades from the age of seven or eight. All that was known of her was, that she had been left by some other little girls in the woods, having been surprised by the snow. The shepherds who found her conducted her to the hospital of Mauléon: she never spoke, nor gave any sign of recollecting the past; they gave her grass and vegetables to eat, but she continued to droop, and in a very short time died of grief for the loss of her liberty.

About twenty years after this a wild man was observed in the same forest: he was very tall, and strongly built, hairy like a bear, active as an izard, and perfectly harmless. His delight was in coursing the sheep and dispersing them, uttering loud peals of laughter at the confusion he created. Sometimes the shepherds sent their dogs after him, but he never suffered them to come up with him. Nothing was known or traced respecting his history, and he appears to have finished his wild career in the forest: probably he was some child left by accident or design in that savage solitude; where, like Orson, some bear nursed him, but who never found a Valentine to restore him to humanity.

Itseaux still presents an immense extent of wood: it covers one side of the mountains of Lescun, fills the valley of Barétous, and joins the great forest of St. Engrace, to the entrance of the Vallée de Soule. It is the largest of the Pyrenean forests.

There is scarcely a valley in the Pyrenees to which some celebrity is not attached. Amongst others, the Vallée d'Aspe resounds with the fame of the pastoral poet, Despourrins: and Ariosto has celebrated that of Gavarnie, where, in the *Tours de Marboré*, he places the abode of some of his heroes.

> "Charlemagne, Agramont, tous leurs fameux héros;
> Les Zerbin, les Roger, les Roland, les Renaud:
> De ces Palais du Temps habitent les ruines.

* * * * * * * *

> Tout parle d'Arioste en ce fameux vallon
> Et comme aux champs Troyens, chaque roche à son nom."

Cyprien Despourrins, though he wrote as one of the people, and *for* them, was not a man of obscure birth; his family was originally of a race of shepherds; but one of his ancestors having made his fortune in Spain, returned a great man to his native valley, the beautiful Vallée d'Aspe, and there bought the Abbey of Juzan, and became a proprietor, with many privileges. The father of the poet inherited his estates, and distinguished himself in the career of arms, being cited for his bravery, the character of which bears the impress of the times in which he lived, namely, the end of the seventeenth century. Numerous anecdotes are told of him: amongst others, that he had had a dispute with three foreign gentlemen; and in order to get the quarrel off his hands at once, he challenged them all three at the same time, and came off victorious in the combat. To perpetuate the memory of his victory, he obtained from the King permission to have engraved, over the principal entrance of his house, *three swords*, which may still be seen on the stone of the old building shown as his residence. After this notable exploit, Pierre Despourrins visited the *Eaux de Cauteretz*, where, in the neighbourhood of Argelez he formed an acquaintance with the family of Miramont, and an attachment to the fair Gabrielle, daughter of that house; through his marriage with whom, he afterwards became possessor of the château of Miramont, near St. Savin, destined to become famous by means of his son, the famous poet Cyprien. The château is still to be seen, and is a great lion in the neighbourhood.

There are constant disputes between the people of Bigorre and Béarn, as to which has the greater right to claim the poet as their own, for he belonged to both; but as he chose the musical *patois* of the latter in which to sing his pastorals, it appears but just that the Béarnese should have the preference. He was born at Accous, in 1698: his two brothers, Joseph and Pierre, became, one the vicar, the other the curate of the village, and *he* was called, *par excellence*, the *chevalier*. There is a curious story told, illustrative of the simple manners of these mountaineer-priests. The two brothers were very musical: one played the flute, the other the violin; and every Sunday their talents were exerted for the benefit of their parishioners. All the young people of the place were accustomed to meet in the court-yard of their house; and, seated at a casement, the reverend pair played to their dancing. As soon as the bell sounded for vespers, the ball was suspended, and all the docile flock accompanied the good pastors to church.

The chevalier had inherited his father's warlike qualities, and was, it seems, always ready with his sword. He was at the *Eaux Bonnes* when he received an affront from a stranger, which—as Sir Lucius O'Trigger has it,—"his honour could not brook." Unluckily, he had not his sword with him, and the affair must be decided at once; he therefore sent his servant to Accous to fetch it, recommending him great promptitude and address in inventing some story to prevent his father from guessing his errand. The servant used his utmost despatch, and thought he had managed very cleverly to avert suspicion: the old knight, however, was too clear-sighted in such matters; and, having divined the state of the case, mounted his mule instantly, and secretly followed the messenger. He traversed the mountains of Escot and Benou, and, braving all their difficulties, arrived at the Eaux Bonnes. On asking for his son, he was informed that he was closeted with a stranger: he repaired thither, and, pausing at the door, heard the clashing of swords. Satisfied that all was as he surmised, the imperturbable old knight remained quietly at his post, awaiting the issue of the combat. At length the noise of arms ceased; young Despourrins came out precipitately, and found his father on the watch, who, embracing him tenderly, exclaimed—"Your servant's hasty departure prevented my setting out with him; but I followed closely, guessing that you had an affair of honour on your hands; and, in case you should fall, I brought my sword with me, which has never yet failed at need." "I am your son," replied the Chevalier; "my adversary is grievously wounded; let us hasten to afford him assistance."

After Despourrins, the son, was established near St. Savin, and the estates of the Vallée d'Aspe were abandoned by his father for his new domain, he seems to have given himself up to the charms of poetry and music, living the life of a shepherd, and familiarizing himself with the habits, customs, manners and pleasures of that simple race, until he spoke with their words, and thought with their thoughts. Whoever has visited the beautiful Valley of Argelez, and wandered amongst the wilds in the neighbourhood of the once famous abbey of St. Savin, can well understand the poet's delight in such a retreat, and will not wonder when he is told that Despourrins often passed whole nights in the woods, singing his verses, like one transformed to a nightingale. Even now the songs he sung are remembered and cherished; and though the *pastous* of his native mountains probably know nothing of the poet, his lays are constantly on their tongues. One of the most famous is a romance, called "La Haüt sus las Mountagnes," which I give entire, with a translation in prose and verse, in order to show the nature of this Troubadour language, which differs from the Gascon dialect, in being softer and less guttural; in fact, resembling rather more the Italian than Spanish language:—

> La haüt sus las Mountagnes, û Pastou malhurous
> Ségut aü pè d'û Haû, négat de plous,
> Sounyabe aü cambiamen de sas amous.
>
> "Cô leüyé, cô boulatye!" disé l'infourtunat,
> "La tendresse et l'amou qui t'ey pourtat
> Soun aco lous rébuts qu'ey méritat?
>
> "Despuch que tu fréquentes la yen de counditiou
> Qu'as près û tà haüt bôl, que ma maysou,
> N'ey prou haüte entà tu d'û cabirou.
>
> "Tas oüilles d'ab las mies, nous dégnen plus meacla;
> Touns superbes moutous, despuch ença,
> Nou s'approchen deüs més, qu'entaüs tuma
>
> "De richesses me passi, d'aünous, de qualitat:
> You nou soy qu'û Pastou; més noùn n'y a nad
> Que noüs surpassi touts, en amistat,
>
> "Encouère que ay praübé, dens moun pétit estat,
> Qu'aïmi mey moun Berret tout espélat,
> Qué nou pas lou plus bèt Chapeü bourdat.
>
> "Las richesses deü moundé nou bèn queda turmen;
> Et lou plus bèt Seignou, dab soun aryen,
> Nou baü pas lou Pastou qui biü counten.
>
> "Adiü, cô de tygresse, Pastoure chens amou,
> Cambia, bé pots carabia de serbidou:
> Yamey noun troubéras û tau coum you!"

TRANSLATION.

High up, amongst the mountains, an unfortunate shepherd
was seated at the foot of a beech, drowned in tears, musing on
the changes of his love.

"Oh light, oh fickle heart!" said the unhappy youth; "for
the tenderness and the affection which I have borne towards you,
is this wretchedness a fitting reward?

"Since you have frequented the society of persons of condition,
your flight has been so high that my humble cottage is too low
for you by at least a stage.

"Your flocks no longer deign to mix with mine; your haughty
rams, since that period, never approach mine but a battle ensues.

"I am without wealth or dignity; I am but a simple shepherd

but there is none that can surpass me in affection.

"And methinks, according to my simple ideas, that I prefer my *berret*, old and worn as it is, to the finest ornamented hat that could be given me.

"The riches of the world only bring uneasiness with them, and the finest lord with all his possessions cannot compare to the shepherd who lives content.

"Adieu, tigress-heart! Shepherdess without affection; change, change, if you will, your adorers, never will you find any so true as I have been."

I here give a metrical version of the same song:

DESPOURRINS.

————

"La Haut sas las Mountagnes."

————

Above, upon the mountains,
A shepherd, full of thought,
Beneath a beech sat musing
On changes time had wrought:
He told to ev'ry echo
The story of his care,
And made the rocks acquainted
With love and its despair.

"Oh! light of heart," he murmur'd,
"Oh! fickle and unkind!
Is this the cold return
My tenderness should find?
Is this a fit reward
For tenderness like mine?—
Since thou hast sought a sphere
Where rank and riches shine,

"Thou canst not cast a thought
Upon my lowly cot;
And all our former vows
Are in thy pride forgot.
For thee to enter in,
My roof is far too low,
Thy very flocks disdain
With mine to wander now.

"Alas! I have no wealth,
No birth, no noble name,
A simple shepherd youth

> Without a hope or claim;
> But none of all the train
> That now thy favours share
> Can bear, as I have borne,
> Or with my love compare.
>
> "I'd rather keep my habits,
> Tho' humble and untaught,
> Than learn the ways of courts,
> With dang'rous falsehood fraught;
> I'd rather wear my bonnet,
> Tho' rustic, wild, and worn,
> Than flaunt in stately plumes
> Of courtiers highly born.
>
> "The riches of the world
> Bring only care and pain,
> And nobles great and grand
> With many a rich domain,
> Can scarcely half the pleasures,
> With all their art, secure,
> That wait upon the shepherd
> Who lives content and poor.
>
> "Adieu, thou savage heart!
> Thou fair one without love:
> I break the chain that bound us,
> And thou art free to rove.
>
> But know, when in thy vanity,
> Thou wanderest alone,
> No heart like mine will ever
> Adore as I have done."

The royal circle of Neuilly has been enlivened sometimes by the sound of the Béarnese minstrelsy; and, on one occasion, listened to a band of mountaineers from Luchon, who undertook, a few years since, a journey through Europe, singing their choruses in all the principal cities. On hearing the above song of Despourrins, the King exclaimed, with his usual ready kindness, —"Your songs alone would be sufficient to make one love your country."

Several celebrated singers, favourites in the Italian world, were natives of Béarn: one of these, Garat, surnamed "the musical Proteus," was born at Ustaritz. Nothing appeared impossible to this prodigious singer: his voice was splendid and his taste exquisite: his only defect was an inordinate vanity—by no means an uncommon fault in artists of this description. A person on one occasion, thinking to embarrass him, inquired how high in the scale he could go; "I can mount as high as it pleases me to go," was his reply. He used frequently to surprise the Parisians by the introduction of Basque and Béarnese airs, whose peculiarity and originality never failed to cause the most lively admiration and enthusiasm; but he did not announce them as mountain songs till he had secured the praise he sought for them, having passed them for Italian productions. A similar *ruse* was practised by Mehul, when he brought out his "Irato," which the public was given to imagine was composed by an Italian *maestro*. Its success was very great, and Geoffrey, the editor of a popular paper, in noticing the opera, exclaimed,—"O, if Mehul could compose as well as this, we might be satisfied with him." When the triumphant composer threw off his incognito, the unlucky critic was not a little mortified. The celebrated singer Jelyotte was from Béarn, and Louis the Fifteenth used to delight in hearing him sing his native melodies: in particular one beginning, "De cap à tu soy Marion," one of Despourrins' most spirited pastorals:—

> "I am your own, my Marion,
> You charm me with each gentle art;
> Even from the first my love was won,
> Your pretty ways so pleased my heart;
> If you will not, or if you will,
> I am compell'd to love you still.
>
> "No joy was ever like my joy,
> When I behold those smiling eyes,
> Those graceful airs so soft and coy,
> For which my heart with fondness dies:
> And when I seek the charm in vain,
> I dream the pleasure o'er again.
>
> "Alas! I have no palace gay,
> My cottage is but small and plain;
> No gold, nor marble, nor display,
> No courtly friends nor glitt'ring train;
> But honest hearts and words of cheer
> Are there, and store of love sincere.
>
> "Why should we not be quite as blest,
> Without the wealth the great may own?
> A shepherd life, methinks, is best,
> Whose care is for his flock alone;
> And when he folds them safe and warm,
> He knows no grief, he dreams no harm.
>
> "If you, dear Marion, would be mine,
> No king could be so blest as I;
> My thoughts, hopes, wishes, should combine,
> To make your life pass happily;
> Caresses, fondness, love, and glee,
> Should teach you soon to love like me."

Another very favourite song is the "Aü mounde nou y a nat Pastou,"[28] in which mention is made of the national dances for which Béarn is celebrated, as well as the *Pays Basque* which produces *baladins*, famous throughout France for

[28] There are two songs beginning with the same words: both favourites.

their feats of agility and grace. There is a great variety of these dances, and those executed by the young men of St. Savin are remarkable in their kind: bands of the dancers go from village to village in the times of *fêtes*, and are much sought after: they appear very like our May-day mummers, or morrice-dancers, and have probably the same, namely, an eastern, origin: instead of Robin Hood, the Chevalier Bayard is the personage represented in their disguise, and a female always appears amongst them, who answers to our Maid Marian: they are covered with flaunting ribbons, and hold little flags in their hands.

SONG.

"There's not a shepherd can compare
With him who loves me well and true;
French he can speak, with such an air,
As if the ways of courts he knew:
And if he wore a sword, you'd say,
It was the King who pass'd this way.

"If you beheld, beneath our tree,
How he can dance the Mouchicou, —
Good Heaven! it is a sight to see
His Manuguet and Passe-pié too!
His match for grace no swain can show
In all the Valley of Ossau.

"Lest Catti, in the summer day,
The noon-day sun too hot should find,
A bow'r with flow'rs and garlands gay,
By love's own tender hand entwined,
Close to our fold, amidst the shade,
For me that charming shepherd made."

There is considerable variety of style and expression in the poetry of Despourrins, although his subject does not change—being "love, still love."

The following might pass for a song by a poet of the school of Suckling:—

SONG.

— — — —

"Malaye quoan te by!"

— — — —

"OH! when I saw thee first,
Too beautiful, and gay, and bland,
Gathering with thy little hand
The flow'r of May,
Oh! from that day
My passion I have nurst—
'Twas when I saw thee first!

"And ever since that time,
Thy image will not be forgot,

And care and suff'ring are my lot;
I know not why
So sad am I,
As though to love were crime—
Oh! ever since that time!

"Those eyes so sweet and bright,
Illume within my trembling breast,
A flame that will not let me rest;
Oh! turn away
The dazzling ray—
They give a dang'rous light,
Those eyes so sweet and bright!

"Thou hast not learnt to love,
But, cruel and perverse of will,
Thou seek'st but to torment me still.
Faithful in vain
I bear my chain,
Only, alas! to prove
Thou hast not learnt to love!"

But, perhaps, one of the most striking of all Despourrins' poems, from the beauty of the *patois* and the pretty conceits, is the "Deus attraits d'ûc youenne pastoure," which reminds one of Ronsard's "Une beauté de quinze ans, enfantine."

POEM.

"Tis to a maiden young and fair,
That my poor heart has fall'n a prey,
And now in tears and sighs of care
Pass all my moments, night and day.

"The sun is pale beside her face,
The stars are far less bright than she,
They shine not with so pure a grace,
Nor glow with half her charms to me.

"Her eyes are like two souls, all fire;
They dazzle with a living ray;
But ah! their light which I desire
Is turn'd from me by Love, away.

"Her nose, so delicate and fine,
Is like a dial in the sun,
That throws beneath a shadowy line
To mark the hours that love has run.

"The fairies form'd her rosy mouth,
And fill'd it with soft words at will,
And from her bosom breathes the South—

Sweet breath! that steals my reason still.

"Her waist is measured by the zone
The Graces long were wont to wear;
And none but Love the comb can own,
That smooths the ringlets of her hair.

"And when she glides along like air,
Her feet so small, so slight are seen,
A little pair of wings, you'd swear,
Were flutt'ring where her step has been.

"Dear object of my tender care,
My life, my sun, my soul thou art,
Oh! listen to the trembling pray'r,
That woos thee from this breaking heart."

A QUARREL.

— — — —

"Adechat! las mies amous."

— — — —

He.—MY pretty Margaret, good day!
　　　The mountain air is chill;
　　　And if you guide your lambs this way,
　　　The cold will do you ill.

She.—No, gentle friend, tho' cold I seem,
　　　The air I need not fear;
　　　It is the chillness of your stream
　　　That runs so fresh and clear.

He.—The cock had not begun his song;
　　　When with my flocks I came;
　　　To meet you here I waited long—
　　　Your haste was not the same.

She.—My lambs and I were in the mead
　　　Before the break of day;
　　　And you, methinks, have little need
　　　To` blame *me* for delay.

He.—My sheep, with many a ruddy streak,
　　　And bells of jocund sound,
　　　Heav'n knows, a lively music make,
　　　Which can be heard far round.
　　　Come, let our flocks be hither led,
　　　Beneath this shade repair;
　　　For you have butter, I have bread,
　　　And we our meal will share.
　　　Feed, pretty lambs, and feed, my sheep,

> Awhile her flock beside,
> And, as on flow'rs ye browse and sleep,
> We'll leave you for a tide.
> Thou, God of Love, who in the air,
> Art hov'ring in our view,
> Guard well our flocks, and to thy care
> Oh! take two lovers too!

She.—No,—farewell till to-morrow, dear,
> I may not now abide;
> For if I longer tarry here,
> My friends will surely chide.

DESPOURRINS.

————

"Y Ataü quoan la rose ey naberè."

————

"When first the rose her perfume threw,
And spread her blossoms to the day,
I saw thee, Phillis, blooming too,
With all the charms that round her play.

"Pure as the sun, thy glace of power,
Thy voice has music's softest swell,—
I saw thee in an evil hour,
Or never should have loved so well!

"Though from thy presence I remove,
While I lament I still adore,—
Oh! what can absence do to love,
But to increase the feeling more!

"Ye simple swains, who know not yet
What pleasure and what pain may be,
Guard well your hearts from Love's regret,
If you would live from danger free."

DESPOURRINS.

————

"Aü mounde nou-y-a nad Pastou,
T'à malhurous coum you!"

————

"No shepherd in this world can be
The child of wretchedness like me:
One would not think it, but I know
No feeling but continued woe;
For Sorrow came into my fold,

And there her dwelling loves to hold.

"It seem'd the joy of Fate,
New pleasures to provide,
And, 'midst my happy state,
A lamb was all my pride.
The sun conceal'd his light,
Whene'er she came in sight.

"I never dreamt of gold,
I lived content and free;
The treasure of my fold,
Seem'd but to live for me.

Alas! those hours that bless,
Not long would time allow,
My joys, my happiness,
Are changed to sorrow now!

"She loved my pipe to hear,
And midst the flock would pause,
And with a smile, so dear,
Would give me soft applause:
And with her music sweet
My notes she would repeat.

"How many jealous swains
Would look, and sigh, and long:
Not one a word could gain,
She only heard my song;
But now that lamb has stray'd
I see her form no more;
My ev'ry hope betray'd,
My fate let all deplore!
My sleep, my rest, is gone,
And I am all undone!"

DESPOURRINS.

— — — —

"Moun Diü! quine souffrance—
M'as tu causat!"

— — — —

"Of what contentment
Those eyes bereft me—
And ah! how coldly
Thou since hast left me:
Yet didst thou whisper
Thy heart was mine,—
Oh! they were traitors

Those eyes of thine!
For 'tis thy pleasure
That I repine.

"Alas! how often
I sigh'd in vain,
And loved so dearly
To purchase pain:
And all my guerdon
To be betray'd,
And only absence
My safety made,
To muse on fondness
So ill repaid.

"But let me warn thee
While time is yet,
Thy heart may soften
And learn regret:
Should others teach thee
New thoughts to prove,
And all thy coldness
Be quell'd by love,
Thou mayst glean sorrow
For future years,—
Beware—false maiden!
Beware of tears!"

DESPOURRINS.

————

"Per acère castagnere."

————

BENEATH a chesnut shade
A shepherd, drown'd in tears,
By her he loved betray'd,
Thus sung his grief and fears:
"Why dost thou smile," he said,
"As all my woes increase?
When will my truth be paid,
And all thy coldness cease?"

The fair one listen'd not,—
And feign'd she had not seen;
But sought a distant spot,
The furze and heath between,
But, as she proudly went,
Thorns, in her path that lay,

Her little feet have rent,
And stopp'd her on her way.

She paused, in sudden pain,
Her pride aside she laid,
And, in soft tone, was fain
To ask her lover's aid;
She bade, in piteous mood,
He would the thorns remove,
And take from gratitude
The kiss denied to love.

That grateful kiss she must
Bestow—tho' she deplore it;
And he had been unjust
Not—doubly—to restore it.

DESPOURRINS.

— — — —

"Roussignoulet qui cantes."[29]

— — — —

OH! nightingale that sing'st so sweet,
Perch'd on the boughs elate,
How softly does thy music greet
Thy tender list'ning mate.

While I, alas! from joy removed,
With heart oppress'd, must go,
And, leaving her so fondly loved,
Depart in hopeless woe.

Ah me! I see before me yet
Our parting and her pain,
My bosom throbb'd with vain regret
To hear her still complain.
My trembling hand she fondly press'd,
Her voice in murmurs died:
"Oh! is not our's a fate emblest,
Since we must part," she cried.

I promised her, whate'er betide,
To love her to the last,
And Fate, my truth has sadly tried,
In all our sorrows past;
But she may trust me, tho' we part,
And both our lot deplore:
Where'er I go, this bleeding heart

[29] This song singularly resembles Burns' charming "Banks and braes" in its opening, though it is greatly inferior as a whole.

Will suffer ever more.

The clearest streams that gently flow,
The river murm'ring by,
Not purer than my heart can show,
Nor have more tears than I.
No book nor scroll can tell a fate
Where sorrows so combine;
No pen can write, nor song relate,
Such misery as mine!

Thus, like the turtle, sad and lone,
Who leaves his mate in pain,
I go, with many a tender moan,
And dream of love in vain:
By all the ties that bound us long,
By all the hopes we knew,
Oh I hear thy shepherd's latest song,
Receive his last adieu!

Anxious to visit a country whose history and traditions had so much excited my interest and curiosity, I accompanied a friend, early in the year 1843, on an expedition to the Vallée d'Aspe, and through part of the Pays Basque. I would willingly have waited for spring, particularly as I heard from everybody in Pau, that to reach the valleys leading to Spain in the month of February was impossible—was worse than folly: in fact, was what none but the English, who are supposed to have taken leave of their senses, would attempt. One French gentleman, who was well acquainted with every part of the Pyrenees, and had twice made the ascent of the Pic du Midi, was indignant at our perseverance, insisting that we should be stopped by the snows—although very little had fallen in the last winter—and that the Basque country was totally uninteresting except in summer. Others told us that it was never worth seeing at any season; but, as I had become aware that persons settled in Pau were bound in a spell, and scarcely ever ventured more than a league from their retreat until, being once in motion, they set forth towards the mountains in the opposite direction, I did not allow myself to be persuaded to remain in the "Little Paris of the South" for carnival balls, and, followed by the pity and surprise of most of our friends, we took our dangerous way, on a sunny morning, as hot as July, towards Oloron.

Oloron, finely situated on a height, is a wide, open, clean, and well-built town, with so much open, fresh air, that, after the enervating and confined atmosphere of Pau, one seemed to breathe new life. The walks are good and extensive, and the magnificent range of the snowy mountains very close. Two rushing torrents divide the town between them—the Gaves of Ossau and Aspe—and from the two bridges which span them the view of their impetuous course is extremely imposing. These magnificent torrents are the charm of the Pyrenees; making the country, through which they hurry, one scene of beauty and animation: they do also terrible mischief by their violence when swelled by rains, as we had afterwards occasion to observe; but, at all times, give a character of singular grandeur to the places where they sweep along in uncontrolled majesty.

The village, or faubourg, of S^te. Marie d'Oloron joins the main town; and here is situated the cathedral, once of great importance, but now, like all the religious establishments in this part of France, preserving little of its ancient glory. The pillars, however, of its aisles are very grand and massive, and are part of the early structure: the form and height are imposing, and the chapels of the choir graceful; but the chief curiosity is the portal, which bears marks of a Saracenic origin. The arch is a wide circle, finely ornamented, and, in the centre, an Indian-shaped pillar divides it into two smaller circular arches: the base of this pillar is formed of two figures standing back to back, stooping beneath the load they bear on their hands and depressed heads: they are covered with fetters, both on their legs and arms: their striped dresses are quite Indian, and they wear a curious, melon-shaped cap: the faces are hideous and exaggerated, the limbs strong and well made, and they are in perfect preservation.

I have not seen any satisfactory account of the cathedral, which might explain these curious supporters: on each side of the portal projects a carved figure—one much defaced, the other representing a leopard or panther. A series of beautiful pillars, forming pedestals to absent saints, fill up the space of the porch, and that beyond is closed by high, open arches—rebuilt, but, doubtless, originally of the same construction as those of the beautiful side-entrance to the cathedral of Bourges, where Moorish carvings also occur.

There are no other antiquities in Oloron; but it is an agreeable, healthy town, and looks flourishing and lively; and, I should imagine, must be a cheap place to live in, and has several advantages over its rival, Pau; this, however, is not acknowledged by the partisans of that exclusive town, which is supposed, by those who patronise it, to bear away the bell from every other in Béarn.

The Vallée d'Aspe begins its winding way soon after Oloron is past; and the magnificent, broad river dashes along its rocky bed, as green and bright and foaming as its rival of Ossau, which it exceeds in volume. Our destination was to Bedous, where we were to rest for the night; and, as the shades of evening were already coming on, we could not long enjoy the beauty of this lovely valley, which we anticipated seeing on our return, after having visited all the wonders of the pass into Spain, as far as Urdos, where the high road, which is remarkably good, ends.

Bedous is a shabby, insignificant, and, at this time of year, desolate-looking town, in the bosom of the mountains, where we were fain to lodge for the night as we best could, having good reason to congratulate ourselves on our precaution in taking provisions, particularly bread, wine, and coffee, as all we found there was bad. There was, however, no want of civility and desire to please; and the attendance, if not good, was, at all events, ample: two of the waiting-maids were extremely handsome—- with dark eyes and fine features, and their handkerchiefs put on very gracefully; but the voices of all the inhabitants of Bedous were cracked and hoarse, and so unmusical, that it was difficult to imagine oneself in the country of Despourrins.

As early as possible the next morning we set forth on our journey further up the valley; and, the weather being fine and the sky clear, we were delighted with the aspect of the snowy mountains above and around us. The plain of Bedous is of some extent, and, in the fine season, must be extremely beautiful, being highly cultivated and very picturesque: seven villages are scattered at distances along its expanse—the most conspicuous of which is Accous, where the poet was born; and on a mound without the town stands a pyramid, lately erected to his memory. Nothing can be more beautiful than this position; and, in summer, it must be a little Paradise. The village of Osse, opposite, is a small Protestant retreat in an equally charming spot: hills, called in the country *Turons*, surround this happy valley—*avant-couriers* of the higher chain, which rise as the Gave is followed into deeper solitude.

Marca, the historian of Béarn, cites, in his work, a curious document relative to this valley. It is dated June 1, 1348, and its title is sufficiently singular; it runs thus.

"Contract of a peace made between the valleys of Aspe and Lavedan, by order of the Pope, who had absolved the earth, the inhabitants and the castle of Lavedan, from the sin committed by the abbé of St. Savin, in causing the death, *by magic art*, of a great number of the inhabitants of Aspe, in revenge for the rapines and ravages they had committed in Lavedan: *in punishment of which crime, neither the earth, the women, nor the herds of Lavedan had borne fruit for six years.*"

The people of this neighbourhood have the credit of being remarkably intelligent, and, at the same time, simple in their habits and manners: there is considerable jealousy between them and those of Ossau: all we could judge of was that the civility appeared equal, and it appeared to us that the beauty of the peasantry was more striking, though in this opinion we are not borne out by that of others. The boasted costumes are rarely seen in winter; but we observed one young woman very picturesquely dressed in an old and faded black velvet boddice, peculiarly shaped, laced with red, which, if it had ever been *new* in her time, might have been pretty. Every article of their dress, however, looks as if it had descended from generation to generation, till every bit of colour or brilliancy had departed from it, leaving only a threadbare rag, which imagination alone can invest with grace or beauty.

The route we were following was the high road to Saragossa, and, occasionally, we met sombre groups of men in black *capotes*, mounted on horses or mules, and others escorting waggons laden with Spanish wool—the chief article of commerce. Flocks of beautiful goats were very frequent, and every object seemed new and singular to our eyes.

We dismounted from our carriage at a little bridge over the Gave, and, under the direction of a guide who had accompanied us from Bedous, we set forth, beside its rushing current, towards the cascade of Lescun, far up in the hills. The loud roar and dash of the beautiful torrent, foaming and splashing over its bed, strewn with huge pieces of rock, was the excuse which our guide gave for declining to sing Despourrins' songs, with which he was, however, well acquainted. *"Ils sont plus forts pour ça en Ossau"* was his remark, in a voice so harsh and coarse that I did not pursue my entreaties. We met a fine old man, whom I took for a shepherd, from his cloak and brown *berret*, and the large Pyrenean dog which followed him, but he turned out to be a rich proprietor of land, showed us part of his domains, and seemed a well-informed man, talking familiarly of England and its *comté de Chester*, asking us our motive for visiting this part of France, which he concluded to be economy, and entertaining us greatly by his remarks. Our walk, or rather scramble, to the cascade was very agreeable, but exceedingly rugged, mounting the whole way between the hills till we reached the spot where the Gave comes foaming over a broad ledge of rock, and falls into the valley below with a thundering sound. It is much interrupted in its descent, and forms new cataracts as it goes: so that the whole side of the mountain is in commotion with its leaps and gambols; clouds of spray, like smoke, curling up from the foamy abyss, and every echo sounding with its hoarse murmurs. It reminded me of some of the falls in the Mont Dore; but without the pines.

Meantime, the snowy peaks of the giants of the valley were seen peering over the lower hills, and shining in light; but scarcely had we reached the highest point of the cascade, and were standing on the bridge which spans it, when clouds came over the scene, heavy drops began to fall, and we found it necessary to hasten our return to the high road, where we had left our carriage.

To descend the stony and slippery ways was infinitely more difficult than to mount; and I soon found that clinging to the tough branches of box, which here grows luxuriantly, and sheds a fine fresh odour round, was not sufficient assistance. The guide now proved, by the strength of his arm in assisting us, and his agility, that he possessed qualities more useful than the Arcadian accomplishment, the want of which had annoyed me as we came, and I forgave him for being unable to sing the praises of *La Plus Charmante Anesquette*, the words of which ditty he nevertheless repeated, with surprise and pleasure at finding they were old acquaintances of ours.

Our way was now towards Urdos, by Cette Eygun, and through Etscau, where the Gave forces its way along the street, and where, on the opposite bank, on a high terrace, stands the antique village of Borce—once of importance and now only picturesque. We did not see the town of Lescun, but the path to it appears most precipitous: the inhabitants are said to be the most daring smugglers in the valley, and the town stands perched like a vulture's nest, closed in by savage hills, and concealed from sight, as if it had much to hide.

The Spirit of the Pic d'Anie was evidently offended at our seeking his vicinity at so unaccustomed a season, and sent down one of his storms of rain which are so frequent in the valley. As the weather, however, continued warm we did not heed his anger, and continued our journey through the most magnificent scenery—grander and more surprising at every step—till we reached the huge masses of rock called Le Portalet, where once stood a fort, built by Henri Quatre to arrest the approach of the Spaniards. A little further on is a wondrous path, worked in the rocks, over a tremendous precipice, for the purpose of transporting timber. A new fort is being constructed here, and the appearance of a little toy-like hut, fastened to the entrance of a cave for the convenience of the workmen who are to blast the rock, is startling and curious.

Urdos is a wild-looking place, at the extremity of the valley, with no interest belonging to it except that it is the end of the road for carriages, and that at this spot the remainder of the way to Jacca must be made on mules. As the weather was unpropitious, and the snows rendered the *trajet* uncertain, we did not allow our curiosity to carry us further, and contented ourselves with observing the remarkable groups crowding round the inn-door at which we stopped. Spaniards, in wild costumes, with white leggings buttoned behind, sandaled feet, turbaned heads, and rough cloaks thrown over their shoulders, carrying large bundles of goods, were lounging by the entrance, waiting till the rain should cease that they might pursue their way. Some women were of their party, whose appearance was very singular, and the colours of their dresses varied and brilliant in the extreme: one had thrown her green gown, lined with red, over her head, like a veil, and her face was nearly concealed by its folds; her petticoat was of two other bright hues, and she stood, in a commanding attitude, grasping a large staff, a perfect specimen of a brigand's wife.

By degrees, as different guests passed in and out of the inn, and were attracted to the door by the appearance of strangers, we were able to form the most charming pictures, till all Murillo's groups seemed combined in the shifting scene within that narrow frame.

At one time, the *tableau* was complete with the following figures, all coloured in the richest manner, and harmonizing most exquisitely:—a very pretty, intelligent young woman, dressed in green, violet, red, and brown, stood leaning against the doorpost, with an infant in pink, grey, and stone-colour, in her arms: her husband—a handsome, dark Spaniard, with a many-coloured handkerchief with ends twisted round his wild, black, straggling hair—raised his face above her: in shade, behind, stood a sinister-looking smuggler with a *sombrero*, dressed in dark velvet, and a large white cloak thrown over his shoulder: occupying the front space, leant, in a graceful attitude, a female who seemed mistress of the inn. She was a very striking figure, and, both as to costume and feature, might have been the original of many a Spanish Sainte Elizabeth, but younger than she is usually represented. Every part of her dress had a tint of red so subdued into keeping, that it seemed the effect of study, although, of course, mere chance; her gown was rich dark crimson, her apron brighter geranium, her handkerchief, sleeves, and boddice, shades of reddish brown; the large hood on her head a chocolate colour: it was formed of a handkerchief tied negligently under her chin; a second, of rich tint, was bound tightly over her brows, hiding her hair, and her beautiful features came out in fine relief; a delicate blush was on her somewhat tanned cheek, and her eyes were full of calm expression: she had very prettily-shaped hands and feet, and was altogether a model for a painter; struggling through this group, almost at their feet, came, from beneath their drapery, a lovely little brown child, all reds and purples, with glossy black hair, ruddy cheeks, and large black eyes fixed upon us with a sly, smiling gaze. The stained stone, of which the house was built, was of a fine cold colour, and the deep rich shade within made a back-ground which completed the whole.

In the door-way of a neighbouring stable was another party watching the rain, nearly as picturesque; and before them was dancing, in grotesque attitudes, a half-crazed old woman, at whose vagaries the lookers-on indolently smiled. Our admiration of the beautiful children quite won the hearts of the mothers, who had, apparently, at first regarded us with a somewhat haughty air, and a few little silver pieces completed our conquest; we, therefore, drove off on our return to Bedous, in high favour with our strange wild friends, and ceased to feel at all alarmed at the possibility of their overtaking us on the mountains.

We were obliged to pass another night at the inodorous inn of Bedous, amidst the noise of a carnival night, and the hideous howls of a jovial party who had that day assisted at a wedding, and who seemed bent on proving that music was banished from the valley. I heard the word "*Roncevaux*" in one of their songs; but could distinguish nothing besides to atone for the discord they made, as they danced *La Vache* under our windows, in the pouring rain, by the light of a dim lanthorn.

I was told by the landlady that in the church of Bedous were formerly two *bénitiers*, one within the aisle, and one in the porch; the latter being appropriated to the use of that unfortunate race—the Cagots—about whom I had been so inquisitive ever since I arrived in Béarn. Accordingly, we lost no time in going to seek for these strange relics; after looking about in vain, and discovering only one *bénitier*, we were assisted in our search by a man belonging to the church, and our female guide; who understood only *patois*, and led to the mysterious spot where the worn stone is to be seen on which once stood the vase of holy water into which the wretched outcasts were permitted to dip their fingers. The recess is now used as a closet, which is closed with wooden doors, and the *bénitier* is removed, "because," said the man, "there is no distinction *now*, and the Cagots use the same as other people,"[30] I inquired if it was known who were Cagot families, and was told "*certainly;*" but little account was taken of the fact. "Bedous," said my informant, "was one of the Cagot villages, but the prejudice is almost worn out now: it is true we do not care to marry into their families if we can help it; not that there is any disease amongst them; it is all mere fancy. Only when people quarrel, they call each other Cagots in contempt; however, we shall soon forget all about it."

On our return through the valley to Oloron, we paused at Notre Dame de Sarrance, a place of pilgrimage, entirely uninteresting as a church, but placed in a beautiful position amongst the hills.

At Oloron, when we passed before, there was no room for us, in consequence of the whole inn being occupied with guests at the wedding of the landlord's fourth daughter, the three others having been lately married. As we arrived the day after the wedding, there still remained sufficient good cheer to supply our wants, and make a pleasing contrast to Bedous.

---

[30] At Utrarítz, near Bayonne, they show, in the porch of the church, a similar recess, where once stood the *bénitier* of the Cagots.

MAULÉON

CHAPTER XVI.

Aramitz — The Play — Mauléon — The Sisters — Words — St. Jean.

Our intention now was to visit Mauléon, and see as much of the Pays Basque as the uncertain state of the weather would allow. The route to Aramitz is very beautiful, with the fine valley of Barétous, and the Bois d'Erreche stretching out at the foot of the bold hills. When we entered the town of Aramitz the whole population was assembled in a great square; some acting, and others gazing at a carnival play, the performers in which were dressed in flaunting robes, with crowns and turbans; while a troop, in full regimental costume, figured away as a victorious French army, headed by a young Napoleon, who ever and anon harangued his troops and led them on to battle against a determined-looking band of enemies, amongst whom were conspicuous *a bishop* and *a curé*, in full dress. A combat ensued, when the heroes on each side showed so little nerve, being evidently afraid of their own swords—which seemed *real* steel, that no child's-play in England could have gone off so tamely: the enemies all fell down at the first attack, and the only comic part was the rushing forward of the fool, and his agonized exclamation of "*O! mon curé!*" as he dragged that reverend gentleman from beneath a heap of slain. We asked our driver how it happened that the clergy of the parish allowed this *travestie*, and how the curé's dress had been procured: he told us that the costume belonged to some one who had *formerly* been in the Church, and as for the representation no one could prevent it, particularly as the sons of the mayor were amongst the actors. "But," he added, "M. le Curé will *have his revenge* next Sunday by preaching them a sermon which he intends shall make their ears tingle; though no one will care a bit about it."

We observed, that it was wrong to turn the ministers of religion into ridicule, to which our lively guide agreed, concluding with the usual shrug and inevitable remark of all Frenchmen—Béarnais and other—"*Mais, que voulez vous!*"

My companion's donation of a franc, was received with rapture by a general and an emperor, who came to our carriage with a plate, in the centre of which was an apple with numerous slits, in which were inserted certain borrowed napoleons, to excite to generosity. We were vehemently invited to mount to a place of honour to view the play at our ease; but we declined, as it was not the dramatic performance that delighted us, but the extraordinary effect of the costumes of the crowd below. All the young girls wore their new and most brilliant handkerchiefs tied on their heads with the utmost care, and exhibiting colours so rich and glowing, that, as they flitted about in the sun, they seemed so many *colibri* with changeable crests of all the hues of the rainbow. The rich colours worn here give an air of gaiety and cheerfulness, agreeably contrasted with the dark and gloomy tints of the head-dresses at and near Pau; which, though gracefully tied, are usually sombre and dim.

The whole town of Aramitz was gay with carnival rejoicings, and as we drove along we came upon another crowd in another square, where we saw a party of six young men in black-and-green velvet dresses, and scarlet sashes, nimbly dancing the *Rondo Basque*; while the gorgeously-adorned young girls stood by, observing, but taking no part in the exercise. They seemed very agile and nimble, and kept up an incessant movement, not without grace; but it had an odd effect to see the men dancing alone, and that circumstance impresses one with the conviction of the dance being of eastern origin. We had not an opportunity of seeing any of the other dances so celebrated in the country, which are precisely similar to our morris-dances still exhibited, occasionally, in the country on May-day.

The Basque country, properly so called, begins at Montory, and a perceptible change, singular enough, is observable in the country: a range of hills, of shapes impossible to describe—so witch-like and irregular is their outline—extends for some distance along the way, ushering the traveller into the pretty plain below.

At Tardets there is a bridge over the charming Gave of *Uhaitshandia*; and now begin the extraordinary names of places, which French, Béarnais, and Spanish alike find so difficult to pronounce or understand. Now the few familiar words which we comprehended in Béarnais were heard no more, and a language of the most singular yet musical sound took its place. The first objects we saw were two Andalusian women, ragged, filthy, and slovenly, to a degree quite amazing, their dingy white woollen gowns thrown over their heads; faded apple-green petticoats in thick plaits hanging from their shoulders, with no indication of waists, bare legs and feet, and bold, savage aspect. They laughed loudly at some remark *en passant* of our driver; who seemed accomplished in languages, being able to speak to all he met. Immediately afterwards we met some Basque women, whose costume had no other distinction but that of their headkerchiefs being white; this, however is rare, except on occasions of *fête*, as we always saw the same beautiful brilliant colours as before, throughout our journey.

Mauléon, one of the chief towns of the Basque country, is charmingly situated in a rich country, on the Gaison Gave, surrounded by the varied hills of the Bois de Tibarène. Of all its former grandeur and strength scarce a vestige remains: one ruined fort, of a commanding height, above the town, alone attests its ancient glory: from this spot is a charming view, taking in all the town and plain and surrounding mountains. The churches, once of great importance, are dwindled to insignificance; and we were much disappointed to discover nothing interesting either at the antique church of Berautte or Licharre. We found, however, an equivalent in the beauty of the scenery round, and the charm of hearing the sweetest of languages from the lips of two pretty little girls of ten and eleven years of age, the daughters of our hostess, who herself had a melodious voice, and peculiarly pleasing manners. These little fairies constituted themselves our attendants during our stay at Mauléon, and as they spoke, equally well, French and Basque, we enjoyed their innocent prattle and intelligent remarks extremely. They were very eloquent in praise of a certain English traveller named *François*, who had stayed some time at their inn, and wanted to take them away to England, and they tried hard to persuade us that he *must* be a relation, because he *talked* and *drew* like us, and because we wanted to take them away too.

I made a little vocabulary of Basque words under their tuition; and it was like listening to music to hear them utter the pretty phrases and words; *maita suthut hanich*—I love you much; *ene-madtea*—my friend; *ama*—my mother; *aita*—my father; *belhara*—grass; *nescatila*—little girl; *minyiate bat*—a fairy; *oheitza*—remembrance.

I procured a Basque dictionary at Mauléon, at a somewhat primitive library, where the usual commodities sold were candles and soap. At one end of the shop was a range of books on a shelf; and while the very civil master was gone to look for those more choice volumes which we required, his housekeeper stood by, in a state bordering on distraction at the sacrilege committed by us, in daring to remove from their positions tomes which her master evidently did not permit her to lay a finger on. In Basque, and all the French she had, did she clamour to us to desist, assuring us it was a thing unheard of, and would derange the whole economy of the establishment; and, certainly, as her anger increased with our indifference, she proved to us that it was possible to make discord out of sweet notes; however, the purchase of the books her master had found silenced and confounded her; and we escaped with our prize, much to the delight and amusement of our little guides, who thought it necessary, *en chemin*, to apologize for the old woman's rudeness.

The father of our favourites we found, though taciturn at first, a very well-informed man; he confirmed all that I had gathered from works I had read on the subject of the Basques—their language and manners; and regretted that the unpropitious state of the weather prevented our witnessing any of the usual out-of-door amusements, common at the season. He described the eloquence and wit of the common people as something wonderful; but their *comedies*, he said, were seldom fitted for more refined ears than their own. The character of their amusements, he added, was grave, as their improvised tragedies prove; the language lends itself to poetry with such singular facility, that poets are by no means rare; and, amongst the lower class, some are, as I had heard before, singularly gifted, but they never write down their compositions, which are, therefore, difficult to collect. The airs of their songs are almost always melancholy and solemn, and require fine voices to give them effect. I have since been told, by a Basque gentleman of taste and information, precisely the same; and, as he sings well, he kindly allowed me to hear some of their melodies, which remind me much of the saddest of the Irish native airs. His opinion was, that there is great similarity in the character of the Basque and Irish; and he tells me, that the *sound* of many of their words is alike; but when they speak together all proves to be *mere* sound; for they do not understand a syllable of either tongue.

The greater part of the language seems to me corrupted by the introduction of French and Spanish words, probably required to express wants, which the original Basque had acquired in the course of time;

"When wild in woods the noble savage ran,"

he did not want much that he afterwards sought for words to express his desire to obtain. But the genuine words, in which there is no mixture of another language, may well puzzle the learned; for they are most singular: as for instance,

Oghia...	Bread	Egura...	Wood
Uhaitza...	River	Eskia...	Hand
Hoora...	Water	Mahatsac...	Grapes
Haicha...	Stars	Sahmahia...	Horse
Hala...	Ship	Etchia...	Habitation
Harhibat...	Stone	Begitatiha...	Face

Our next destination was to St. Jean Pied de Port; and we took our way across the mountains of Musculdy, the scenery the whole way being exquisitely beautiful, and richly cultivated in the plains. We continued mounting without cessation for nearly two hours; and as we walked the greatest part of the time, we met with a few adventures by the way. We were joined, in a very steep part, by a party who were travelling from Mauléon to St. Just. We had been struck with the brilliant colours of the young woman's dress as we passed her and her mother, and a boy accompanying them; she was leaning against a stone wall, where she had rested her large white bundle, and her attitude was free and graceful in the extreme, as she bent her head on her hand evidently fatigued. She wore a headkerchief of deep chocolate-colour, striped with blue, and bordered with bright yellow; her stuff petticoat was scarlet, edged with black velvet; she had tucked up her green-striped gown, and thus displayed its crimson lining; her shawl was of fine red merinos, embroidered in glowing colours, of Spanish manufacture, as she afterwards informed us, *and smuggled*; her legs were bare, but she wore black shoes; and her umbrella, the constant appendage, was brown; her gait, as she walked along the road, with her white package on her head, was that of a heroine of a melo-drame. I never saw a more striking figure; for she was, though not pretty, remarkably well-made and tall, and all her motions were easy and unconstrained. She did not seem so communicative as her mother,—a pretty little *old* woman, whose pride was evidently gratified by our admiration of her daughter's finery, and our pleasure in sketching her as she stood; her gratitude was so great on our allowing her boy and her bundles to be put on the carriage, that she became quite enthusiastic in our praise; and the present of a small piece of silver enchanted her. She actually cried with pleasure; and yet we found she was not poor; but had been to see a son, who had amassed several hundred francs and set up in a *cabaret* at Mauléon: this explained the gorgeousness of his sister's costume, which, at the risk of spoiling, she continued to wear on her journey home to their village, aware of the sensation her macaw-like appearance created wherever she passed.

BASQUAISE

On a high hill, opposite that we were mounting, we observed a chapel, which we found was dedicated to the Sainte Madeleine, and held in much reverence throughout the country: pilgrims coming from great distances to visit her shrine, and sick persons thronging there in the hope of a miracle being performed in their favour. The same occurs at another chapel, on a neighbouring height, dedicated to St. Antoine; but there, it seems, the young men resort, in order, by the saint's intercession, to obtain an exemption from the chance of conscription. They entreat of Heaven that they may choose a *good number*, and be allowed to remain at home; and so firmly are they convinced of the efficacy of the saint's prayers, that hundreds had, we understood, lately taken their way to the holy mountain; for this was the season for the fatal lots to be drawn.

ARNEGUY

CHAPTER XVII.

Arneguy — The Cacolet — Rolando's Tree — Snow-White Goats — Costume — Sauveterre — The Pastor — Navarreux — Spanish Air.

WE arrived at St. Jean Pied de Port late in the day, and the aspect of affairs at Le Grand Soleil, where we stopped, was by no means exhilarating. Having passed through the black, dirty kitchen, and climbed the dingy staircase, we were shown several rooms, which we *could not have*, by a very sour-looking old woman, who tried to persuade us to content ourselves with apartments without fire-places. This we resisted determinedly, suggesting that ladies had a right to supersede male travellers, and, assisted by the eloquence of our invaluable *cocher*, we at length obtained possession of the disputed chambers. As it was soon discovered that we meditated remaining several days, no further opposition was made to our convenience, and the fat landlady, having reproved her thin sister into good humour, we were allowed to command, in the worst of all possible inns, where good-will held the place of performance in most instances, and where carelessness seemed carried to a perfectly Eastern excess.

We began to make immediate enquiries as to the possibility of entering Spain, of visiting the convent of Roncesvalles and the neighbouring mountains; and every sort of contradictory information was given us, enough to bewilder an ignorant traveller into giving up the projected expedition altogether. However, as we resolved that we would not be altogether disappointed, and recollected all the romances invented to deter our daring, by our friends at Pau, we ordered a guide and *cacolet* and mule to be sent on before, and on the following morning set forth in the carriage as far as Arneguy, the last French town, from whence we were to cross the Gave of Bihobi, and trust ourselves to the perils of a Spanish journey.

Accordingly, we pursued the very good road to that frontier village—one of the most miserable I ever beheld, filled with soldiers and mud and ruin: here we alighted, and walked across the little bridge which divides the two kingdoms. Once *in Spain*, and having made a drawing of the spot, as a souvenir, we mounted our mule; seated comfortably in the arm chairs, slung at each side of the patient animal, and, with our muleteer and two servants on foot, began the scrambling ascent of one of the most rugged paths I ever beheld.

Every step, however, exhibited new and startling beauties; and the further we advanced the more sublime the mountains became: the foaming stream rushing beneath us, the deep ravines and precipices, the wooded hills and enormous trees, all possessed a character quite unlike that of the two valleys of Béarn, which we had already seen; both of which led into Spain, as did this pass of Roncesvalles; but we now felt ourselves really in another country; and, as we passed the opposite village of Ondarol, and heard that the last houses in France were left behind, and all the mountains, on each side of the ravine, belonged to Spain, there was something singularly agreeable in the idea. Our *cocher François* had, at the village of Valcarlos, an opportunity of exhibiting his knowledge of Spanish; for the officer there, who took cognizance of us, could not understand either *patois* or French.

We wound along the beautiful ravine of Valcarlos, by a road more stony and rugged than can be described, trusting to our mule, who kept his feet in a manner perfectly surprising; it was like mounting a ruined staircase, so steep was the path in many places; but, going slowly and carefully as we did, and seated in our comfortable panniers, we felt no inconvenience, and were scarcely conscious of the difficulties, sensibly understood by all our companions, who toiled through the mud, and over the stones and torrents with infinite cheerfulness and perseverance.

The beeches and chesnuts here grow to an immense size, and look so old in their winter guise that one might almost believe they had spread the shade over the paladins of Charlemagne. We could not do otherwise than indulge in this idea, when we reached a spot where an enormous *plateau* of rock seemed to bar our further progress; and, beside it, we rested beneath a gigantic chesnut, which threw its naked arms far across the ravine below, and, when covered with leaves, must have been a majestic tree. A huge stone lay amongst others near it, and this was pointed out by our guide as the identical stone thrown by Rolando in his anger when his horse's foot slipped over the rock at the edge of which we stood. The print made by the hoof as it slid along the surface is *clearly visible* to poetical eyes, and this is one of the numerous *Pas de Roland* so celebrated in the Pyrenees, where the great hero's course is marked in many directions.

ROLANDO'S TREE

As we desired to avoid the possibility of a similar accident happening to us, we dismounted from our *cacolet*, and walked across the ledge to some distance: and, after a short repose beneath the shelter of the overhanging rocks, which a violent shower made most convenient at the moment, we prepared to retrace our steps; satisfied with having advanced so far on the same route taken by "Charlemagne and all his peerage."

The return was infinitely less easy than the advance, for we had now to descend; and we felt the motion much more, for the mule could not so well keep its feet in spite of the guide's assistance. We had sundry adventures by the way at

Posadas—tasted the bitter Spanish *ordinaire* wine from a wine-skin, and the excellent maize bread and cream cheese of the country, and returned to Arneguy, much gratified with our trip.

These mountains must be exquisitely beautiful in summer, when all the fine trees are in full grandeur, for I never saw any larger or more flourishing. It is the custom for the French to decry everything Spanish, even to the natural productions; and I had often been told that the moment the French side was quitted all was barren and worthless; I found, however, on the contrary, that the mountain-scenery greatly increased in sublimity the nearer we advanced towards Roncesvalles, and on our return that which had looked well on our way had dwindled into tameness in comparison with what we had left. Our driver, in the true spirit of his country, laboured to convince us that even the Basque on the Spanish side was inferior to that on the French—a fact we were not in a condition to decide on, as readily as we could with respect to the scenery. I think, as a general rule, that a foreign traveller may always be sure, if a country is abused in France, it possesses attractions for him, and *vice versâ*; for the "toute beauté" of a French amateur is invariably a piece of formality or common-place, unendurable to the lovers of the really beautiful.

Flocks of snow-white goats, with long hair, were climbing up the steepest parts of the mountains; and a few stragglers, with their pretty kids, greeted us on our rugged road: a party of Zingari, with scowling brows but civil demeanor, hurried past us, with a swiftness rather unusual to their indolent race, unless indeed they were afraid of pursuit—as our muleteer seemed to hint by his exclamation of alarm as they appeared. Besides these, and a traveller mounted on a mule, who was, we understood, a rich merchant of Pampeluna, who constantly made the *trajet* by that bad road, we were little disturbed in our solitude. The Gave sounding far below, the smaller brawling cataracts crossing our rocky path, the overhanging rocks and gigantic trees, the constantly-changing scene, and the novelty of the whole, made our wild and strange journey altogether delightful. We were congratulated on our return that the rain, which overtook us on our way, had not been snow; for in these regions the path is sometimes obstructed in the course of half-an-hour; and a sad story was related to us of a courier despatched to Roncesvalles in sunshine, having been overwhelmed by the snow on his return the same evening. Whether this was a *mountain* fable we could not be sure; but we had heard so many terrors, and experienced none, that we found it difficult to give credit to all the histories of travellers eaten by wolves and destroyed by avalanches, such as had arrived at Pau from the heights of Gabas and Urdos throughout the winter, only to be contradicted after they had had their effect for the given time.

From St. Jean Pied de Port—where the female costume is pretty, and whose arsenal, and the fine view from it, are all that claim the slightest attention in the most slovenly of ugly towns, and whose church portal tells of former magnificence long since swept away—we took our departure by St. Palais to Sauveterre, crossing the Pays Basque, which is perfectly lovely as to scenery, and, in fine weather, is worth a long journey to visit—so varied, rich, and agreeable is the country in all directions. Sauveterre is a neat, clear, respectable town, finely situated, well-enough paved, and having many attractions—particularly a magnificent ruin of a strong castle, which is called that of the Reine Jeanne, but is, evidently, originally of much more ancient construction. One high tower is very commanding, and must have been formidable in its time: that of the church, on still higher ground above, is of the same date, and is very curious: on the whole, Sauveterre is as picturesque a town as any we had seen, and we were sorry that bad weather a good deal masked its beauties.

COSTUME OF SAUVETERRE

We paid a visit to the Protestant church; and the minister's wife, a very simple, kind person, who deeply regretted the absence of her husband—gone to look after his scattered flock, which is dispersed, in distant hamlets, all over that part of the country towards Navarreux. This excellent man is in the habit of walking many leagues, in the severest seasons, to visit his people, who reside by twos and threes in villages far remote; and he seems to spare no pains in his vocation. His establishment is of the simplest and most primitive kind, evidently quite unknown to luxury; and the sight of the good pastor—which we were fortunate enough to get on the morning of our departure—confirmed our preconceived opinion of his benevolence, if countenance be a faithful index pf mind. Our interview happened in this sort.

We had decided to leave Sauveterre early, fearing the weather, and were just starting, when, at the carriage-door, we beheld two figures, which we at once recognized as the returned pastor and his wife: a violent shower greeted them; but, mindless of it, there they stood, under their umbrellas, determined to make our acquaintance, and to thank my companion for a donation she had sent to the poor Protestants under his charge. His fine open, healthy countenance, and cheerful, good-humoured expression, gentlemanlike manners, and easy address, pleased us extremely; and the unassuming little wife, dressed in a cap like a *bourgeoise*—joining him in kind exclamations of sorrow at losing their friends of the moment—equally amused and gratified us with the *naïveté* of the whole proceeding. I have no doubt that our apparition in that solitary town was quite an event, and one which the good minister would have been sorry to miss. He had come back late the night before, through a deluge of rain, and by the most difficult cross-roads—of course flooded—after walking twenty or thirty miles; yet he had energy to rise early, dress himself in his best, and come to meet the strangers, before their departure.

I think he must really be a pattern of a minister, and is a worthy example for many richer and less zealous clergymen. The French government is not able to allow more than a thousand francs a-year to the Protestant ministers, and out of this he no doubt gives much in charity, for almost all his flock is poor, and I believe he has a family to support besides: yet he seemed cheerful and contented, and probably thinks himself well off, happy in the exercise of his duty, and in relieving the sufferings of his fellows.

Navarreux is a strongly-fortified little town, looking extremely warlike, filled with troops: it would be difficult to say why, as it is so far from the frontier; but, probably, they are ready, as at Pau, in case of an outbreak on the part of the Spaniards, which seems improbable, but is talked of.[31] From hence to Pau the country is pretty; but the nearer approach to the wide, marshy lands round, renders the prospect infinitely less interesting, and the air less refreshing.

I had now accomplished, however imperfectly, a long-entertained intention of *visiting Spain*; and, although I had merely breathed Spanish air *for a few hours*, yet it has given me a sort of assurance that I shall, one day, be able to put my favourite project in execution—of travelling over that most poetical and interesting of all countries—at a time, I trust, when its government shall be well established, and peace and order so prevail, that the fear of brigands may not deter strangers from seeking its romantic cities, and crossing its wild and wondrous mountains.

For the present, I take leave of my readers; hoping that, in my next tour, they will indulgently accompany me to Madrid and the Alhambra.

THE END.

---

[31] This has since occurred, and Espartero is in England and Queen Christine in Spain.

Lector House believes that a society develops through a two-fold approach of continuous learning and adaptation, which is derived from the study of classic literary works spread across the historic timeline of literature records. Therefore, we aim at reviving, repairing and redeveloping all those inaccessible or damaged but historically as well as culturally important literature across subjects so that the future generations may have an opportunity to study and learn from past works to embark upon a journey of creating a better future.

This book is a result of an effort made by Lector House towards making a contribution to the preservation and repair of original ancient works which might hold historical significance to the approach of continuous learning across subjects.

HAPPY READING & LEARNING!

LECTOR HOUSE LLP
E-MAIL: lectorpublishing@gmail.com

9 789390 294893

www.ingramcontent.com/pod-product-compliance
Lightning Source LLC
LaVergne TN
LVHW091146180726
843490LV00004B/1334